Nonviolent Action and Social Change

Nonviolent Action And Social Change

Edited by

Severyn T. Bruyn

Boston College

and

Paula M. Rayman

Brandeis University

Preface by

David Dellinger

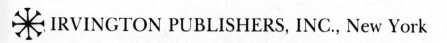

☀ IRVINGTON PUBLISHERS, INC., New York

To Alfred McClung Lee, our deep appreciation
for giving this book its initial inspiration.

CONTENTS

Part III. International Social Change Movements

Part IV. The Future of Nonviolent Action

CONTRIBUTORS

Susan Abrams received her Ph.D. in German from Yale and has taught at Swarthmore College and the University of Virginia. An activist with the women's and peace movements, she was media coordinator for the United Farm Workers' New England Office in 1974—1975. She is currently a freelance writer and radio commentator on social change issues in Boston.

Joseph Amato is an Associate Professor of History at Southwest Minnesota State College, Marshall, Minnesota. He visited Dolci in Sicily in January, 1972 and was host to Dolci for one day during his spring trip to the U.S. Aside from writing two other essays on Dolci, his doctoral dissertation on Emmanuel Mounier's Personalism has been published by the University of Alabama Press under the title of *Emmanuel Mounier and Jacques Maritain: A French Catholic Understanding of the Modern World.*

Louise Muenzer Bruyn teaches dance at Boston College and in Newton and works at present with the Mobilization for Survival. In 1971 she became nationally known for a personal witness against the Viet Nam War, a solitary walk of 450 miles from her home in Newton, Massachusetts, to Washington, D.C. Four years later, she was one of nine persons who were deported from South Vietnam for demonstrating against continued U.S. support of the Thieu government in front of the American Embassy. In 1974 she received a Masters degree in Theater for Social Change at Cambridge-Goddard Graduate School for Social Change.

Severyn T. Bruyn has been active for many years in the Civil Rights movement and most recently has been organizing producer cooperatives with unemployed workers. He has held various offices in the Society for the Study of Social Problems and was recently elected to the Council in the Section on World Conflicts of the American Sociological Association. He has served as a consultant to agencies involved in new town planning, mental health services, and crime prevention programs. His books include *Communities in Action: Pattern and Process* (1963); *The Human Perspective in Sociology: The Methodology of Participant Observation* (1966); and *The Social Economy: People Transforming Modern Business* (1977). He is now bringing together a journal of his experiences in Puerto Rico, focusing on the issues of self-governance in institutional life.

David Dellinger, a draft resister during World War II, was a principal figure of the anti-war movement in the 1960s. For many years an editor of *Liberation* magazine, today he edits the magazine, *Seven Days.* David Dellinger is the author of *Revolutionary Nonviolence, More Power Than We Know,* and numerous articles concerning social change struggles.

John P. Hunt is a student in the Ph.D. Social Science Program at Syracuse University where he holds a University Fellowship. He is currently teaching a course on nonviolence in America for the Program in Nonviolent Conflict and Change.

Neil H. Katz is Director of the Program in Nonviolent Conflict and change at Syracuse University and Assistant Professor of Public Affairs in the Maxwell School. At the University of Maryland he wrote his doctoral dissertation on "Radical Pacifism and the Contemporary American Peace Movement: The Committee for Nonviolent Action, 1957—1967." He has published articles in several peace studies, journals and books including PEACE and Change: *A Journal of Peace Research in History, Priorities, and Doves and Diplomats* (forthcoming).

George Lakey is author of *Strategy for a Living Revolution* and co-author of *A Manual for Direct Action* and *In Place of War: An Inquiry into Unarmed National Defense*; he is a member of The Movement for New Societies, Philadelphia Life Center.

Paula Rayman is an Assistant Professor of Sociology at Brandeis University. She has been actively involved in the nonviolent movement with particular emphasis on issues of the Middle East and feminism. She has done research and writing on the development of the Israeli Kibbutz, urban communes, and social change strategies. Her present research concentrates on labor issues confronting economic conversion programs.

Mary Roodkowsky is acting director of the Boston Industrial Mission, where she works on the issues of world development and economic justice with Church and community organizations. She is especially interested in identifying the root economic and social causes of war, and in developing viable alternatives to them. She is also active in feminist concerns. Some of her recent publications include, "In Agribusiness We Trust," in *Beyond Survival*, Dieter Hessel, (ed.) Friendship Press, 1977; and with Lisa Leghorn *Who Really Starves? Women and World Hunger*, Friendship Press, 1977. She studied at Wellesley College, and holds a Master's degree in Theology from Harvard University.

Gene Sharp, D. Phil (Oxon.), is Professor of Sociology and Political Science at Southeastern Massachusetts University, and has recently been Lecturer, Department of Psychology and Social Relations, Harvard University. He was a Research Fellow of the Center for International Affairs, Harvard University, 1965—1972. He was previously attached to the Institute for Social Research, Oslo, Norway and the Institute of Philosophy and the History of Ideas of the University of Oslo. He is a Life Member of St. Catherine's College, Oxford. His major work, *The Politics of Nonviolent Action*, was prepared under the auspices of Harvard's Center for International Affairs.

David J. Toscano is an Assistant Professor of Sociology at Nichols College, Massachusetts; Acting Director, Boston College Program for the Study of Peace and War; co-editor of the forthcoming, *American Colonial Struggles 1765—1775*, Porter Sargent (Boston).

Charles C. Walker is founding member of the World Peace Brigade, Chairman of its training section; staff member for pacifist and Quaker organizations; four years Director of Field Studies, Nonviolent Action Research Project, Haverford College; Director of workshops on nonviolence in South during the civil rights movement, in India for the Gandhian movement, in England for peace movements; founding editor of Liberation Magazine, author of handbooks and monographs on nonviolent action; organizer for action projects in Puerto Rico, Panama, Cyprus and U.S.A.

Harvey Wasserman completed an 18-month around-the-world tour, gathering and dispersing facts on the spread of nuclear energy.

In 1967 he was co-founder (along with Marshall Bloom, Ray Mungo, and others) of the Liberation News Service, and is author of *Harvey Wasserman's History of the United States*, New York: Harper and Row, 1972. Wasserman currently lives on an organic communal farm in western Massachusetts and is very actively involved with the Clamshell Alliance, dedicated to halting construction of a nuclear power plant in Seabrook, New Hampshire.

Paul Wehr is an Associate Professor of Sociology at the University of Colorado at Boulder. He is also director of the Environmental Conciliation Project in the Institute of Behavioral Science. His teaching and research currently focus on the development of conflict regulation methods and their application to environmental and international conflict.

PREFACE TO THE PAPERBACK EDITION

Since this book was originally issued, world events have moved the entire "spaceship" of earth precariously closer to the spectre of nuclear holocaust. On the day this new introduction was written, the media reported that a computer at the nation's missile-warning center erroneously put U.S. strategic forces on alert against a purported Soviet missile attack. This is not the first time this type of "error" has taken place. These events remind us that social stability cannot be built upon institutions which foster unequal power and lack of trust. Unequal power—whether between the Western nations and the Third World, between the urban and rural communities, between blacks and whites, between men and women—sets up a have and have-not struggle, with the fallout of violent cycles we witness daily.

These acute crisis events have occurred both domestically and internationally. On the domestic front, the Three Mile Island crisis brought nightmares into reality, caused grave mental anguish to Pennsylvania residents and raised fears for all American (and world) citizens. In the late 1970's, Love Canal forced President Carter to declare the nation's first man-made disaster. Emergency relief finally reached the victims of toxic wastes left behind by chemical companies and the army in the 1960's. This opened the door to discoveries of the dangerous disposal methods for hazardous wastes all over the country.

Domestic crises in the beginning of the 1980 decade also reflected the worsening economic situation. Riots in Miami spotlighted the continued poverty situation stemming from racism towards blacks. The lives of unemployed autoworkers and steelworkers in the Midwest evidenced the link between economic insecurity and individual and social stress.

Internationally, political tensions erupted into terrorism in the Middle East, in the flight of refugees from Vietnam, in escalating human rights violations in Argentina, as well as the Soviet incursion into Afghanistan. The May Korean uprising of unarmed stu-

xii   Preface to the Paperback Edition

dents and workers tightened the knot of martial law restrictions which had been in effect since the assassination of President Park Chung Hee.

In thoughtful moments, we realize the absurdity of waging war to insure a peaceful settlement of these crises. Our common sense informs us that weapons do not bring genuine security, that we cannot advance ourselves by reducing others to daily death toll numbers. We share the knowledge that we are social beings. When we resort to undermining another person's, another race's, another nation's humanity, we lose our own.

—Paula Rayman

Waltham, Mass.
July 1980

PREFACE

When on April 4, 1968, Martin Luther King Jr. was killed by an assassin's bullet, many people who were engaged in the struggle for social justice in this country concluded that the cause of nonviolence had failed. A black colleague with whom I had been arrested in nonviolent actions on both sides of the Mason-Dixon line said at the time: "Martin was the most nonviolent [black] man in the country and they killed him. Nonviolence doesn't work."

On December 4, 1969, less than two years after King's death, Fred Hampton, chairman of the Illinois section of the Black Panther Party was killed by police in a pre-dawn raid that we now know was a setup for murder. The police riddled Hampton's body while he slept in bed, heavily sedated by a drug that apparently had been slipped into his evening coffee by an FBI agent who had infiltrated the Panthers and served as Hampton's security chief. A few hours later, at Panther headquarters, a Panther said to me: "Now you can see, Dave, why everyone has to pick up the gun. Nonviolence doesn't stand a chance against people like them."

Leave aside the fact that the man who said that was one of "them," the security chief who later was revealed to have been in the employ of the FBI. Leave aside what that may say about whether the armed defenders of the status quo find it easier to combat opposition that is violent or militantly nonviolent. At the time, I didn't know whom he worked for. In my sorrow, all I could think of was that Martin Luther King Jr., who practiced nonviolence, had been murdered, and that Fred Hampton, a gentle man whom I admired at least as much as I admired King, had been influenced by King's death to believe in the necessity of armed self-defense, and now he too lay dead.

It is common in our culture to have a double standard about casualties incurred in the struggle for justice. If they occur during a campaign in which "our side" employs some violence (anything from beating up "scabs" or attacking "pigs" to armed struggle) they are taken for granted as part of the price we must pay for engaging in the struggle. We may condemn our opponents *for their violence* (in itself a double standard) but rarely is it argued, except by the fainthearted whom no serious revolutionary wants to follow, that the casualties prove that violence does not work. But let a nonviolent movement suffer a death or two and immediately the cry goes up that nonviolence has failed and must be replaced by "stronger methods."

It is usually said at such times that the latest atrocity proves once again that those who hold power in the existing society will not relinquish their privileges without resorting to violence and that therefore those who want to change existing power relationships must also turn to violence. Although the first proposition is true—at least up to a point—the second proposition does not follow automatically from the first. The fact that those who cling to the status quo choose violence as the most effective method to defend it does not necessarily mean that those of us who want to change the status quo should choose violence as the most effective method to change it. After all, as Gandhi pointed out, why should we allow our opponents to decide not only which weapons they will use against us but also which weapons we will use against them.

When I say that the first proposition is true, but only up to a point, my purpose is to remind us that nothing in life is absolute, including the violence that can be utilized effectively by those who are seeking to maintain unjust privileges. A number of variable factors affect the extent, intensity and continuance—ultimately the success—of the violence they can rely on. These include defections and tactical splits (both existing and potential) in the ruling class. They include variations in the ability of the most calloused members of that class to command the obedience of those outside their class who must carry out the violence if it is to be extensive and prolonged enough to subdue an aroused and resolute populace. A third obvious variable is the attitude of normally nonpolitical people (the so-called silent majority) whose support or opposition, apathy or disgust, can become an important swing factor.

Only the most romantic revolutionaries, to whom explosive violence offers a temporary personal escape from the burdens of patience, discipline and the complexities of coalition building, will fail to weigh these factors before deciding to engage in violence.

On the other side, of course, only romantic pacifists will ignore these crucial determinants and indulge in symbolic acts of individualistic or small group nonviolence without attention to whether the political situation at the time calls for such acts or not. Both sets of romantics apparently prefer the satisfactions of dramatic personal acts (including for some, the ultimate satisfaction of martyrdom) to the turbulence, confusion and demanding relationships of disciplined mass actions.

I think back to the Chicago Democratic Convention in 1968 with thousands of aroused, basically nonviolent protestors in the parks and streets, only a tiny minority taunted the police or threw sticks, stones or bags of shit at them. This gave vent to their anger and temporarily relieved their feelings of political impotence. But it also clouded the issues and convinced an important section of the public, however erroneous, that the demonstrators were "no better than the police or Mayor Daley." On the other hand, a group of forty or fifty pacifists kept themselves aloof from the major actions, thereby separating themselves from the dynamic tactics of tens of thousands of fellow opponents of the war. They marched symbolically toward the convention amphitheater and passively submitted to arrest. Together these two groups helped produce a paradoxical and politically debilitating situation. At the very time when a majority of the country turned at last against the war and demanded that it be ended, a high percentage of them also turned against the anti-war movement.

Having said all this, I want to add a caution, in the interests of a necessary humility. Even the most experienced and astute tacticians cannot always accurately appraise in advance the effects of a symbolic act, whether violent (the assault on Batista's Moncada on July 26, 1953) or nonviolent (Rosa Parks' refusal to move to the back of a segregated bus in Montgomery, Alabama, on December 1, 1955). We should always make the effort to develop politically responsible collective processes and to make available within them a range of activities, including some that provide dramatic opportunities for those whose anger or impatience has reached the boiling point. And we should recognize that if there is an uncertainty principle in the science of physics, there is an unpredictability in the science of politics. That realization should temper our annoyance at those who seem to be "going it alone," apart from the dominant organizations or coalition of the time.

The question of whether we must resort to violence because they resort to violence requires far more careful analysis than is customary in a society that has stressed *macho* values and responses for so long that even opponents of the status quo have been poisoned—or at least intimidated—by them. The analysis needs to be based on a far wider range of data and information than normally comes to us through either the establishment media, the traditional left, or the simplistic homilies of utopian pacifists.

The distinction of the present book is that it supplies a wealth of just such information and analysis. It does so without succumbing to either of the illusions that commonly debilitate the unwary on either side of the debate about the merits of violent and nonviolent actions. It weighs the accomplishments and shortcomings of a number of key nonviolent movements of the last 40 years (including some little known successes of nonviolent resistance to the Nazis in occupied Norway) without suggesting, as some pacifists do, that all the changes our society needs can be accomplished without prolonged conflict and bloodshed. And it clearly rejects the notion of some advocates of armed struggle that nonviolent action is ineffective because, at one stage or another of the struggle, it cannot prevent bloodshed.

For example, we read that nonviolent forces in India suffered 1200 dead and 3600 wounded at Amritsar, in 1919, when British troops machine-gunned demonstrators protesting the imprisonment of Gandhi. But we read on to discover that the Indians continued their nonviolent actions, strengthened rather than demoralized by what happened at Amritsar. They continued in a protracted nonviolent struggle, through many victories and many defeats until independence had been won. So much, by the way, for another illusion about nonviolence; namely, that it worked against the English because they were so humane, but wouldn't work against less civilized races. And what about the racism of those who attribute the successes of Gandhian nonviolence to the humanity of the English rather than the courage and discipline of the Indians?

This is not a shallow book that indulges in one-sided propaganda in favor of anyone's favorite cause. It brings us much valuable data, insights and organizing hints from the Gandhian campaign. But David Toscano, who brings us much of that material in a chapter entitled "Gandhi's Decentralist Vision," does not hesitate to say not only that independence failed to result in economic justice but that it failed in part because of Gandhi's "overly idealistic belief in the inherent goodness of the owners of capital, an assumption . . . (which) contrasted sharply with the actual social and economic situation in India during his lifetime." This blindness on Gandhi's part led him to champion the idea of "trusteeship." In Gandhi's own unfortunate words, trusteeship meant that "the rich man will be left in the possession of his wealth, of which he will use what he reasonably requires for his personal needs and will act as trustee for the remainder to be used for the society."

Fortunately the editors and most of the authors in *Nonviolent Action and Social Change* harbor no such illusions about the existing economic system. Severyn Bruyn and Paula Rayman say at the very beginning that "the primary task of nonviolent action is to address the violence of the present system." Traditionally most advocates of nonviolent action give at least lip service to a similar concern for the violence of the system. But in practice, too often the active emphasis is on the violence of armaments and war and the violence by which society's victims try to liberate themselves by "whatever means (seem) necessary." But the concern in this book is far from perfunctory and illuminates areas that cannot be neglected if nonviolent action is to offer hope and a practical strategy for those who suffer poverty, exploitation and powerlessness.

Equally refreshing, the authors tackle questions concerning the violence of the system without thinking that it is limited to purely economic matters. They challenge the violence of sexism, of hierarchical command systems, of centralized decision-making (which is destructive even if the decision-makers are elected); of any patterns, customs and relationships that prevent people from achieving their maximum human potential. In applying these standards, a number of authors write brilliantly about the achievements of a Daniel Dolci (in Sicily), a Caesar Chavez (and the United Farmworkers) and other charismatic leaders but also take note of serious shortcomings in their work. They are not afraid to say that "Mohandas K. Gandhi and Cesar Chavez, for example, helped negotiate settlements between labor and management and thus maintained the disparity of power between these two industrial classes." They don't make this statement in a nit-picking way, to discredit heroes or indulge in a utopian stance but to show how complex and persistent violence is, how persistent and sophisticated participants in nonviolent action must become.

After the media's glamorization of that great, flawed man, Martin Luther King, to the neglect of the hundreds of dedicated, gifted organizers in the South and the unknown thousands of inspired participants without whom the mass actions could not possibly have taken place, I was grateful for a recurring theme in this book that the charisma of the unknown participants is at least as important as the charisma of the well known leaders—and far less dangerous. Severyn Bruyn writes of the importance of turning followers into co-leaders, a reversal of the process by which the media and a hierarchically oriented society rewrite history to make it appear as if the co-leaders were followers—and often succeed in influencing contemporary movements in this unhealthy direction.

Let us return for a moment to the question of the nonviolent resistance in Norway to the Nazis. Paul Wehr describes successes that should give pause to anyone who mechanically cites Nazism as the ultimate proof that nonviolent action cannot cope with the depths of depravity that tyrants are capable of. Of course a case can be made that the Nazis were the logical outgrowth of a world that was addicted to violence and eventually overdosed on it in Germany. And one can point out that when any addiction gets that bad, nothing can prevent immense suffering; in this case overthrowing the Nazis by a surfeit of violence did get rid of Hitler the man, his most notorious lieutenants (Goering, Goebels, et al) and the German Nazi Party. But in the course of helping rid the world of Hitler the United States developed the nuclear bomb, a weapon whose existence makes it unlikely that the human race would survive any future World War. In a sense this has become, in its turn, the ultimate argument why we must develop nonviolent action as an alternative to the military way of combatting tyranny.

In any case, unlike those who ignore the historical causes that produced Nazism, Wehr refuses to claim more for the successes of nonviolent action in Norway than is historically valid. He carefully points out the historical as well as spiritual reasons for its accomplishments, showing that in Norway victories were won that were impossible, at least in the short run, in Czechoslovakia when that country was invaded by troops from the Soviet Union and Warsaw Pact countries in 1968. He says that

> There were widely disparate international and geographical contexts in the two cases which determined that one would survive and the other crumble. The Norwegian movement had support from the Allies, the promise of eventual liberation, links by sea with friendly nations, and a long common border with Sweden, which provided comfortable exile. Czechoslovakia, by contrast, could expect nothing but moral support, and its geographical position, surrounded as it was on all sides by hostile governments save one, was hopeless.

Although Wehr points out that in one sense nonviolent resistance in Czechoslovakia was hopeless and therefore crumbles at least in the short run. Gene Sharp supplements Wehr's analysis by explaining that military resistance was *even more hopeless* and would have accomplished even less. Saying that "we learn from lost military wars and we can learn from lost nonviolent wars," he points out that

> The Russians anticipated military resistance from the able Czechoslovak army, and expected they could overcome it and install a puppet government within four days. . . . Instead an unprepared, improvised nonviolent resistance occurred which despite serious problems and apparent major strategic errors . . . managed initially to frustrate completely the Russian efforts to install a puppet government . . . and maintained the Dubcek regime, so hated by the Russians, in power (after forcing their release from arrest and imprisonment) until April of 1969—eight months!

Being an anthology, *Nonviolent Action and Social Change* is perforce uneven. If you are like me, you will find some chapters more rewarding than others. But on the whole, this is a revolutionary book of high quality. It focuses our attention on questions that we must deal with both scrupulously and imaginatively if we want the human race to survive. One must deal with these questions of conflict, if we want not only to survive but to achieve a society of liberation for which we strive even in the present violent state of affairs.

Dave Dellinger

INTRODUCTION

**Severyn T. Bruyn and
Paula Rayman**

*Over the expanse of five continents throughout the
coming years an endless struggle is going to be
pursued between violence and friendly persuasion,
a struggle in which, granted, the former has a
thousand times the chances of success than that of
the latter. But I have always held that, if he who
bases his hopes on human nature is a fool, he who
gives up in the face of circumstance is a coward.*

Albert Camus

We have never been in more of a need for understanding the
power of nonviolent action. Our world today exists under the
constant shadow of technology geared far more for destruction
than creation. We live our daily lives knowing that sophisticated
weaponry will not bring us closer to genuine security, knowing
that a single nuclear accident could lead to the deaths of family,
friends, communities and nations.

A few statistics provide evidence of the extent present governments rely upon the nuclear arsenal for "conflict resolution": the
atomic bomb that destroyed Hiroshima in 1945 had the explosive
power of 15,000 tons of TNT. Today, the U.S. arsenal includes
weapons that range from .5 kiloton to 25 megatons or 25,000,000
tons of TNT. In round figures the U.S. and Soviet Union together have 20,000 strategic nuclear bombs and warheads primed

1

for use against each other.[1] The recent descent of a nuclear-re-actor satellite to earth not only triggered fears of radioactivity but also raised the lid on the probability of similar incidents in the future.

In the thoughtful moments of our lives we realize the absurdity of producing these weapons to bring security, of waging war to insure peace, of promoting ourselves by reducing others' lives to daily death toll numbers. We have the knowledge that we are social beings and that when we resort to undermining another person's, another race's, another nation's humanity, we lose our own.

Yet, we live in a reality where conflict is an integral part of human experience—with social, economic and political dimensions. Conflict is an undeniable human force. It can either be a thruway to further human potential or result in a dead-end of dogmatism and destruction. Tied to the process of change, conflict can signify the variety of possibilities in human life and the struggle each unique individual faces in becoming socialized.

Humankind will continually face circumstances of conflict. The critical questions, therefore, confronting us are twofold: Does the result of a particular conflict affirm human goals and meet human needs? Is there a particular method of conflict that best serves these ends?

It is these questions that form the focus of this book as we explore nonviolent action. Joan Bondurant considers the question of conflict the gravest challenge confronting social and political theorists:[2]

> ... there is rapidly developing a demand hitherto neglected by social and political theory. This is the demand for solutions to the problem of conflict—not for theoretical systems of end-structure aimed at ultimately eliminating conflict, but for ways of conducting conflict when it arises: ways which are constructive and not destructive.

It is our hope as we take up this challenge, that a convincing argument is made for the study and practice of nonviolent action.

We begin with the assumption that nonviolence involves an active, not passive, posture, that it offers many strategies for dealing with conflict, and finally, that it is both practical and vision-ary—practical since it is a direct response to a given reality, visionary since its implementation sows seeds for a more liberating future.

In the remaining sections of the introduction we will look at definitions of violence and nonviolence, the principal conceptual themes which weave their way through the various chapters, and lastly, a brief discussion of the chapters themselves.

Definitions of Violence and Nonviolence

The concept of violence is understood in everyday life as the destructive use of physical force against property or people. It has also begun to mean the use of physical force to maintain systems of oppression and domination. The linguistic change in the term "violence" from its original reference to physical destruction to include now "systems of oppression" is a sign of the broadening consciousness of the social origins of physical conflict in the context of society.

In the first chapter by Severyn Bruyn, the distinction is noted between "physical violence" and "structural violence." Structural violence is located in the organization of society and leads toward physical violence. Structural violence is present when "human beings are being influenced so that their actual somatic and mental realizations are below their potential realizations." Utilizing Johan Galtung's definition, violence is "the cause of the difference between the potential and the actual." More specifically, "violence is that which increases the distance between the potential and the actual, and that which impedes the decrease of this distance."[3]

Our task, in this anthology, is to formulate some of the terms which define the direction of nonviolent action. A great deal of attention has been placed on separating those who emphasize ideal values from those who emphasize a pragmatic orientation. There is no doubt that many look at nonviolent action as an ethical way to live or reach humanitarian ends. It is also true that others concentrate on the methods of nonviolent action as the critical dimension. In the study of nonviolent action we prefer to think in terms of a dialectical perspective which keeps both principles in mind in research on the subject.

We assume that there are practical forms of social action which people can take to bring about change. Nonviolent action may, thus, be thought of in terms of strategy for change having various techniques—i.e., protest, noncooperation, intervention at its disposal. Political theorist Gene Sharp lists 198 different methods within the general category of nonviolent action:[4] He illustrates the method of boycott, for instance, with the example of how Czechs and Slovaks in 1968 ostracized Soviet soldiers in their resistance movement. As an example of protest, he notes how Vietnamese Buddhists in 1966 erected altars in the middle of streets although this was banned by the government. He also describes nonviolent intervention on the part of nations to protect their sovereignty.

Research on nonviolent action suggests a perspective of development which includes individual resources as well as the resources of a society as a whole. An order of freedom is created through social networks which reinforce the emergence of individual growth. Essential resources for "living the good life" are internalized so that the needs of the community and those of the individual are integrated. People join together to produce those resources necessary for well-being and security. Necessary resources found outside of a given society are made accessible through mutual patterns of interaction. The goals of nonviolent action have historically been concerned with the challenge for social justice and new forms of culture.

Principal Conceptual Themes

While the chapters of the anthology offer different levels of analysis and various viewpoints concerning nonviolent action, there are a number of themes that are consistently raised. The three key themes which link book's chapters are (1) affirmation of the individual, (2) building of community networks and (3) creation of a decentralized political economy. All of these have been part of important discussions in the fields of sociology, political theory, economics and philosophy. As they are often generally emphasized in the ethical framework and are often approached in the pragmatic analysis of nonviolent action, we feel they are critical to the study of the field.[5] The degree to which these themes are stressed by participants in nonviolent action generally represents the extent to which the action falls within an ethical framework which is described in the first chapter as the radical tradition.

Affirmation of the Individual

We live in an age where mass technology undermines the recognition of the value of each individual. The ultimate importance of every human life is an essential feature of nonviolent action. Nonviolent leaders including Gandhi, Martin Luther King Jr. and Dorothy Day have stressed the equal rights of all persons to affirm individual potentials.

Nonviolent action in the radical tradition moves against the sense of *anomie* and alienation so prevalent in modern times and embraces the worthiness of each human being. The focus on individual integrity encourages each person to "standup" for one believes. A central aspect of the power of nonviolent action is a willingness of individuals to hold unto the power of convictions. Commenting on Gandhi's term *satyagraha*—translated as "truth force"—Barbara Deming provides insight on the power of this approach:[6]

> . . . one has to cling with one's entire weight. One doesn't simply say, I have a right to sit here, but acts out that truth—and sits here . . . One brings what economic weight one has to bear, what political, social, psychological, what physical weight.

The affirmation of the individual has another component that is linked to the power of nonviolent action—the expectation that the nonviolent activist is not a coward but one who successfully confronts fears of death. Gandhi held that "Just as one must learn the art of killing in the training of violence, so one must learn the art of dying in the training for non-violence."[7] A great deal is, therefore, expected of the individual engaged in a nonviolent struggle—an insistence of acting out one's own will without injuring the opponent. This calls upon a level rationality and courage which is not necessary in violent action.[8]

The nonviolent activist strives for a rational analysis of the social reality and how social change can be best effected. Attention is directed to the institutions and systems which perpetuate the injustices of oppression, exploitation and de-humanization. An analysis of the institutional network of a given society is essential for a viable nonviolent movement. The energy of the nonviolent activist is channeled into deciding upon and utilizing the various methods of nonviolent action needed to press for change.

Building of Community

Nonviolent action rejects a wholly determinist outlook by focusing on the power of the individual to bring about change. At the same time it also avoids the problem of ethical relativism by setting up a way for objective consideration. The testing-out of individuality is done in the social milieu of the community. Just as society rests upon individual affirmation, the individual's well-being and growth depends upon the building of community. Nonviolent action recognizes and supports the fact that human beings are social-beings.

In the above section we discussed the importance of each person holding on to convictions. What happens then when convictions clash? What happens when your search for truth follows the sounds of a different drum than ours? It is at this crucial point that the relationship between the individual and the larger community becomes all important. It is here that the need for creative nonviolent action is most significant.

The answer to the second question is complex but it is buried in the work of such radical nonviolent activists as Mohandas K. Gandhi. Gandhi believed that no individual could ever know truth in the absolute sense. Therefore, individuals need to remain open to the possibilities of an alternative definition. Distancing themselves from dogmatism of any kind, individuals are open to each other's struggle.

When convictions do clash they are tested out in the context of community: "The search for truth cannot be prosecuted in a cave."[9] Each person can then experiment with various options and resolve choices within the community. Nonviolent action becomes the dynamic by which people maximize their separate life-experiences while simultaneously expressing human social ties. In a conflict situation nonviolent action in this Gandhian tradition supports the greatest degree of individual openness with the greatest degree of community solidarity.

The strain between the individual and demands of society has long been a focus of sociological, political and philosophical argument. Sociologists Durkheim, Weber and Mead have discussed the problems of alienation arising in contemporary society. The individual increasingly faces the dilemma of being lost in the crowd, cut off from traditional networks of security and paradoxically, experiences less freedom to act than before.

When nonviolent action provides for affirmation of the individual within community it is a force of integration. By encouraging community relations nonviolent action offers an alternative to the continuing fragmentation inherent in violent clashes. Paraphrasing the eloquent philosopher Martin Buber, nonviolent action encourages "I and Thou" relations—relationships of subjective encounters rather than objectified separations.[10]

It is clear that the building of community ties, community trust, community support systems, particularly in our age, is not an easy task. Many of the chapters in this book look at struggles to promote these ends—i.e., Abrams article on the United Farm Workers and Roodkowsky's on Feminism. However, the roots of nonviolent action are inherently linked to the development of community and the question of how nonviolent movements have encouraged this development leads us to the next theme of decentralization.

Decentralized Political Economy

Based upon studies of nonviolent action, including those in this anthology, decentralization of our political economy appears as a constructive pattern of social organization. Decentralization offers a promise for creating new designs of individual-community synthesis.

In the industrially developed nation, decisions concerning all critical dimensions of daily life are made within a highly centralized bureaucratic order. Communities lose their ability to organize around human needs and instead become filters for decisions made "from above." Individuals in turn, are divorced from the decision-making processes and feel impotent to confront the bureaucratic complexity. In pressing for a reshaping of the social order along decentralized lines, nonviolent action can institute the revitalization of the community and re-emergence of the individual.

Pressing for such a reshaping, social analysis of nonviolent change challenges three salient myths of our present society: the myth that power emanates from the top, the myth that violence is only committed by those outside the established order and, the myth that there are unlimited natural resources for humankind to manipulate.

First, nonviolent action rests on the definition that power is the capacity to effect social change and development. Power is potentially in the hands of the people: individuals, separately and collectively have the final authority to retain or entrust power. Power is, therefore, not like a cake which a centralized leadership can slice up and dish out at its discretion. Any person can chose to relinquish or hold back his/her individual power; people can effectively join together to regain power which those at the top have improperly used against them. Radical nonviolent activists perceive power as flowing from people as individuals to their leadership rather than visa versa.

Second, the principal participants in violence are not those classified as rebels. The basic fact, in A. J. Mustes's words is, "that the economic social and political order in which we live was built up largely by violence, is now being extended by violence and is maintained only by violence."[11] People have permitted the centralized institutions of the state to perpetuate violence in the "legitimized" battlefields of World War I, the extermination camps of World War II, and the tiger cages of the Indochina War. On a more daily basis, states legitimize the continuation of racism, sexism, and growing worldwide hunger. The primary task of nonviolent action is to address the violence of the present system. Working to build a decentralized order offers a progressive response.

Third, the prevailing system utilizes natural resources as if they were income rather than an irreplaceable capital. For example, the people of the United States today constitute about 6 percent of the world's population but consume 40 percent of its resources. Consumption is considered the chief purpose of all economic activity and the U.S.A. "standard of living" is measured by the amount of national annual consumption. However, since the resources we are using are finite, and other peoples are justly demanding their rightful share of what is available, the existing system leads to a dead end.

Economists who have studied the field of nonviolent action are concerned with the quality and measured use of goods for consumption and how societal resources can be used to attain maximum well-being.[12]

> As physical resources are everywhere limited, people satisfying their needs by means of a modest use of resources are obviously less likely to be at each other's throats than people depending upon a high rate of use. Equally, people who live in highly self-sufficient local communities are less likely to get involved in large-scale violence than people whose existence depends upon world-wide systems of trade.

Viewing consumption as a means to a liberating end is a new way of thinking for most of us and presents a clear challenge for nonviolent activists. A nonviolent movement needs to create alternative forms of technology in the context of cross-cultural contacts. Further research is necessary for formulation of a political economy which reduces the narrow tendencies of provincialism without destroying autonomy. We need to explore how to establish decentralized forms of decision-making which allow individuals to experience a greater sense of participation in the events which shape their lives. Decentralization and nonviolent action, therefore, are tightly interrelated.

Contributions of the Chapters

The chapters which follow express an orientation to social studies of nonviolent action which expands our understanding of its role in the world today. One or more of the primary three themes—affirmation of the individual, community building, and decentralization—is discussed in each chapter. The chapters focus on the themes from three dimensions: Part One presents theoretical and research models; Part Two covers social change movements first in the United States and second, from an international perspective; Part III, the final section, integrates the major themes as it emphasizes prospects for a future nonviolent society.

Each section will hopefully stimulate further questioning and practice of nonviolent action. Together, the chapters remind us of its continuing and important history, not only on the international scene, but within our own society. People have too often swiftly dismissed the potential of nonviolent action in conflict situations while allowing violence to continue. Since the study of human experience demonstrates the many failures of violence to solve societal problems, the time for the study of creative alternatives has arrived.

Notes

1. *WIN MAGAZINE*, January 29th, 1976, page 9.
2. Joan Bondurant, *Conquest of Violence: the Gandhian Philosophy of Conflict*, University of California Press, 1971, p. XIII.
3. John Galtung, "Violence, Peace and Peace Research," *Journal of Peace Research*, 1968, pp. 5—6.
4. Gene Sharp, *The Politics of Nonviolent Action, Part II*. Peter Sargent, 1973.
5. For example Sharp discusses the concept of decentralization in his chapter on redistribution of power; Ibid, Part III.
6. Barbara Deming, "Revolution and Equilibrium." *Liberation*, February 1968.
7. Bondurant, op. cit., p. 29.
8. For a fuller discussion of the interplay between the thinking of Franz Fanon and nonviolent action see Deming, op. cit.
9. Gandhi as quoted in Bondurant, op. cit., p. 22.
10. Martin Buber, *I and Thou*, New York. Charles Scribner, 1970.
11. Nat Hentoff, editor, *The Essays of A. J. Muste*, New York: Simon and Schuster, 1967, p. 180.
12. E. F. Schumacher, *Small is Beautiful: Economics as if People Mattered*, New York: Harper and Row, 1973, p. 55.

Part I.

A Social Science Framework

Nonviolent theory and action are closely interwoven as we will see in the following chapters. In Chapter One, Severyn T. Bruyn traces the variety of ways in which nonviolent action can be interpreted in sociological theory and, conversely, how theory can illuminate nonviolent action as creative conflict in society. In Chapter Two, George Lakey reviews the social mechanisms by which nonviolent action can be expressed in actual cases. David Toscano then demonstrates in Chapter Three how a sociological theory of nonviolent action is drawn partly from the actionists themselves like Mohandas K. Gandhi.

The basic principle of theory-building in this section is drawn from classic European thought applied to modern social research. The work of the great German sociologist, Max Weber, for example, emphasized the subjective life of people to be of vital importance to the formulation of hypotheses and generalizations. Nonviolent action thus becomes the basis for generalizing and conducting research on the social process, the social structure, and the typological development of society.

Part I

A Social Science Framework

Chapter 1

Social Theory of Nonviolent Action: A Framework for Research in Creative Conflict

Severyn T. Bruyn

Social theory is an important part of the critical study and practice of nonviolent action. It offers guidelines for interpreting the nature of nonviolent action in society; it supplies a foundation for analyzing the successes and failures of nonviolent action; it serves as the basis for appraising nonviolent social movements that have changed the course of history. In fact, as we shall see, social theory can even serve as a guideline for practicing nonviolence in everyday life.

At first nonviolent action is a personal experience and participants can have different interpretations of what it means to them. These interpretations are all important to any understanding of the subject, and are indeed essential for building a comprehensive theoretical framework of the subject. Together they help us define the general nature of nonviolent action and provide a basis for testing its veracity. Its veracity is determined in part by the people who engage in it; they define its terms in practice and discover its meaning in their own experience.[1]

At the same time, nonviolent action is a social process that can be studied by historians, psychologists, economists, and sociologists. Its veracity in this case can be tested by outside observers who compare different cases and study the process of action with its political consequences in society. The picture that is given to us by insiders is then complemented by outsiders who have another perspective on the subject.

The quest for the truth about nonviolent action in the final analysis involves the method and philosophy of participant observation. We need to understand both the subjective and the objective dimensions of this type of social action through our own experience. We must evaluate its history against our experience with the facts, judge their inconsistencies, and eventually bring them together into an integral perspective. This task may seem complicated but its importance becomes quite evident as we proceed. The truth is only approximated in research and practice. Nonviolent action is understood only gradually through both the intuitive experience of participants and through systematic observations and statistical studies of the action process.

Mohandas K. Gandhi saw nonviolent action as both a subjective and an objective process which involved fact-finding, negotiations, meditations, attempts to persuade and dissuade opponents, critical self-examination, education, and finally, barring no success in these efforts, intensive direct action involving such techniques as civil disobedience.[2] The process of nonviolent action for Gandhi was essentially a quest for truth. He did not separate scientific inquiry from nonviolent action but rather included it as an integral part of the process.

The first academic treatment of nonviolent action was in 1923, by the sociologist Clarence Case. His book, *Nonviolent Coercion*, was used extensively by Gandhi. Dr. Edward Ross found the book in Gandhi's library marked with personal notations. In fact, Ross concluded that it was among the most used books in his (Gandhi's) library.[3] A scientific orientation was important to Gandhi as was a religious orientation. He was interested in that spirit of inquiry that could be tested in action. Any enterprise that could enhance life and develop human resources was of vital interest to him. Now, many decades later, we continue the inquiry with contemporary perspectives of social theory and research.

Perspectives

We begin with the notion that nonviolent action is creative conflict which can be studied from a pragmatic and radical perspective. The pragmatic perspective generally focuses on the use of such techniques of action as intervention, noncooperation, and protest.

The pragmatic applications of action are not seen so much in the beliefs and values of the participants as in the successful utilization of techniques which match forces with the opposition. Gene Sharp has examined the pragmatic dimension in great detail in his classic work on *The Politics of Nonviolent Action*.[4]

The radical perspective in nonviolent action, on the other hand, focuses on the capacity to treat the causes of violence and offer a direction to human development. Our task in this theoretical section is to look more carefully at this radical perspective and its implicit theory of social change in society.

The study of nonviolent action from this perspective draws its theory from the activities of many people who claim that their work is based on the principles of nonviolence. We are interested in the social nature of this type of action and seek to clarify its direction in society.

The most notable people who have been engaged in radical, nonviolent action have been Mohandas K. Gandhi in India and Martin Luther King in the United States. But others have also been very active including Danilo Dolci in Sicily, Lanzo del Vasto in France, Thich Nhat Hanh and Cao Ngoc Phong in Vietnam, Dom Helder Camara in Brazil, Betty Williams, Mairead Corrigan, and Ciaran McKeown in Northern Ireland, Cesar Chavez and Dolores Huerta in the United States, Vinoba Bhave in India, Kagawa in Japan, and others around the world. We believe these movements are a 20th century development of major social significance.

This type of study is related to the study of techniques on nonviolent action in the pragmatic tradition but does not focus its attention there. It considers such techniques as strikes, boycotts, embargoes, lockouts, mutinies, sitdowns as important in relation to the idea of nonviolence. However, we are interested especially in the character of "principled" nonviolent action so that we can clarify its problems as well as the values contained in this tradition.

We hope to initiate a provisional framework for social-scientific studies by interpreting nonviolent action as creative conflict in society. Our interpretations should not be considered definitive since they are only intended to set guidelines for research and offer a basis for theoretical discussion on this very complex subject.

The Concept of Conflict: The Way It Is Usually Defined

The definition of "conflict" varies among writers in the field as well as in its everyday usage. The Webster dictionary defines its common usage as "strife for mastery," "a struggle," "a clash of opinions," and "a collision." Professional researchers have sought to define it further. Kenneth Boulding, an economist, states that "conflict is a goal-directed activity designed to improve the position of one party at the expense of the other."[5] Morton Deutsch, a social psychologist, states that "a conflict exists whenever incompatible activities occur," and that "an action which is incompatible with another action prevents, obstructs, interferes with, injures, or in some way makes it less likely or less effective."[6] Lewis Coser, a sociologist, defines conflict as "a struggle over values, and claims to scarce status, power and resources, in which the aims of the opponents are to neutralize, injure, or eliminate their rivals."[7]

The cases of conflict involving nonviolent action in the radical tradition, however, do not conform to these concepts of conflict. The differences begin with the motive or intent of nonviolent actionists.

The Meaning of Nonviolence: Ground for Creative Conflict

It was not the intent of such leaders as Mohandas K. Gandhi or Martin Luther King to defeat their opponents or to conquer them at their expense. Rather it was to seek the truth underlying the conflict, and if possible, to win the understanding and friendship of their opponents. Their ultimate aim was to help develop a new order of social institutions. Gandhi and King sought the kind of social order in which power could be shared and human resources could be developed in society.

Gandhi spoke repeatedly of "ahimsa" which meant the refusal to do harm to any living creatures. He emphasized its active side in the quality of love that would do good to the evil-doer. Nonviolence involved conscious suffering in the process of social intervention or noncooperation. (It did not involve "passive resistance" which implied a lack of a capacity to employ violence and tended to be a preliminary step to violence). It involved a firm grasping of the truth and an active feeling of respect for the opponent. The purpose was to become free of fear, resentment, and revenge. The final test of this feeling of regard for the opponent was in what Gandhi called "tapsya," or self-suffering.[8]

This type of intent and motive of course challenges the traditional definition of conflict that has been based on the notion of a struggle among parties to overcome each other. It also changes the conditions thought to underlie the opposition. It requires us therefore to re-examine our traditional theory of conflict to build a framework for studying nonviolent action.

Martin Luther King also acted on grounds that do not conform to the traditional meaning of conflict. The basic aspects of nonviolence for him were consistent with the radical thought and practice of Gandhi. In defining the terms of nonviolence, King states first that nonviolence is "active," not passive, it is not for cowards. Second, nonviolence "does not seek to defeat or humiliate the opponent but to win his friendship and understanding." Third, "the attack is directed against the forces of evil rather than against persons who happen to be doing the evil." Fourth, it accepts suffering without retaliation believing that "unearned suffering is redemptive" and has "tremendous educational and transforming possibilities." Fifth, nonviolence "avoids not only external physical violence but also internal violence of spirit. The nonviolent resister not only refuses to shoot his opponent but he also refuses to hate him." The essence of nonviolence, King continues, can be best defined by the Greek term *agape*, a disinterested love, which seeks "to preserve and create community. . . . It is a willingness to forgive, not seven times, but seventy times seven to restore community." Sixth, nonviolent action "is based on the conviction that the universe is on the side of justice. Consequently, the believer has a deep faith in the future."[9]

On the basis of the traditional theory of conflict, it would seem that such major figures as Gandhi and King were never in conflict. Their basic aims were not to injure, eliminate, or even simply to neutralize their "rivals" but rather to gain their friendship. Their aims implied a desire to cultivate human resources and to develop new forms of social governance.

Yet we know that conflict did exist in the course of action of these leaders. When Gandhi walked with untouchables down a road that was forbidden to them, they were attacked by orthodox Hindus and then given prison sentences. It was only after a lengthy period of creative resistance that the orthodox Hindus were finally persuaded to let the untouchables walk down the road past their sacred temple. Similarly, Martin Luther King was sent to jail for participating in illegal marches and it was only after lengthy negotiations and in some cases a change of heart that white establishments opened their doors to blacks.

The differences between this form of conflict and the standard forms include:

1. The refusal of the nonviolent actionists to retaliate against their opponents with physical violence.

2. Their intent not to dominate their opponents.

3. Their effort to act on the causes of the violence.

To act on the causes of violence is no easy matter. It requires starting with old patterns of domination and building a new social order based on mutual exchange and decision making. It also involves some measure of social transformation. A new set of attitudes must be developed and new social structures created to contain and express those attitudes. It is a subjective change on the one hand, involving a transmutation of old energies based on hate, indifference, and prejudice into new energies based on a sense of community. It is an objective change, on the other hand, involving the destruction of an old command system and the construction of a new organization based upon a greater degree of mutual exchange and democratic decision making. Nonviolent action in this tradition involves establishing a new order of social relations. Nonviolent action in this sense is creative conflict. It is the reformation of reality—subjective and objective—releasing new human resources for social development.

We will discuss the theory behind all this later but it is clear that the meaning of conflict in such cases must be seen in a broader context of human values than social scientists had originally defined it. Conflict refers to a contest of opposing forces most visible in the incompatible activities that occur in the same place at the same time. But the incompatibility does not define the motive or intent of the participants nor does it tell us anything about the processes of social interaction. The truth-seeking quest of Mohandas Gandhi and the disinterested love of Martin Luther King may exist in the midst of the opposition to help change the condition and the definition of conflict.

The extraordinary powers of charismatic figures are helpful to understand how major conflicts are resolved but that is not the key point here. The point is rather to stress the importance of subjective factors in defining the character of conflict. All conflict is defined in subjective terms as well as objective terms. The subjects of the action are often more important than most scientists realize and this requires special attention of social researchers in the study of creative conflict.

Morton Deutsch stresses the importance of the subjective factors when he talks about the conflict between himself and his wife over the closet space in their bedroom. It appears to him at first that "the more closet space that my wife uses for her clothing, the less space there is for my files." It was a simple case of a conflict over scarce resources. It appeared to be determined by objective conditions, that is, a conflict that was unresolvable without one party winning over the other one. Nevertheless, the resolution turned out to be contingent upon subjective factors including the discovery that "her clothes and my files can both fit if I remove some shelves from the closet that are rarely used."

Deutsch notes further that "even the classical example of pure conflict—two starving men on a lifeboat with only enough food for the survival of one—loses its purity if one or both of the men have social or religious values which can become more dominant psychologically than the hunger need or the desire for survival."[10]

The Concept of Power: The Way It Is Usually Defined

The concept of power has also been defined by social scientists without taking account of the character of nonviolent action in the radical tradition. Robert Dahl, a political scientist, defines power very much in the intellectual framework of Max Weber who saw it as a contest of "wills" between people. Dahl says, "A has power over B to the extent that he can get B to do something B would not otherwise do."[11] Richard Emerson, a sociologist, suggests that all people are interdependent and that power resides "implicitly in the other's dependency."[12] Gene Sharp defines power in *The Politics of Nonviolent Action* as "the capacity to control the behavior of others, directly or indirectly, through action by groups of people, which action impinges on other groups of people."

Each of these definitions suggests a tendency to associate power with forms of social control or domination over others. This is understandable in the sense that all societies have shown patterns of domination. However, the cases of radical-nonviolent action point to another basis for understanding the nature of power.

Gene Sharp gives us some insight into this problem by describing two opposing views on the origins of power. One view holds that power emanates from the government and people are dependent upon the good will of their government leaders; the other view holds that power emanates from the people and the government is dependent upon them. Here Sharp begins to distinguish power as a latent force that can be exercised under special conditions from either the top or the bottom of the society. Force becomes manifest, in part, through the patterns of authority that are defined to be legitimate in society.

Sharp continues to describe the sources of power in the types of authority (right to command), human resources, skills, knowledge, material resources, sanctions (such as fines or imprisonment) and intangible factors such as habits and attitudes of submission. Implicit in his analysis is the notion that the development of new patterns of authority, knowledge, skills, attitudes, and the like will prove to be the basis for changing the forms of domination and exploitation in society. However, the direction of that development is never fully explored because the focus of his study is on cases of nonviolent action interpreted within the pragmatic tradition.

The Purpose of Radical-Nonviolent Action: Creative Power

If we focus on cases of nonviolent action in the radical tradition, we see these definitions of power challenged and at the same time we see a direction for nonviolent development. The aims of such leaders as Gandhi and King were not to "control the behavior of others" or to "exercise power over them" or even "to make them dependent" in some manner. Indeed, their objective was virtually the opposite of what is implied in these definitions. Their object was to create the conditions that would liberate and free people to exercise their own independent will and judgment. The aim was to end the systems of domination and release the deeper energies of self-governance.

The capacity to help people take steps toward self-governance and their own independent authority becomes the measure of power in this radical tradition. The exercise of power in nonviolent action is not measured by an increase in the authority over people but rather by an increase in the level of independent authority of everyone. The aim is not to maximize the power and authority of oneself over others but rather to create the conditions whereby power can be shared. *The purpose is to create the conditions in which each individual's opportunity to exercise power is maximized in the context of the larger community.*

This review of purposes in radical-nonviolent action leads us toward a theory of social change based on two key principles: self-governance and social development. These principles can be found embedded in the philosophy and practices of nonviolent action taken by leaders in different parts of the world.

Social Theory of Nonviolent Action

In the course of nonviolent action in India, for example, Gandhi appropriated key words in the culture and coined other words to describe the purposes of his work. One of those words was *swaraj* or self-rule. The concept of self-rule was applied to all levels of social and political life in India. Gandhi emphasized self-rule for the individual as well as for the community and the nation as a whole. Swaraj became the guiding principle in the independence movement. It was a long struggle toward political self-rule but it was finally achieved through the power of nonviolent action.

This major principle of self-rule in Gandhi's campaigns is equally important in other nonviolent action movements elsewhere in the world. Self-rule or self-governance refers to the ability of people to manage their own affairs at all levels of institutional life in society. The major purposes of nonviolent action according to this principle is to increase the capacity of people to govern themselves effectively and properly within the social, political, economic, religious, and educational institutions of the community.

To achieve self-governance requires a theory and practice of social development. Social development, in turn, involves a very complex dialectical process of change. It calls, at best, for a decentralization of authority from the top of an organization and a taking of power from below at the same time. It requires a decentralization of rights and privileges and a cultivation of social responsibility among all the parties that permits the change to take place successfully.

Emile Durkheim saw the dilemma clearly at the turn of the 20th century. The major problem of modern society lay in decentralizing and multiplying the "centers of communal life without weakening national unity." It was not a simple process.

> The only really useful decentralization is one which would simultaneously produce a greater concentration of social energies. Without loosening the bonds uniting each part of society with the State, moral powers must be created with an influence, which the State cannot have, over the multitude of individuals. Today neither the commune, the department nor the province has enough ascendency over us to exert this influence; we see in them only conventional labels without meaning.[13]

Mohandas K. Gandhi saw the same complicated process in decentralizing authority within the British empire by taking power through methods of massive noncooperation. The quest for self-rule in India involved a widespread withdrawal of support for the colonial powers. The process was so threatening to the unity of the nation that it was labeled "seditious" by the British because it seriously threatened the stability of the nation. Gandhi acted independent of the theoretical work of Durkheim but said the same thing in the field of action: Indian withdrawal and decentralization of authority should be in proportion to "their ability to preserve order in the social structure.[14] The degree of withdrawal of all assistance to an outside government was to be measured by the degree of internal government that was being established to create a new social order. Otherwise the result would be chaos and most probably a new dictatorship.

The establishment of a new order of self-government required not only the decentralization of power but at the same time the constant cultivation of human resources. In general, this means the development of personal and social responsibility, sensitivity, confidence, trust, knowledge, and skills so the people can manage the new political order. The cultivation of these human resources then becomes our subject of study as nonviolent action seeks to increase the levels of self-governance within individuals who can co-manage the key institutions and organizations of society.

The key institutions involved those of the state (e.g., political parties and governments), economy (e.g., enterprises and unions), religion (e.g., churches, and temples), education (e.g., schools and universities). The organizations of each key institution function today with a contradiction. They each function in part to help liberate people and to cultivate human resources. Yet, they also function to dominate and exploit people. It is in these tendencies toward domination and exploitation that the seeds of rebellion are born and the cause for nonviolent action is found.

The Direction of Development: Decentralization and Emergence

Decentralizing authority from above and assuming new authority from below at the same time is a very complicated process. It generally requires thoughtful planning and training in new skills. Such changes may be approached wisely by some leaders in nonviolent movements and unwisely by others. It requires considerable study to determine the manner in which it can be done effectively and in a lasting manner.

In some cases, a charismatic leader in a nonviolent movement can be a hindrance to the decentralization of authority and the cultivation of self-governance. The adoration and even idolatry that may surround great leaders can drain away the inner power and self-governance of their followers. Indeed, when the great leader fails to measure up to standards or is defeated in battle, the ground may exist for mass disenchantment and hostility. Gandhi saw this early in the nonviolent movement when he found himself to be the object of growing adulation among the multitudes.[15]

A major concern of Gandhi was not only to find the way to decentralize authority within national institutions but to "de-charismatize" his effect on people. He sought to cultivate the charisma or grace of authority and self-rule among his own followers even though he was not always successful. Max Weber, the sociologist, would have said that his problem was to "routinize the charisma" that was developing in the leader-follower pattern created by the Indian movement for independence. The cultivation of human resources among "followers"—so that they become co-leaders in a nonviolent movement—becomes as important as cultivating resources among the underclass within the hierarchical organizations of the society.

With this in mind we want now to look at the problem of overcoming dominance in the social structure of modern society. It is the larger expression of the problem of overcoming dominance in the structure of the nonviolent movement itself.

The Study of Radical Social Development

Social development refers to the amplification of human resources so that people are able to become more self-governing. By human resources we mean authority, imagination, responsibility, leadership, sensitivity, and the structures that support society without state regulation. An increase in the level of self-governance at any level of association implies an increase in the resourcefulness and the responsibility of people in that association. It implies a new measure of self-reliance, self-control, and social accountability.

Social development in the radical tradition is a special case because it is a broadening of human resources that leads toward the social transformation of institutional life. Social transformation means ultimately the fundamental alteration of reality as it is defined in the daily life of people. Radical development changes the way we see the world and the way people organize in society. Accepting the principles of nonviolence requires an outlook that leads to fundamental changes within the individual and the society at the same time.

The principles of nonviolence challenged the whole life-being of people like Gandhi, King, Dolci, Camara, Kagawa, and others. It meant finding the courage to face one's own death in social action and a deep faith in the eventual working-out of basic changes within the society.

The radical ideals maintained by these leaders by no means suggest that they succeeded in attaining them, or that they are paragons of virtue themselves or that they follow all the principles they propose all the time. Martin Luther King was criticized constantly for his strategies of social action. His major strategy, for example, was to concentrate on self-governance in the political order rather than self-governance in the economic order, and only late in his life did he begin to see the importance of the business system as a target for change through nonviolent action. Gandhi was constantly under criticism for failing to measure up to his beliefs and was constantly admitting his failures. Nonviolent actionists today are under similar pressures from critics.

A tension exists between radical leaders who have different outlooks on strategies and goals appropriate to a political order. Different types of social consciousness and degrees of radicalism pervade these movements giving cause for the development of critical theory that can help leaders think about their direction and priorities for action.

The Sociology of Self-Governance

Society is a web of relatively self-governing associations that coexist on different planes with some measure of consensus. Each association is highly interdependent with other associations for its degree of self-governance in the society. Metropolitan or local associations like the church, Chamber of Commerce, YMCA, Art Club or Communist Party, are interdependent with their larger regional and national federations. Each federation differs in the degree of self-governance that is permitted for its units at the local level. The same is true of the political order in both capitalist and socialist nations. Towns are interdependent with states; states are interdependent within their nation. Each larger affiliate permits, restricts, limits, or encourages self-governance for its unit-associations according to political and legal policies.

The key fact about this for our purpose is that individuals are finally members of these various associations and are dependent upon them for their own level of self-governance. The authority of an individual as a supervisor in a local factory, a parishioner in a local church, a member of a political party (Republican or Communist), a citizen in a local village, is dependent upon the relationship these local associations have to their national affiliates. The degrees of self-governing power of a person working in a factory, worshiping in a church, speaking in a political party, and living in a village, will depend upon the vertical structure of authority of these local associations. The authority and self-governing power of the individual is largely defined in these institutions. The authority of the individual is dependent in large part upon the connection of one's self to the institutional roles taken within the community.

This social fact is important to follow because it gives direction and meaning to research in the radical tradition. Radical action aims to increase the level of self-governance of individuals in the context of their society. This means that actionists must take serious account of how individuals are connected to associations and how those associations augment or lessen their level of self-governance as "worker," "worshiper," "politician," and "citizen." A major task of research then is to identify the factors that contribute to increasing the self-governance of local associations.

Our theory is that an increase in the level of self-governance of a local association in the context of its national association should then increase the level of self-governing power of individual members. We see the "self" as determined partly by the complex institutional roles taken in associational life. Our self-identity is closely connected with being a "worker," "politician," "citizen," and so on. An increase in initiative, freedom of conduct, responsibility, authority, and power in these various roles should feed back to expand the self and its capacity to be whole and self-governing in society.

This is a complex proposition. Its resolution is dependent upon overcoming many variables including organizational structure, social norms, communication systems, political economy, among others. Our purpose here is to begin identifying some of the important variables. In the radical tradition, these variables are defined broadly in what has been called "structural violence."

Structural Violence

Johan Galtung distinguishes "physical" violence from "structural" violence in a manner that is important to a theory of social development. The concept of violence is normally understood as the destructive use of physical force against people. Galtung suggests, however, that a "structural violence" is located in the organization of society. He argues that the organization of society can help cause physical violence.

Structural violence is present when "human beings are being influenced so that their actual somatic and mental realizations are below their potential realizations." For Galtung, violence is "the cause of the difference between the potential and the actual." More specifically, "violence is that which increases the distance between the potential and the actual, and that which impedes the decrease of this distance."[16] Galtung is saying, in effect, that structural violence is any organized impediment to human development.

Johan Galtung and others have diagnosed the problem in general terms and it is now time to become more definitive about the solution. We need to think more about how to increase the "human potential" in the context of society. We need to formulate a theory of social development that offers guidelines to nonviolent action.

We start with the idea that Galtung's structural violence begins with structural dominance within major institutions.[17] We define dominance existing when one group of people maintains the right to control the behavior of others without seriously attempting to create the conditions that cultivate or encourage self-governance.

Modern institutions express structural violence, for example, when democratic forms are lacking in an organization (e.g., business conglomerate or state socialist corporation) or when an organization becomes so large (e.g., a nation-state) that democratic forms become meaningless in the face of a huge command bureaucracy with no conscious attempt to decentralize power and authority.

This condition of course does not become a social problem until people see it to be so. A large, bureaucratic state can be remote from its citizenry and even far removed from direct control by its elected representatives and it may all be accepted until its power and administrative sprawl becomes clearly oppressive to people. At the point where people become conscious of the dominance, it is essential to have the alternative at hand. Social research on institutional behavior thus becomes critical in providing the essential information for developing specific alternatives.[18]

The general alternative in this case involves the decentralization of authority from the top and the taking of power from below through the cultivation of human resources. This alternative to dominance then becomes a major theme for social theory, research, and nonviolent action.

Structural Dominance in Modern Institutions

Structural dominance can be seen in all modern institutions including both state capitalist and socialist nations. It can be seen in the business economy when large corporations are permitted to lay off workers en masse while they still have capital reserves or are still making profits. Structural dominance can be seen in big unions when oligarchies can repress the free speech of local members and when top union leaders can exploit union pension funds for their own use. It is visible in the capitalist or socialist-based church that can suppress the right of women and minorities to become ministers and priests. It is seen in the capitalist or socialist-based university that can suppress radical courses or bar minorities from faculty positions. It is seen in the state whose agencies can censure, prosecute, and even secretly kill dissident citizens in the face of civil rights that are written into a constitution.

The institutional patterns of subordination that exist in all modern societies are now being questioned with good reason. It is not simply the broad class subordination of laborers versus capitalists in the business system that become important forms of dominance. There are parallels in all institutions: the church (clergy/laity); the corporation (manager/worker); the school (teacher/student); medicine (doctor/patient); law (lawyer/client); the professions (therapist/client); and the family (parent/child). This institutionalized form of class-status control is beginning to show clear patterns of dominance that are becoming the basis for creative conflict in both capitalist and socialist societies.

There are complicated questions about social structure that need to be answered in social research. We need to look at how nonviolent action functions—or does not function—as a social process to decentralize power and cultivate human resources among the subordinate class. We are especially interested in how ordinary people act to increase their level of self-governance over the structures of dominance in these modern institutions.

Sociology of Creative Conflict

We look now at conventional areas of social theory and indicate how they apply to the study of nonviolent action conceived as creative conflict. We are especially interested in the principles of self-governance and social development interpreted in the radical tradition. They help us define the research problems ahead and suggest propositions that must be tested in action.

Nonviolent action becomes an expression of social action in many ways but here we can deal only with certain sociological dimensions: social movements, normative life, systems of com-

munication, symbolic interaction, formal organization, and political community. These are diverse areas around which sociological
thought has been developing and against which nonviolent action
can be tested. The first four areas of theory (social movements,
normative life, communications, and symbolic interaction) fall
roughly into problems of *social process* while the second two areas
(formal organization and political community) fall into problems
of *social structure*. In each case we will pose some basic propositions
about nonviolent action as creative conflict. Our purpose is to
clarify how nonviolent action functions as a social phenomenon.
At the same time we want to see how radical nonviolent action
challenges the traditional premises underlying social theory today.

Social Process

Leaders of movements based on nonviolent action in the radical
tradition stress that the process or the "means" are as important
to study as the "ends." The ends and means have always been
considered equally fundamental since they are so closely interdependent in determining the outcome of any action. However,
the social process that accompanies any major transformations in
the institutional life of society has always been disputed by radical
theorists.

The theory that violence must always accompany changes in
major institutions of society is still contended in the literature and
becomes a part of our concern here. For example, the 19th century theory of class warfare took the form of a believable myth
even though its principal contender, Karl Marx, cautioned followers to constantly review the course of history to assess theory
against social reality. The reality today does not remove the possibilities of class warfare or the likelihood of violence but it does
offer a new basis by which to examine history and the basis for
making of major transformations in society.

Gene Sharp has begun the refutation of the myth of violence
with the help of his impressive collection of cases of nonviolent
action down through history. The record demonstrates how major changes in the social structure of society have been accomplished through social movements based on nonviolent action in
the pragmatic tradition. The question of whether violence is es-

sential to revolutionary change in society is still open to investigation. The meaning of "revolution" and the level of human resources available to initiate basic changes become the critical elements of research.[19]

The power of collective-nonviolent action to act upon the most fundamental problems of a society has yet to be fully studied in history and social research. For example, there is good reason to propose that there was a greater reduction in the institutional patterns of prejudice and discrimination in the United States following the nonviolent movement of the Southern Christian Leadership Conference and other like-minded organizations than had occurred as a result of the whole tragic and bloody civil war.

The radical-nonviolent movement tends toward what Andre Gorz has called "revolutionary reform," that is, reform which represents significant advances toward the basic transformation of society. Actionists do not always achieve this ideal in their work but their efforts and writings point clearly in this direction of social change.

The radical goals of nonviolent actions are aimed generally at transforming structures of dominance and it is becoming increasingly clear that a major target area is the political economy. Major changes made in the structures of the political economy are critical to making changes in the rest of the society. Changes in the structure of business and the corporate command systems of both capitalist and socialist countries are crucial to making changes in other institutions such as the government, political parties, churches, schools, trade unions, and other voluntary associations. At the same time they are perhaps the most difficult structures to change in society.

An example of a significant step toward revolutionary reform in the structure of American business would be nonviolent action that led to the federal chartering of all large corporations so that they function legally in the public interest. Federal chartering in this case would also encourage corporate decentralization and employee self-management. A major legal change in corporate charters by itself, however, is not sufficient to constitute revolutionary reform; basic changes are also needed in the attitudes of employees who are accustomed to work for profits and wages in their own self-interest. The enlargement of a social consciousness among employees is also vital to revolutionary change. However, the process is very complex and gives reason why nonviolent action is so important to revolutionary reform.

An example of revolutionary reform at the micro-level would be the successful takeover of a single enterprise by the employees so that they can manage it as a public trust in the interest of the community as well as themselves. The employee takeover of a firm of course can be as revolutionary in a state socialist system as in a state capitalist system. State command systems in modern socialist countries can be as domineering and repressive to local employees as the command systems of a big business conglomerate. The origins of power in a state command system can become bureaucratically and professionally established in big cities quite remote from the local plants themselves. Again, a broad social consciousness of employees must be developed while recognizing a need for local self-direction in the plant takeover; the plant has a larger social accountability to the society even while it increases the level of its own local authority and self-governance. Such developments have begun to occur in some socialist countries (e.g., Yugoslavia) and in capitalist countries.

The philosophy underlying radical-nonviolent action suggests that such basic changes in the charters of large-scale corporations and the development of social (not state) ownership of property advances us significantly toward the nonexploitive society. This process of nonviolent revolutionary reform has many complicated dimensions that must be studied from a social-scientific perspective.

Let us now look at what happens during nonviolent action in the light of sociological theory. We want to see the extent to which it is a method of revolutionary reform in the institutional life of society.

Social Movement Theory

Theories of social movements have been influential in sociology but as a rule they are not adequate to comprehend the course of nonviolent action in the radical tradition.

Neil Smelser's *The Theory of Collective Behavior* can illustrate this problem most aptly. Smelser assumes that people typically develop a "generalized belief" in their social movement that keeps them from taking the essential steps to achieve their goals. The social movement is then "short-circuited" because the generalized belief becomes a myth that contains magical thinking and develops feelings of omnipotence among the members. The members envision a future of unlimited bliss and believe that their particular reform or revolution will solve the problems of the world. The myth then blurs the intermediate steps that are necessary in the practical politics of social change and the movement comes to an end.[20]

However, this dismal view of a social movement fails to take account of all the facts about them. Indeed, it tends to discredit social movements in general by its assumptions of irrationality among the people who engage in them. Some cases of nonviolent action in the radical tradition would probably fall into his characterization but many of them do not. In fact, it is more probable that most of them contradict these traits. Therefore it is important to examine here in some detail the character and direction of a specific social movement in the radical tradition of nonviolent action.

Our purpose is to suggest how a theory of social movements may be developed on alternative grounds. Cases of nonviolent action have taken account of the "intermediate steps" toward a solution and often involve "negotiations" with the opposition. More important, however, they can be examined typically on the basis of the extent to which they decentralize authority and cultivate human resources.

We will look at a brief summary of what happened in the Salt Satyagraha in India to see how these traits apply in reality. The reader can then refer to other social movements in the radical tradition to determine the extent to which such movements also express these traits.

The Salt Satyagraha*

The Salt Satyagraha was part of a year long civil disobedience movement led by Mohandas K. Gandhi in 1930—31. It was a collective action with long-range objectives to bring about the political independence of India and short-range objectives of removing the "undesirable" salt laws imposed by the British. The

*Satyagraha is most often translated as "truth force."

Salt Acts made it illegal in India for people to make salt and at the same time provided for the government monopoly of salt. The laws were seen to work as a hardship on the poor and they symbolized an unrepresentative "alien government" which needed to be overthrown. The following description of that social process draws heavily upon the research of Joan Bondurant.[21]

Primary Phase

1. **Preparation.**   At the beginning of the campaign, participation is limited to members of Gandhi's Ashram. They are "steeled to the disciplines and hardships" of a 200 mile march on foot to the sea. Prominent members of the Indian National Congress participate as organizers of the movement in parts of India. Satyagrahis (leaders) start training courses in nonviolent action and develop methods for controlling large crowds. Gandhi prepares to lead a march to the sea where leaders will prepare salt from sea water in violation of the law. One leader is chosen to prepare people along the way on the objectives of the march, instructing them in the principles of nonviolence. Pledges to nonviolent civil-resistence for the Independence of India are made.

2. **Preliminary Action.**   A public notice of the march is given. Gandhi writes a letter to Lord Irwin, the Viceroy, apprising him of the plan and its purpose. He notes that nonviolent action could be "an intensely active force" and urges a negotiated settlement. He also notes the exact day upon which the march would begin. He further states that his letter is in no way a threat but a "simple and sacred duty peremptory on a civil resister."

3. **Action.**   Gandhi and co-satyagrahis leave Ahmedabad for Dandi on the sea coast on March 12, 1930. They urge villagers along the route to pursue constructive work and remain nonviolent. The march attracts nation-wide attention. On April 5 they proceed to the beach and prepare salt from sea water, thus breaking the salt laws. They publish instructions on how to manufacture salt. Nehru wrote: "It seemed as though a spring had been suddenly released. Everywhere people began to make salt." Satyagraha leaders are arrested, and throughout the country shops close in sympathy for the leaders. Headmen

in villages voluntarily resign in large numbers in sympathy with the movement. Dramatic demonstrations are conducted in the cities with an "effigy" of the Salt Acts cast into the sea symbolizing the death of British law on the land. In some areas a program of nonpayment of taxes is initiated. Gandhi then notifies the government of his intention to occupy government salt-depots. Gandhi is arrested. Indian notables march to occupy the salt depots. Many are struck down by the police and others step in to take their places. One raid results in 320 injured including many people rendered "insensible with fractured skulls." First aid units are organized in other raids. Police begin refusing to continue the fight against waves of volunteers moving in. Civil disobedience then begins taking other forms of action including the boycott of foreign made products. Cloth and liquor shops are picketed. The campaign continues throughout the year.

4. **Negotiations.**   Through the early months of 1931, civil disobedience is met by arrests, firings, and forms of "police force." Settlement talks finally begin between Gandhi and the Viceroy. The salt laws are not repealed but a new official interpretation is effected in the settlement which specifies "For the sake . . . of giving relief to certain of the poorer classes, the Government will extend their administrative provisions, allowing people in areas adjoining locations where salt can be collected, to make salt but not to trade with individuals living outside their areas. The government agrees to an amnesty for all persons convicted of civil disobedience, a withdrawal of restraining ordinances, and a restoration of confiscated properties. In return the civil disobedience is to be ended including any continued "organized defiance" of the law." The settlement includes a statement that further discussions on constitutional reform should involve Congressional representatives and that in a future Round Table Conference, that such questions as federation, financial credit, and the position of minorities would be discussed. The settlement provides that the Congress should participate in conferences to consider constitutional questions involved in the advancement of India along the road toward full independence.

Secondary Phase

A secondary phase of action then involves the participation of Congress in the Round Table Conference, the discussion of constitutional questions, and the remaining steps taken in the process of achieving political independence.

This brief account of the Salt Satyagraha oversimplifies a very complicated process in reality but it does offer the reader a sense of the intensity in the events and the risk taken by the participants. All key participants risked their lives in the action; some participants were killed and many Indians were gravely injured. The personal risk, the courage, the suffering of participants must be considered part of the social process of transformation that overcame the opposition in this case.

The transformative process is complicated and not altogether known. We can say theoretically, without reference to detailed documents, that a new sense of inner authority emerged among participants in the process and that the action generated a great feeling of self-confidence among Indian citizens as the campaign revealed collective strength in the face of British troops. A new inner feeling of dignity and honor must have emerged in the process of confronting the superior colonial powers. A new feeling of power emerged collectively among the leaders of the social movement toward political independence. The new resources that were released among Indian leaders and citizenry can then be understood as a "force" entering into the subsequent conferences and political activities leading finally to the withdrawal of British troops.

Another example of nonviolent action as a social movement is illustrated in Chapter Eight of this book where Joseph Amato describes the life-world of Danilo Dolci. Here we see the primary phase developing in Dolci's response to the hunger, disease, illiteracy, and unemployment in the slums of Western Sicily. We see that these conditions were connected to the organization of the Mafia and political corruption; we see also how people had been taught by "the force of centuries" to accept the inevitability of their misery and domination.[22] Dolci brought to this condition a whole set of nonviolent methods including demonstrations, sit-ins, and strikes. The nonviolent action in each instance involved a great risk to his own life because he opposed the power of the Mafia which had frightened people into submission all these years. Dolci personally confronted the Mafia-power, unarmed, exposing its roots. His courageous action woke up people to their own personal resources. They found their own power, authority, and courage to change the virulent conditions.[23]

The capacity for nonviolent social movements in the radical tradition to develop human resources and decentralize authority seems evident in these cases. However, the conditions of revolutionary development that underlie this process of social change need to be specified in more detail.

Let us now summarize some of the propositions contained in the theory of social movements that may be involved in such research. Our purpose is not to try to capture the essence of the theory but rather to stimulate thought about some of the issues of research.

1. Nonviolent action which is designed to overcome political dominance can lead toward a sharing of material resources and an increased feeling of confidence and fulfillment in the personal lives of the participants.

2. When the opposition (e.g., police) see some legitimacy in the dedication and collective determination of unarmed people, they show strong tendencies to refuse to do violence to their opponents.

3. When leaders risk their lives to overcome conditions of social domination and exploitation, the action leads others to understand the seriousness of the cause and brings them toward collective action themselves.

4. The more the basic principles of the movement (e.g., self-rule) are grounded in the larger values of the society itself, the more likely it will receive widespread legitimacy and support.

Normative Theory

Social theorists differ on how "norms" (the rules of social order) function in society. For example, according to Emile Durkheim, the legal norms perform an integrating function for an otherwise differentiated, highly specialized society. He believed that the creation of legal norms by the State were due to structural strains in the society and that they helped maintain social solidarity. Max Weber, on the other hand, believed that the invocation of legal norms to resolve conflicts or strains within society was not always wise. He was greatly concerned about the authoritarian tendencies of the State to make all the rules resolving social or political conflicts. He questioned the effectiveness of legal norms applied generally or exclusively to the resolution of conflicts between opposing parties in society.[24]

Karl Marx took still a third position on legal norms. He saw them largely as defending the inequities between social classes. He would perhaps have agreed with Durkheim's premise that they represented part of the "collective conscience" giving solidarity to the society, but he would have shown how they create a false consciousness before the real injustices existing in the industrial state. He would have agreed with Weber in abhorring the authoritarian tendencies of the State. But he wanted to participate in a new social movement that would set the conditions for the dissolution of the State.

The theory of norms implicit in radical-nonviolent action stands partly outside these theories even though it is closely associated to each of them. Radical nonviolent action begins first with the assumption of Marx that the most important norms are created outside the power of the State. It assumes that legal norms are based, in the final analysis, on fear as much as on consensus. Furthermore, insofar as the rules are based on fear rather than respect for others, they cannot serve as the primary basis for self-development. Second, radical-nonviolent action assumes that social norms can point toward the basis for self-development and self-governance. The social norms created in the process of non-violent action should lead directly toward the cultivation of human resources and the reduction of the need for a State. Third, action seeks to create social norms (rather than legal norms of the State) that will lead in the direction of a decentralized form of communal life.

The cases of nonviolent action in the radical tradition offer evidence for developing this type of normative theory. It is possible to formulate a more systematic statement on this question from a study of many cases but let us look at the norms in the case of Satyagraha in India. They were later followed by Vinobe Bhave in his movement for land reform and illustrate this tendency in radical nonviolent action.

The following social norms are drawn from research by N. K. Bose who sought to depict the general character of campaigns of Satyagraha. They are simplified for our purposes and summarized below:[25]

1. Self-reliance at all times. Outside aid may be accepted in proper circumstances but should never be counted upon.

2. Initiative in the hands of the Satyagrahis. Maintain constructive leadership.

3. Propagation of the objectives, strategy, and tactics of the campaign. Keep educating the opponent and the public to the purpose of the action.

4. Reduction of demands to a minimum consistent with truth. Continue to assess the situation to make adjustments on demands without compromising principles.

5. Progressive advancement of the movement through steps and stages determined to be appropriate within the given situation. Static conditions must be avoided and direct action launched only after all efforts to achieve an honorable settlement have been exhausted.

6. Examination of weaknesses within the Satyagraha group. The morale and discipline of leaders must be maintained and constant awareness of any breakdown of nonviolent attitude.

7. Persistent search for avenues of cooperation with the adversary on honorable terms. Every effort should be made to win over the opponent by demonstrating sincerity to achieve an agreement rather than a "triumph."

8. Refusal to surrender essentials in negotiation. Satyagraha excludes all compromise which affects basic principles of valid objectives. Care must be taken not to engage in bargaining or barter.

9. Insistence upon full agreement on fundamentals before accepting a settlement.

Given such guidelines devised by participants, the action itself can be studied for adherence to them as a "model." The Salt Satyagraha in India can be examined in terms of these nine guidelines. However, the interpretation of the action by participants becomes a crucial dimension in the study of such cases. It requires, where possible, the observer's own participation in the action.

The code of discipline which participants impose upon themselves may also be the point of inquiry concerning the actual course of action. For example, the following norms or rules are paraphrased from a code developed for volunteers in the 1930 Salt March:[26]

1. Harbor no anger but suffer the anger of the opponent. Refuse to return the assaults of the opponent.

2. Do not submit to any order given in anger, even though severe punishment is threatened for disobeying.

3. Refrain from insults and swearing.

4. Protect opponents from insult or attack, even at the risk of life.

5. Do not resist arrest nor the attachment of property, unless holding property as a trustee.

6. Refuse to surrender any property held in trust at the risk of life.

7. If taken prisoner, behave in a exemplary manner.

8. As a member of a Satyagraha unit, obey the orders of Satyagraha leaders, and resign from the unit in the event of serious disagreement.

9. Do not expect guarantees for maintenance of dependents.

The psychology underlying the formation of such norms has yet to be investigated. We do not know enough yet about how such a norm as "harbor no anger" could be introduced into the training of a Satyagraha without some repression of normal instincts. The norms could lead toward psychological "domination" and neurosis rather than "sublimation" and an integrated personality. Gandhi himself acknowledged feelings of anger at times but claimed that he would not vent them on people. Martin Luther King recommended venting frustrations and anger at the "forces of evil" or the system rather than toward the individuals in the system.

In any case, many propositions have yet to be investigated in normative theory including the following:

1. Social norms can be formulated in the process of nonviolent action that lead toward the cultivation of individual resources and an increase in the capacity of people to manage their own affairs without legal norms.

2. The ends and the means of nonviolent action in the radical tradition are mutually involved in the norms of a campaign.

3. Nonviolent actionists can learn how to express their deepest feelings without harboring anger and fear.

Social Network and Communications Theory

Social scientists who study the diffusion of influence through social networks and the diffusion of knowledge through informal systems of communication could find a wealth of data in the many events of nonviolent action. These theorists are aware that the infrastructure of formal organizations can be more important for expressing power than any formal decision-making apparatus.[27] It is typical of nonviolent action that it functions outside the established processes of decision-making and so this mode of theory becomes critical to understand its field of operations. Social network theory and communications theory contribute to our understanding of how nonviolent action imparts ideas, feelings, and purposes in the context of society.

Social theory of "nonverbal communication" is especially important here because we know that nonviolent action extends well beyond the expression of words themselves. For example, the feelings behind the words are generally communicated by other channels of expression that make up what Edward Sapir called "that elaborate and secret code that is written nowhere, known by none, and understood by all." The tone of the voice, the use of silence, the tension of the body, the expression of the face, the rhythm of movements, the use of space, gestures, and many other signals play a crucial role in human communication.[28]

In this book we find numerous cases in which the field of "communications" becomes connected to our key principles of self-governance and social development in nonviolent action. Here we can illustrate how communications theory becomes important to self-governance at the level of the individual, the community, and national associations.

The principle of self-governance is significant for the individual under all circumstances of nonviolent action but it becomes dramatized at the point of a violent physical attack. Here the need for self-reliance and self-control becomes paramount since no one else may be able to deal so directly with the attacker as the person who is attacked. Note the following brief story about Toyochik Kagawa, Christian pacifist, who was speaking to an audience following a church service in Tokyo, Japan:[29]

> Following the church service, a number of youths raced up to his platform and beat him with large bamboo sticks. Kagawa chose to receive the blows showing no fear or anger in his expression toward them. After the attackers had expressed their feelings with the sticks, he invited them to talk with him about what they felt. The attackers accepted Kagawa's invitation and they spoke together about the need to change the conditions of poverty that existed in the neighborhood. Before long the attackers apologized for their action. Kagawa then became involved in an active campaign to organize neighborhood cooperatives to improve the economic well-being of the community.

Kagawa took no physical action to stop the blows in this case but he communicated with his attackers simply by the way he governed himself in the face of the attack. In this case we do not know fully how that communication took place.[30] The medium of communication with an attacker can be merely a "look" or a slight physical movement indicating one's own feelings. We also do not know fully what stopped the attackers from beating him to death. He may have communicated something of his own personal discipline and integrity that became convincing to the attackers. It could have been a fear of reprisal from the audience. In any case, we see here the elements of creative conflict. The personal resources of the parties in conflict were preserved first of all in the sense that no one was killed in the event and, secondly, that no one went to jail. Furthermore, their resources were increased by Kagawa's self-determination to overcome the violence and later by the efforts of people to act cooperatively to stop the deterioration of their neighborhood.

This case suggests how the qualities of self-governance such as initiative, self-reliance, self-control, are expressed in a very critical situation. We do not know all the components of character that become important in the mature life of a nonviolent activist such as Kagawa. There seems to be an inner democracy, a balanced use of resources, an integrity of intellect, spirit, imagination, and sensitivity that becomes evident in the life of such nonviolent activists. This has yet to be understood more fully and is part of our search for the meaning of self-governance.

The principles of self-governance, however, also operates at the community level. Nonviolent action in the community can help initiate changes needed at the level of the society-at-large. In Chapter Eight of this book, for example, we learn how unemployed workers in a Sicilian community created a "reverse strike" to dramatize the need for jobs. They decided to repair a road and to work without pay in opposition to police orders. They succeeded in raising a national issue over the "right to work" guaranteed in the Italian constitution. The local action set off a chain reaction. It was a nonviolent protest that was made in the public interest and resulted in a legal case to implement the constitutional principle of the right to work at the national level.

It is often believed that nonviolent action at the local level cannot have any significant affect at the national level but many such cases of nonviolent action suggest the opposite. The key to change in the society-at-large rests on networks of communication that help to dramatize the dominance or exploitive conditions that is felt by the public.

The experience of blacks in "sit-ins" at the beginning of the civil rights movement in the United States demonstrates how community action can carry the meaning of local oppression to the national level. These civil actions burgeoned into "pray-ins," "wade-ins," "sleep-ins," "walk-ins," and other similar actions that spread across the nation like a wild flash fire. These local actions struck at the public character of such "private enterprises" as restaurants, ice cream parlors, department stores, bars, night clubs, churches, and swimming pools. They set in motion a multitude of court cases and changed the character of federal and state laws.

The principle of self-governance also applies to national associations that may need themselves to overcome domination and oppression. Paul Wehr describes in Chapter Ten, for example, how the Nazi occupation of Norway in 1941 resulted in an attempt to control all national organizations. Teachers, educators, and administrators, however, developed an informal network of communication that became the basis for collective resistance. They organized systems of correspondence to resist Nazi mandates. They dramatically transformed the violence-prone conditions of direct military dictatorship over the schools by substituting an alternative governing body that operated so effectively that the Nazis could not rule. They became a hidden government. They communicated so quietly and powerfully at the national level that they were able to stop military controls and resist Nazi terror and domination.

These cases suggest many propositions about how nonviolent action functions within a society. A few theoretical propositions are suggested below for further investigation:

1. The more fierce and widespread a military oppression, the more deep and widespread is the resistance if the populace establishes a communication system to express it.

2. The more clearly alternatives for conflict-resolution are communicated, the more likely a resolution will be forthcoming.

3. The more clearly actionists communicate with opponents on a nonthreatening and friendly basis, the more likely opponents will respond in a similar fashion. (Similarly: the more directly actionists communicate with attackers on grounds that respect the human dignity of the opponent, the more likely opponents will respond favorably to help resolve the conflict. Conversely: the more actionists communicate hostility and fear, the more likely the attackers will respond in like fashion.)

Symbolic Interaction Theory

Symbolic interaction theorists arose partly to oppose the classic scientific view of "positivism" which interpreted people as "objects" instead of "subjects" of social action.[31] George Herbert Mead and Charles Cooley were early theorists in this tradition and more recent theorists include Herbert Blumer and Peter Berger. Theories of symbolic interaction are based on such propositions as the following:

1. Human beings act toward things on the basis of the meanings that the things have for them.

2. The meaning of such things is derived from the social interaction that people have with one another.

3. People are largely what they think themselves to be.

4. The world of everyday life is taken for granted as reality by the ordinary members of society; it originates in their thoughts and actions and then is maintained as real by them.

Symbolic interaction theory must be understood in relation to Marxist thought if we are to understand radical-nonviolent action. The Marxist views subjective meanings as created largely by the social structure and not created simply through the medium of social interaction in everyday life. The collective positions which people take as "owners" and "workers," for example, generate meanings that are not created basically out of their daily social intercourse. They are transmitted from the society as a whole in its historical period. They are generally thought to be "reality" and part of the "natural world" but in the Marxist perspective they actually constitute a false consciousness. For Marx, the reality is emerging through a new social consciousness of the exploitive character of the modern political economy.

Let us now look at how significant traits of nonviolent action can be formulated as an ideal type (or research model) keeping in mind symbolic theory and the truth in Marxist thought. We can then apply our model to a hypothetical case of nonviolent action. We are not intending to be rigorous here; we are simply illustrating how symbolic theory can be applied to interpret nonviolent action.

What are significant traits of nonviolent action conceived within symbolic theory?

First, the actionists use symbols that alter the way people perceive the conflict situation. For example, traditional conflict is often charged with words that prejudice the truth about people. Such loaded words as "racist," "pig," "capitalist," and "communist" rule out the fact that people are also individuals and human beings. Such terms do not become useful in creative conflict and destroy the basis for communication with each other on truthful terms.

Second, radical-nonviolent action is generally unconventional and basically communal in its intent. It is outside the customary or institutional way of doing things; it is not necessarily abnormal but it is often unconventional. It functions outside the symbolic meanings of separate classes and yet it goes to the heart of the larger community latent within the society. It functions within the Marxist tradition in this respect; actionists become like a "class" which Marx once said:

> . . . has radical chains, a class in civil society which is not a class of civil society, a class which is the dissolution of all classes, a sphere of society which has a universal character because its sufferings are universal, and which does not claim a *particular redress* because the wrong which is done to it is not a *particular wrong* but a *wrong in general*.[32]

Third, the action is *praxis* in the sense of converging "practical" action with correct theory in a manner that strikes at the root of the problem. The practical self-interests of the actionists are mixed with the broader interests of the community-at-large. In radical-nonviolent action, the root of the problem involves overcoming the objective conditions of dominance in society while respecting the subjective life of the opponents. Praxis requires seeking a synthesis of these two conditions of social action.

Radical nonviolent action is understood in part by the level of awareness that people have for overcoming the contradictions that are built into a conflict situation but it does not always require adults who are sophisticated in their knowledge of society and the nonviolent tradition.

Let us take a case of boys playing basketball on a schoolyard. They are suddenly faced by bigger boys of the same age who tell them to get off the court because they want to play and there is not enough room for everybody. It is a case of raw domination but the smaller boys may act quickly and nonviolently in the situation. Instead of running away or getting their heads beat in, they use their wits to face the tough boys with a new "definition of the situation." They tell them of a new movie playing down the street which they have been waiting to see . . . it starts in a few minutes. Or, they may tell them they are practicing for a game with a competitive school and they need their help to win. The feeling of common loyalty as opposed to the sharp rivalry between the two schools overcomes the desire to dominate the situation. It could lead to a friendly game of "training" teams mixed between the big and small boys.

The Marxist picture is important here because we know from sociological studies that the class structure can supply the key meanings to this situation. Let us say that the big boys, in this case, are from the working class and the small boys from the middle class. The big boys have been facing domination in the school all day long from middle class teachers. Their parents have not taught them to appreciate the virtues of disciplined study; they have not been taught the values of book learning and the restraints of the middle class. They have been taught instead the virtues of spontaneity. They do not hold the same awe and respect for property as do the middle class teachers. They suffer from penalties of low status inside the school and so they are ready for some revenge in the schoolyard. The middle class boys sense this fact even though they have not read about class structure in their schoolbooks.[33]

Let us say the problem of the basketball court is not yet resolved and the small boys still want to solve it on their own without getting hurt unnecessarily. They begin to take steps toward what might be called radical action. They have not heard of "nonviolence" but they have a sense of their own nonviolent direction. They talk to others who feel the domination of the big boys. They talk to some girls who live in the working class section of the community about their common problems of being dominated. The girls are interested in learning to play basketball and suggest that the boys teach them. Together they organize mixed teams (male-female) to practice after school hours. They know they will be facing the big boys on the court after school and prepare themselves. They are thus creating a new condition for attacking the inequality in power on the school grounds. The big boys see the girls playing basketball with the smaller boys and refuse to do violence to them. The big boys' perception of the situation is radically changed. They do not want to appear as bullies in front of girls in whom they have some personal interest. The big boys are invited to help the mixed teams learn the game better. Now the rudiments of nonviolent action begin to be expressed in the situation with new "matching forces" on the school grounds.

The class structure and the meanings they supply do not wholly determine the new "definition of the situation" as Marx himself would acknowledge. The people who are being dominated (here: middle class boys and working class girls) may respond collectively to create the conditions for ultimately sharing human resources and skills. The boys and girls in this case act on the class system as they learn basketball together.

The roots of the class structure of course, are much deeper. The action therefore becomes even more innovative when it leads toward communal learning in the class room. If all students begin to learn together inside as well as outside the school building as a result of the basketball experience, we see the elements of radical change taking place. The boys and girls now begin to talk more openly with the teacher about the existence of family poverty in the midst of family wealth within the community. Teachers respond with readings for the youngsters about the economic conditions under which they are living. The teachers realize that they have not been teaching directly about economic injustice which is close to home and begin to discuss the subject in social studies. The tough boys are now interested; they want to learn more about the "class structure" of the community and ultimately their "historical roots" in the society. They want to learn how to overcome the historical conditions under which they live.

Let us now look at a few propositions that express the key ideas underlying symbolic interaction theory in the light of nonviolent action in the radical tradition.

1. Human meanings originate in the thoughts and actions of people in the social interaction of everyday life and are generally maintained as real by them.

2. Human meanings also originate in the structure of society

within its historical stage of development and are generally maintained as real by people in the social interaction of everyday life.

3. While the subjective world of daily life is generally taken for granted as "reality" by ordinary members of society, a new "definition of the situation" can be introduced which changes the way people perceive that reality.

4. The causes of violent action are always partly symbolic. (e.g., the school hated by lower class boys who suffer low status in it).

5. The causes of violent action can be treated by the introduction of other symbols and meanings. (e.g., the rival school equally disliked by all boys in spite of their differences in status on home grounds).

Social Structure

Organizational Theory

If nonviolent actionists are interested in removing the barriers to the development of human potential by increasing the level of self-governance, they must study the structure and power of large-scale bureaucracy. They must eventually face the problem of how to overcome bureaucracy in the modern corporate state. The basic question is how to eliminate bureaucratic command systems without substituting other command systems.

Max Weber, the great German sociologist, warned of the growing impersonal and de-humanizing effects of bureaucracy in modern society but he never described how to eliminate those effects. He never told us how to de-bureaucratize the corporate state.

We know now that the answer is complex for both capitalist and socialist systems. The collective attempt to de-bureaucratize the big corporate and state systems could simply lead to other authoritarian systems. However, if done nonviolently, it could lead to a more individually resourceful and a decentralized society. We are now talking about a society that is governed in the nonviolent tradition.

We have referred to Satyagraha campaigns in India that helped overthrow colonial command systems and substituted a system of self-governance in the Indian nation. We noted how it resulted in an increase in domestic authority and personal self-reliance relative to what had existed under the British empire. We can now ask a broader question for social research: Can we carry the meaning of this nonviolent action into a general theory of how to decentralize large-scale organizations in the post-modern society?

Can we say that decentralizing the command system of the multinational corporation so that its foreign subsidiaries become increasingly self-governing would in turn increase the personal self-reliance of the host employees? Could a nonviolent action help decentralize authority effectively in the subsidiaries of a large business corporation so that economic trade could be maintained between the two nations? Could the action encourage employees to develop a broader outlook on the social purposes of the corporation in society? Could nonviolent action help increase the workers' level of community responsibility, add to their knowledge of corporate administration, and result in an expansion of themselves as persons? Could the corporate decentralization offer workers a greater control over the forces that play upon them in a corporate state?

The big business and the big state are not the only bureaucracies in modern society. The "corporate church" in the United States reveals different degrees of democratic bureaucratization in its different denominations. These denominations have not yet been studied for their effect on the feelings of self-worth and the personal growth of their laity. Many questions, therefore, remain unanswered: Is the lack of decentralized church authority related to the refusal of certain denominations to admit women into the priesthood and minorities into the higher levels of their organization? Is a gain in the power of the laity in the social organization of the church consistent with the purposes of the church? If so, does decentralization then become a priority for nonviolent action?[34]

To study these questions, we must first describe the traits of bureaucratic organization. We need to specify principles that characterize its structure of authority and then we can suggest alternative principles of organization as the basis for experimental change.

The table below contains principles of bureaucratic organization based on a "command authority" in contrast with principles of small-scale organization based on "mutual authority." The large-scale organization is founded on "rational rules" defining the duties of each office and emphasizing professional knowledge as important to its higher offices. The ultimate power rests at the top of the organization. The authority to act on behalf of the larger organization becomes increasingly limited as one passes down through the ranks to offices of lesser authority and power. In the contrasting system of traits in small-scale organization, the rules are jointly made with the intent to optimize the authority of each person in the work environment. Everyone has equal authority on overall decisions based on consensus or an electoral system. The main tasks are designed to be simple enough for everyone in the organization to assume personal responsibility for them. The model suggests a line of transition from left to right through nonviolent action.

ORGANIZATIONAL DEVELOPMENT

Principles of Authority

Command Authority		Mutual Authority
	1. Governance	
Bureaucracy———————————————————		Self-Management
	2. Status	
Hierarchy———————————————————		Equality
	3. Process	
Competition———————————————————		Cooperation
	4. Relations	
Formal ———————————————————		Informal
	5. Knowledge	
Professional———————————————————		Laity
	6. Ethic	
Duty ——————————————————— (obligation)		Responsibility (Rights)

While a system of "mutual authority" may at first seem very utopian to suggest as an alternative to large-scale organizations in society, we can see a fundamental change taking place already within many major institutions which suggest this kind of development. Organizational research in schools, corporations, hospitals, prisons, churches, voluntary associations, show definite trends in the direction of developing self-reliance and personal authority. For example, schools have been experimenting with cooperative work-tasks which reduce the competitive emphasis on grades, searching for more informal learning environments, and looking for ways students can self-manage their education. In the church, we can see the large-scale movement to "laicize," or "de-professionalize" as well as "de-formalize" activities. The concern is to reduce the amount of hierarchy and command authority in denominational and ecclesiastical organization. In business, we see a definite trend toward self-management, cooperative work tasks, profit-sharing, and employee ownership.[35]

A significant experiment in this direction of developing an organization based upon mutual authority was conducted in a highly competitive and hierarchical business. The pet food plant of General Foods Corporation was entirely re-organized with the purpose of eliminating hierarchy and competition, formality, bureaucracy, and the "duty" of work. The experiment shows similarity to what a Chinese factory might be doing under the guidance of the Communist Party although this factory exists within the business tradition. With initiatives from management in the interest of higher productivity and from workers in the interest of higher wages, teams were organized for employees to learn the whole assembly line operation of the plant. Employees planned a way to circulate all work-teams periodically throughout the plant assembly line to reduce the tediousness of performing the same jobs repeatedly. They have come to learn the whole assembly line system and to set their own schedules of work democratically through their teams. There are no supervisors and no formal hierarchies in the plant. Workers have in effect created a set of "collectives" which function without the bureaucratic command system formerly operating within the plant.[36†]

This development of worker power and authority is part of a larger process of basic change that has been taking place quietly in the business system. Local workers and managers have been taking control of whole factories and plants in the United States for various reasons and under various conditions for many years. For example, the workers in the plywood industry in the Northwest United States have owned and managed their own mills since the 1920s. Today there are about 18 plywood producer cooper-

†This major step toward self-management would take a more revolutionary turn if General Foods were to charter itself to operate in the public interest. It also becomes revolutionary at the plant level if the workers are granted full control over its operations.

atives operating autonomously in that region. In that same period of the 1920s the owner of the American Cast Iron Pipe Company gave his stock to the workers for what he said were Christian motives. Today this plant is operating with 3,000 worker-owners in Birmingham, Alabama. The President of the Milwaukee Journal did likewise, phasing out his ownership of the stock to the workers in the 1940s. Today this company is operating with about 1,400 employee-owners under an internal organization based in part on principles of self-management. In more recent years, workers have begun to take over plants that have been shut down by conglomerate corporations. For example, the employees of the South Bend (Indiana) Lathe Company bought out their plant with the help of loans when they were shut down. The employees at the Vermont Asbestos Plant and separately the employees at the Saratoga Knitting Mill in New York bought their plants independently when the conglomerates that owned them decided to shut down. These plants have done remarkably well, making profits for their workers in the succeeding years.[37]

While there is no socialist consciousness that seems to exist among the workers in these cases they are nevertheless examples of innovative steps toward self-governance. The take-overs are mostly the result of an employer's ideals or employee responses to breakdowns in the corporate system; yet they still represent the kind of transformations that are involved in nonviolent development. The employees in these plants increased their level of authority and self-governance over their own affairs. They increased their own authority over production and have pioneered a method of revolutionary reform within business enterprise.[38]

These cases fit our organizational theory of nonviolent action better than do some cases drawn from the better-known figures in the radical tradition. For example, Mohandas K. Gandhi and Cesar Chavez helped negotiate settlements between labor and management and thus maintained the disparity of power between these two industrial classes. The basic principles of nonviolent action, however, point toward organizing to eliminate this stratified system of work by helping employees to own and manage their own enterprise in the interest of the society as well as themselves.

Gandhi developed this principle later in his life calling it "aparigraha" (Nonpossession). He formulated a method for organizing trusteeships which would bring property into a common ownership. (This concept is discussed by David Toscano in Chapter Three.) However, this same principle of trusteeship developed independently among a number of worker-owned enterprises in the United States on the basis of their own experience.

Some propositions in organizational theory that require further research and clarification as as follows:

1. Self-directed change from a "command authority" toward a "mutual authority" in organizational life increases the personal resources and power of people in the organization. (e.g., Plywood companies).

Corollary: Changing a structure based on "hierarchy" to a structure based on "equality" is accompanied by a feeling of self-confidence when the process includes employees making the change themselves.

2. The process of eliminating hierarchy in formal organization creates a challenge for people who must now call on their own resources to deal with social problems that had been solved previously by professionals. (e.g., arbitration experts, collective bargaining lawyers, and so on.)

Corollary: The redesigning of tasks so they can be done by nonprofessionals may be threatening to the professional for a possible loss of status and also to the nonprofessional for the added learning and responsibility that is associated with the new tasks.

Political Theory

Nonviolent action is basically community action, and it should be seen in the context of the *polis*, the community of people who are related to one another in terms of power and territory.[39] The concept of the *polis* in ancient Greece suggests not only a real community but also the development of an ideal within it. It assumes that people want to determine their lives more fully and fairly together.

Political theory in the radical tradition is drawn from the principles of nonviolence and their practice. Two basic principles we noted earlier are self-governance (*Swaraj*) and nonpossession (*Aparigraha*). Community self-governance refers to the capacity of individuals to organize associations effectively together with a common bond and within a common territory. The principle of nonpossession refers to the freedom from being personally attached to material things. Gandhi felt that nonpossession could not be fully realized in this world but that it could be put into practice and approximated in human experience. He spoke of the creation of community land trusts and the "equitable distribution" of goods as part of the means for achieving this principle.

The *Community of the Ark* is an example of an attempt to put these principles into practice. It was established by Lanzo del Vasto in Southwestern France on nonviolent principles. Del Vasto had been a disciple of Gandhi in 1937 and lived in Gandhi's Ashram for three months. He swept the premises, emptied latrines, learned to spin, and listened to Gandhi talk about the satyagraha campaigns. A year later he left India to create the "first Ashram of the West." Today there are two such communities in France, another in Grenoble, and affiliated communities on other continents.[40]

Members of the community are trained in nonviolent action and then leave periodically to help others confront political crises. The training occurs on a daily basis in the community in contrast to training conferences that are conducted on location in nonviolent campaigns. The community seeks to be self-governing in daily life and it is in such places that the basic principles of a nonviolent polity are born.

There are three basic concepts of the master principle of self-governance that we should examine: autonomy, viability, and democracy.

Autonomy (Self-Control)

Autonomy means the capacity of people in a community to be independent of external controls and to express their own authority in society. It is observed in the degree to which individuals in a community are free from outside decision-making. It can be seen in the degree to which a community can make decisions internally without an arbitrary will imposed upon them from the outside. It is also seen in the degree to which communities within a larger unit such as a federation of communities share power and authority equitably with each other. These suggest really complicated variables and one can easily see how difficult it would be to achieve full autonomy for any community.

The political autonomy of any organization is especially important to observe in connection with its economic ties to the outside. Too much financial support coming from the outside is destructive. For example, the autonomy and integrity of Dr. King's Southern Christian Leadership Conference was challenged when it received a large gift from the Teamster's Union. Also, when Chavez's United Farm Workers accepted financial support from the treasury of the AFL-CIO, serious issues were raised in regard to the way outside controls might be exercised on these otherwise autonomous organizations. Any large donation can make a campaign or a nonviolent organization indebted to the donor even without any formal contractual agreements.

Viability (Self-Sufficiency)

The concept of viability means the extent to which people can solve their own problems without outside help. The principles of material self-sufficiency and diversification are important here to clarify the meaning of the principle of viability.

In the *Community of the Ark* we see the notion of self-sufficiency applied to its extremes. All clothing in the community is homespun, handwoven, and even sewn by hand or the treadle machine. The community produces most of its own wheat, vegetables, fruit, and dairy products. To pay for necessities it cannot supply itself (such as rice, transportation to other communities, hospital services), the community sells its own home-made products on the market. The community is maximizing its capacity to meet its own economic needs.

The principle of diversification also applies here. The notion of a nonviolent model of *polis* is different than that of most towns, cities, and nations. The modern "polity" is organized around the democratic state but the nonviolent community is organized around a network of associations based on a consensus community. The "general will" of the community is not expressed through the institution of the State, but through all institutions of the community. Charles Cooley, a sociologist, captures the spirit of this idea in his definition of the "public will":[41]

> The view that many hold that public will must be chiefly if not wholly identified with the institution of government is a just one only in a certain narrow sense . . . only a small part of the

will of society is of this sort. In a larger sense it is a diversified whole, embracing the thought and purpose of all institutions and associations, formal and informal that have any breadth of aim . . . Surely the true will of humanity never has been and it is not likely to be concentrated in a single agent, but works itself out through many instruments, and the unity we need is something much more intricate and flexible than could be secured through the state alone.

There is an interest in maintaining both diversity and unity in the experimental communities established by nonviolent leaders. In fact, it is said that diversification of institutional life is essential to maintaining unity and solidarity in this type of polity. But the basis for maintaining unity must go beyond the unifying power of the charismatic leaders or else the community loses its self-governing power. Mohandas K. Gandhi and Lanzo del Vasto were both aware of this fact and sought to reduce the tendencies of followers to rely heavily on them even though reports from members of their Ashrams indicate only limited success in achieving this goal.

More recent communities based on nonviolent principles, therefore, have sought to build their organization on a broad base of leadership at the outset. For example, the Philadelphia Life Center is part of a network of nonviolent action communities in the United States and a half dozen in other countries. In West Philadelphia, the 150 or so members range in age from sixteen to sixty and include some twenty preteen children. They live in about twenty communal houses. Each communal house is autonomous, but is responsible to the others for sharing ideas and experiences, making decisions that affect the whole network, and extending mutual aid in times of crisis.[42]

Democracy (Self-Accountability)

The distinction between the concept of autonomy and the concept of democracy in defining self-governing communities is important here. Autonomy refers to the political will of the community that is independent in some measure of outside controls. Democracy refers to the political will of individuals and groups within the community that is fully and fairly represented in the body politic. The idea of autonomy is opposed to external dominance while the idea of democracy is opposed to internal dominance.

The tendency toward internal dominance or autocracy is generally fought against in nonviolent campaigns for practical reasons. Cesar Chavez refrained from imposing the idea of nonviolence on participants because it had to be learned by them as a self-governing principle:[43]

> And so we now have 10,000 people on strike in seven different places and in almost every single case—with 98 percent of the people—they've never had the experience. That's difficult.
>
> You have to deal with them in such a way that you don't *impose* the idea of non-violence on them but that they *accept* it. Because if you try to impose it in a situation as difficult as this one, a situation that's so charged up, they'll reject everything.

Two different types of democracy can be observed in the nonviolent action community. They may be observed as "electoral politics" and "consensus-making." The pattern of electoral politics is traditionally expressed by secret ballot and decisions for the whole community rests on majority opinion. This is customary practice for modern states. But it does not necessarily characterize the practice of many nonviolent communities. Instead an ideal is often practiced on seeking open consensus or achieving total agreement of members through mutual persuasion.

The following outline summarizes our discussion of key criteria that "measure" the extent to which a community is based on the principles of a nonviolent polity.

The Nonviolent Polity: Measures of Self-Governance

1. *Autonomy* (Self-Control)
   a. Independent Decision-making
   b. Independent Authority

   Opposed to External Domination (Imperialism)

2. *Viability* (Self-Reliance)
   a. Self-sufficiency
   b. Diversification and Unity

   Opposed to Excessive Dependency (Colonialism)

3. *Democracy* (Self-Accountability)
   a. Electoral Politics
   b. Consensus and Persuasion

   Opposed to Internal Domination (Oligarchy)

The following propositions are associated with this model and warrant further study:

1. A relative degree of autonomy in a nonviolent action community may be achieved without too much viability and democracy.

2. A relative degree of democracy may be achieved without too much viability.

3. A relative degree of viability may be achieved without too much democracy.

Conclusion: Social Theory and Research for the Future

The radical nonviolent movements of the 20th century that have originated in the United States, Japan, India, Brazil, France, Northern Ireland and other parts of the world, suggest that a new methodology for social change and development is emerging without precedent in history. These contemporary movements are an expression of traditional values but they constitute a new synthesis of opposing interests such as the "secular" and the "sacred," and the "individual" and the "community."[44] They require, on the one hand, a fundamental change in the personal outlook of the individual that is close the religious or sacred tradition, expressing a spiritual view that sees all people as precious beings bound in one human community, believing it is wrong to kill anyone in conflict. However, they do not stop with this sacred view of things or with radical ethics on personal well being of the enemy. They also see the importance of radical social action to overcome the secular systems of dominance and exploitation in the modern community. They focus on rapid social change toward self-governance in the organization of society. They would translate the higher quality of life experienced inwardly by the individual into revolutionary social change in society.

There is a new direction for social thought and theory that is implicit in this radical tradition. It can be developed systematically to stimulate new social policy and social practice. It can help people think about the direction of social change and choose the priorities for social action today.

We have noted a key principle within these movements as "self-governance." This principle helps to clarify the meaning of both the process and the structure of nonviolent action in the radical tradition. It represents the ends and means of a nonviolent social movement. It is a goal in the sense of seeking to create optimum self-governance for all human beings. At the same time it is the means expressed in rules and norms of the movement itself. People are encouraged and taught to be self-reliant in the action process.

The concept of self-governance is simple and yet complex in its convolution within the organized life of society. It is first of all implicit in the structure of social action in the sense that all bodies of people are to some extent self-governing. At the same time it is the unfolding principle, the direction toward which all social bodies are developing. Its ideal expression is seen in that action of the community that leads toward the full realization of the self-potential in the context of society.

The task now is to bring the attention of social research to this integral perspective. These social movements bring together the meaning of social and personal development in ways that the church and the state have not been prepared to undertake. They suggest in effect a model for acting on oppressive systems in state capitalist and state socialist nations.

Our purpose in the remainder of this book is to examine the factors involved in this wide-ranging phenomenon of nonviolent action. We want to see how its principles bear on research and practice at all levels of society. Social theory and research may then begin to contribute something of value to people who are engaged in the great social change of this century. The social sciences may offer a human perspective and sensitive critical studies to the experiments in nonviolent action. Together they may help create the conditions leading to a more nonviolent society for the 21st century.

Notes

1. Mohandas K. Gandhi, *An Autobiography*, Boston: Beacon Press, 1957; A. J. Muste, *The Essays of A. J. Muste*, Nat Hentoff, (ed.), New York: Bobbs-Merrill, 1967; Arthur and Lila Weinberg (eds.), *Instead of Violence*, New York: Grossman, 1963.

2. Mohandas K. Gandhi, *Nonviolent Resistance*, New York: Schocken Books, 1975.

3. Clarence Case, *Nonviolent Coercion*, New York: Century, 1923; see also, Paul Hare and Herbert H. Blumberg, *Nonviolent Direct Action*, Cleveland, Ohio: Corpus Publs., 1968, p. 319—320.

4. Gene Sharp, *The Politics of Nonviolent Action*, Boston: Porter Sargent Publisher, 1973.

5. Kenneth E. Boulding, "The Power of Nonconflict," *Journal of Social Issues*, Vol. 33, Number 1, 1977.

6. Morton Deutsch, "Conflicts: Productive and Destructive," *Journal of Social Issues*, Vol. XXVI Number 1, 1969.

7. Lewis Coser, *The Functions of Social Conflict*, New York: The Free Press, 1956, p. 8.

8. Joan Bondurant, *Conquest of Violence*, Berkeley: University of California, 1969.

9. Martin Luther King, *Stride Toward Freedom*, New York: Harper & Bros., 1958.

10. Deutsch, op. cit., p. 9.

11. Robert Dahl, "The Concept of Power," *Behavioral Science*, 2, July, 1957, pp. 202—203.

12. Richard Emerson, "Power Dependence Relations," *American Sociological Review*, 27, No. 1, Feb., 1962, p. 32.

13. Emile Durkheim, *Suicide*, Glencoe: The Free Press, 1951, pp. 389—390.

14. Gandhi, op. cit., p. 127.

15. Mohandas K. Gandhi, *Young India*, 1922, p. 135, quoted in Arne Ness, *Gandhi and Group Conflict*, Oslo: Universtetsforlaget, 1974, p. 13.

16. Johan Galtung, "Violence, Peace, and Peace Research," *Journal of Peace Research*, pp. 5—6, 1968.

17. For a sophisticated treatment of "dominance," see Trent Schroyer, *The Critique of Domination: The Origins and Development of Critical Theory*, New York: George Braziller, 1973.

18. See Paulo Freire, *Pedagogy of the Oppressed*, New York: Herder and Herder, 1973.

19. The argument that violence is essential to make revolutionary changes in society has already begun in Marxist theory and socialist thought. For example, Karl Kautsky was an early follower of Marx who noted that the distinction between reform and revolution cannot be made on the basis of violence or force. Violence may or may not accompany either process. The constitution of the dele-

gates of the Third Estate at the National Assembly of France on
June 17, 1889, was a revolutionary act with no apparent use of
force. However, in 1774 and 1775 this same France had had great
insurrections for the unrevolutionary purpose of changing the
bread tax to stop the rise in the price of bread. See Karl Kautsky,
The Social Revolution, Chicago: 1902.

20. Neil Smelser, *Theory of Collective Behavior*, New York: The Free
Press of Glencoe, 1962; William Gamson also refers critically to
Smelser's work on this point. See, William Gamson, *The Strategy of
Social Protest*, Homewood, Ill.: The Dorsey Press, 1975, pp.
132—133.

21. Bondurant, op. cit. This is my summary of her characterization of
the process.

22. The primary phase of nonviolent action in Dolci's case shows how
personal risk involved others in the process of transforming the
conditions supporting "privileged access" to human resources. The
secondary phase involved the development of human resources
through new organizations. In this case it involved the creation of
wine cooperatives at Menfi, Sciacca, and Partinicio as well as housing cooperatives, building, and irrigation cooperatives organized
elsewhere. Here we see the broadening of democratic controls over
political life replacing political corruption. This is shown in the
successful effort of people to democratize Sicily's water supply including the building of the Jato Dam. We also see an increase in
material resources measured by the "substantial number of new
tillable acres, a longer growing season, and more varied crops."

23. In Dolci's case we can observe the nonviolent action increasing
human resources at three levels of development: First, the greater
abundance of material goods more widely distributed in the new
order of relations; second, the growth of new social organizations
in the form of federations and cooperatives reducing the rigid
stratification and permitting the resources in the area to be shared;
third, the development of the subjective life through an increase
in social authority, a new sense of freedom and responsibility. As
a result of this "social transformation" we see Sicilians in this case
sponsoring seminars in art and music, organizing a handicraft shop,
and generally developing a cultural life which had not existed before.

24. Sociologists have examined the way in which legal norms have been
expressed in India's industrial disputes on the basis of these theories of Durkheim and Weber. B. C. Cartwright and R. D. Schwartz,
"The Invocation of legal norms: An Empirical Investigation of
Durkheim and Weber," *American Sociological Review*, Vol. 38, Num-

ber 3, June, 1973, p. 340ff.

25. N. K. Bose, Studies in Gandhism, 2nd ed. Calcutta: Indian Associated Publishing Co., 1947, p. 157 (Quoted in Bondurant, op. cit.)

26. D. G. Tendulkar, Mahatma, Vol. III, Bombay: Jhaveri and Tendulkar, 1952, p. 17 (Quoted in Bondurant, op. cit.)

27. See Mark S. Granvetter, *Getting a Job: A Study of Contacts and Careers*, Cambridge: Harvard University Press, 1974; Diana Crane, *Invisible Colleges*, Chicago: University of Chicago Press, 1972.

28. Lawrence Wylie and Rick Stefford, *Beaux Gestes*, New York: E. P. Dutton, 1977.

29. Allan Hunter, *Courage in Both Hands*, New York: Ballantine Books, 1962; Margaret Baumann, *Kagawa: An Apostle of Japan*, New York: MacMillan, 1936.

30. The manner in which such an attack is met nonviolently is discussed by Richard Gregg, *The Power of Nonviolence*, New York: Fellowship Publications, 1959.

31. For a more detailed analysis of these propositions, see: Richard Lichtman, "Symbolic Interactionism and Social Reality: Some Marxist Queries," *Berkeley Journal of Sociology*, Vol. XV, 1970.

32. T. B. Bottomore and Maximillan Rubel, (eds.), *Karl Marx: Selected Writings in Sociology and Social Philosophy*, London: C. A. Watts & Co. LTD, 1956, p. 182.

33. This hypothetical case is drawn from situations studied by Albert Cohen, *Delinquent Boys*, New York: Free Press, 1955.

34. Social scientists usually describe three different types of denominational structure based on the following order of decentralized authority: 1. congregation (high), 2. presbyterian (medium), 3. episcopal (low). The question is whether an administrative change from an episcopal type of low decentralization (with strong controls exercised at the top by the priesthood) toward a congregational type of high decentralization (with strong controls by local laity over property and the choice of ministry) produce at the same time a higher level personal self-direction and self-reliance in the spiritual life of members.

35. David Jenkins, *Job Power*, New York: Doubleday & Co., 1973.

36. R. E. Walton, "Alienation and Innovation in the Workplace" in J. O'Toole, (ed.), *Work and the Quality of Life*, Cambridge, Mass.: M.I.T. Press, 1974.

37. Severyn T. Bruyn, *The Social Economy: People Transforming Modern Business*, New York: John Wiley Interscience, 1977.

38. Paul Bernstein, *Democratizing the Workplace*, Kent State U. Press, 1976.

39. Krishnalal Shridharani, *War Without Violence*, Bombay: Bharatiya Vidya Bhavan, 1962, p. 110ff; Anders Boserup and Mack Andrew, *War Without Weapons*, New York: Schocken Books, 1975.

40. Marjorie Hope and James Young, *The Struggle for Humanity: Agents of Nonviolent Change in a Violent World*, New York: Orbis Books, 1977, pp. 41—70.

41. Charles Cooley, *Social Organization: A Study of the Larger Mind*, New York: Scribner's, 1920, pp. 402—403.

42. Hope and Young, op. cit., p. 11ff.

43. James Forest, "An Interview with Cesar Chavez," *Fellowship*, September, 1973.

44. The movements are not the same as the sacred Christian Crusades of the Middle Ages or the secular political revolutions of the 18th and 19th centuries. While they do express something of the underlying values that supported both types of movements, they are of an entirely new order. They constitute a new synthesis of attitudes and a philosophy peculiar to this century. The picture of the "new society" toward which people in this movement believe they are headed is discussed in: Susanne Gowan, George Lakey, William Moyer, Richard Taylor, *Moving Toward a New Society*, Philadelphia: New Society Press, 1976.

Chapter 2

Sociological Mechanisms of Nonviolence: How It Works*

George Lakey

An old man, his thin hair lifted by the breeze, steps forward on the Boston scaffold and waits patiently while the noose is fixed around his neck. A young Negro with hornrimmed glasses tries to pray while behind him someone puts out a cigarette on his neck. A minister of foreign affairs tells Bismarck that, rather than yield to unreasonable demands, he will allow his beloved France to be occupied by German armies. Jewish leaders prostrate themselves before Pilate, saying that, before he places the insignia of Caesar in the temple enclosure, he will have to remove their heads.

These events, separated by centuries, have something in common—all are cases of nonviolent action. We use this term "nonviolent action" because, though the behavior of the persons described is determined enough, and even in its own way forceful, it is without physical violence. As it happened, the nonviolent action was successful in these cases—the Quakers were given religious liberty by the Puritans, the sit-ins integrated the Nashville lunch counters, Bismarck backed down, and Pilate relented.

Evidently, nonviolent action has some kind of power, even when

*Acknowledgement is hereby made to the author and to Pendle Hill, Wallingford, Pa., for permission to quote from George Lakey's "Non-Violent Action: How it Works" (Pendle Hill Pamphlet 129, 1963), 3—16.

the action is not very spectacular. The question then arises, what is this power? Some people say, "It is the power of God"; others say, "It is the power of love." Either answer leads to further questions, for just as the astronomer does not feel his task is done when he hears the stars defined as "the wonders of nature," so we are not content with a philosophical description of nonviolent action. The task of this chapter is to discover the "how" of nonviolent action.

We want to know how nonviolent action works, and so we look at the opponents of the nonviolent campaigners to see what their reactions are to the campaign. From these reactions we may begin to work toward an understanding of the process or mechanism[1] involved. A difficulty immediately arises: instead of reacting in only one way to a campaign which finally proves successful, the opponents react in various ways. The opponents sometimes change their minds completely about the issue, deciding that the campaigners were right after all. But then sometimes the opponents believe to the end that the campaigners are wrong, and yet they bow to the demands of the campaigners. Let us examine an example of the latter case.

In the 5th century B.C. the Roman peasants were suffering greatly as a result of the unjust social and economic systems of the time. The great landowners, or patricians, had all the political rights and most of the wealth. The plebeians resorted more and more to loans to maintain their families and pay the taxes. Finally, nearly crushed beneath the weight of these debts and frequent imprisonments, they left Rome in great numbers and camped on Mons Sacra, declaring they would not return until they were given a share in the government and in the common lands. No matter how reluctant the patricians were, they were forced to make concessions to the plebeians. They could not wage war or till the crops without the laborers.

Here is an example of what can fairly be called coercion. The plebeians actually took away the ability of the patricians to maintain the status quo, although they took away that ability by a nonviolent method. The patricians were coerced into lessening the injustice of their behavior.

Whether or not coercion of the opponent is a possible result of nonviolent action depends mainly on how dependent the opponent is on the nonviolent campaigner. The labor strike is a powerful weapon because the employer is dependent on the employees for his own goals. The boycott, too, usually depends for its effectiveness on the fact that the producer depends upon the purchaser for his own economic existence. The producer may not change his mind about the issues involved, but if the boycott is complete he is forced to concede.

In about 1531 the Portuguese began settling in Brazil. They met resistance from the Indians, as did most colonists, but in Brazil the tribes, particularly the Chavantes, were more ferocious than most. In 1650, an expedition in search of gold and diamonds entered the territory of the Chavantes. The Indians regarded this as an infringement of their hunting rights and massacred the expedition as it was crossing the river. To this day the river is called the River of Death.

Relations with the Indians continued to be stormy until 1910 when in that year Colonel Candedo Rondon took up the responsibility for relations between the government and the Indian tribes. As a soldier he had fought against the Indians, but in spite of this his Indian Protective Service began a radical new approach. Even in self-defense, firearms were not to be used. Rondon instructed his men: "Die if you need to; but kill, never."

One of Rondon's first responsibilities was developing the telegraph system in Brazil. Before 1910 even heavy garrisons at outpost stations had not been able to protect the lines from the embittered Indians. Rondon withdrew the garrisons, began giving gifts to the Indians as the line was built, and in every way possible showed the good will of the Indian Protective Service.

Twenty-six men were sent into Chavante territory to establish friendly contact. At first contact six were killed; a few days later the remaining twenty were massacred, but not one fired back in self-defense.

A second expedition was sent into the territory and was unmolested. The unarmed men spread around visiting encampments with gifts, and bit by bit hostility decreased. Finally, 400 Indian warriors came to their encampment, spears blunted as a token of friendship, to make peace with the "tribe of white Indians." Instead of chopping down telegraph poles, the Indians soon began to report the incidence of fallen trees on the lines.

This little known case of nonviolent action shows a real change of heart in the opponents. As a result of the actions of the nonviolent campaigners, the Indians came around to a new point of view which embraced the ends of the campaigners; this mechanism we will call *conversion*. Conversion usually demands a great deal of patience from the campaigners. The classic Vykom Temple Road Satyagraha in India required 16 months of standing at the barricade before the Brahmans were fully converted by the campaigning Untouchables. Such patience is rewarded, however, by gaining cooperation from the opponent.

Sometimes situations occur in which one cannot say that the opponents have been coerced, for they could continue to oppose if they wanted to; but we cannot call it conversion either, for the opponents do not accept the point of view of the campaigners. Nevertheless, the campaigners succeed in achieving their aims. The opponents can be overheard saying, "Let them have what they want; it's too much of a nuisance to continue the fight."

Midway through the Indian Salt Satyagraha of 1930—31, many in the Bombay English community were reported by correspondent Negley Farson to be changing their attitude to the campaigners. Many were "appalled by the brutal methods police employ against Mahatma Gandhi's nonviolent campaign." The very Englishmen who six weeks before were the "damn-well-got-to-rule" type saying, "Well, if the Indians are so determined to have dominion status as all this, let them have it and get on with it."

These Englishmen still believed in the Empire, but the Empire was not worth treating the Gandhians the way police were forced to treat them in order to repress them. They could have continued to support harsh action, but there was something about the behavior of the Indians which persuaded them not to do so. Let us, then, call this mechanism *persuasion*.

The American movement for woman suffrage found the same response on the part of some important political figures. The militant suffragists, impatient with the slow progress of "suffrage education," formed the Woman's Party under the leadership of Quaker Alice Paul. They began by picketing the White House, and for some months this did not create much public notice—what there was seemed impartial or mildly antagonistic. The World War was being fought, and suffrage seemed a very minor issue. However, the picketing continued with ever more uncompromising slogans, demanding that the right to vote be given, asserting that the United States was no democracy if it kept its women in bondage. The public became increasingly antagonistic, and when the signs appeared to the crowds to be unpatriotic, there were riots and demands for repression of the women.

Those who were picketing were taken to jail and prison sentences became longer and longer, but the picket line grew with each measure of repression. Ladies of high prestige, including White House dinner guests, were sentenced to foul prison conditions, but when they were released many immediately went back to the picket line.

The public continued to dislike the picketing but there was increased sympathy for these women who were suffering for their beliefs. Representative Volstead of Minnesota was reported as saying, "While I do not approve of picketing, I disapprove more strongly of the hoodlum methods pursued in suppressing the practice."

Dudley Field Malone, who said that he had first been irritated by the picketing, resigned as Collector of Customs for the Port of New York because of the treatment of the pickets.

Finally the issue of suffering became stronger than that of suffrage, and one congressman is reported to have said, "While I have always been opposed to suffrage, I have been so aroused over the treatment of the women at Occoquan (a prison) that I have decided to vote for the Federal Amendment."

Some of the opponents were apparently persuaded that, even though the women were wrong, they were not really so bad as to justify long prison sentences. The women, like the Gandhians, were using the mechanism of persuasion.

It now appears that there are three mechanisms of nonviolent action: coercion, conversion, and persuasion. A friend, who has been looking over our shoulder all this time, is nevertheless unsatisfied. "All you have done," he says, "is to classify actions by their results. You find out that someone changes his mind about the campaigner, but not about the issue, and call that persuasion. If he changes his mind about the issue, too, you call it conversion. What I want to know is why he changed his mind. What does the campaigner do that causes such a change?"

Our friend has asked a forthright question, and it is one we will not try to evade. In order to answer it, though, we must again look at people and try to understand why they are willing to use violence in the first place.

All men, no matter how debased they may seem, treat well the members of their own group. Even the famous gangs of cold-blooded thugs who terrorized the highways of India received intense loyalty from their members. For these criminals the persons who "counted," who were their true fellowmen, were the other thugs. Their victims they despised as weak, foolish beings who only deserved to be exploited. Indeed, these thugs saw the travelers not as human beings, but merely as objects who no more had human feelings than the victims of the flyswatter.

In history we see again and again that violent persons do not regard their opponents as fully human. The Greeks, it seems, waged war only against "the barbarians;" for the Massachusetts Puritans, the early Quakers were "ravening wolves;" African slaves were thought to be animals; Himmler repeated again and again that Jews were vermin, and vermin must be exterminated; and the Nazis, in turn, were "mad dogs."

On the other hand, sociologist E. Franklin Frazier notes in his history of slavery that "where human relationships were established between masters and slaves, both slaves and masters were less likely to engage in barbaric cruelty toward each other." It is also known that debtor slaves were as a rule treated with more consideration than were foreign slaves obtained by capture and trade.

In sum, it is easy to be violent against those who are seen as either inhuman ("mad dogs") or non-human (foreign slaves, unseen faces). The task of the nonviolent campaigners, then, is to get the opponent to see them as human beings. To understand how this is done we must look at close range at an actual case of nonviolent action—the case of the Quaker "invasion" of Puritan Massachusetts.

The story begins with the image the Puritans held of the Quakers; these now-gentle folk had been described in a letter from England as "railing much at the ministry and refusing to show any reverence to magistrates." Quakers of both sexes were reported to have danced together naked. They were said to be plotting to burn Boston and kill the inhabitants.

Puritan hostility to Quakers was not only because they appeared to be such monsters—to admit groups like the Friends would have meant the end of theocracy and surrender of the Puritan "way of life" in a political sense.

In July, 1656, the first Quakers, Mary Fisher and Ann Austin, arrived in Boston. They were greeted as though they carried the plague and were sent out by the next ship. However, two days after these first two sailed out of Boston harbor, eight of their co-religionists sailed in. In spite of harsh penalties, the number of Quakers coming to Massachusetts constantly increased.

These formidable zealots carried the battle to the Puritans, avoiding devious means of spreading their message. They attempted to speak after the sermon in church, made speeches during trials and from jail windows during imprisonments, issued pamphlets and tracts, held illegal public meetings, refused to pay fines, and refused to work in prison even though it meant going without food.

Sixty-year-old Elizabeth Hooton came back to Boston at least five times, being expelled each time, and she was whipped four times through neighboring towns. Even the death penalty did not deter the Quakers. While William Leddra was being considered for the death penalty, Wenlock Christison, who had already been banished on pain of death, calmly walked into the courtroom. And while Christison was being tried, Edward Wharton, who also had been ordered to leave the colony or lose his life, wrote to the authorities from his home that he was still there.

The public did not go unaffected by all this. The jailer's fees were often paid by sympathetic citizens and food was brought to the prisoners through the jail window at night. A number of colonists were converted to Quakerism by witnessing the suffering. For example, Edward Wanton, an officer of the guard at the execution of Robinson and Stephenson, was so impressed that he came home saying, "Alas, mother! we have been murdering the Lord's people."

When Hored Gardner prayed for her persecutors after her whipping, a woman spectator was so affected that she said, "Surely if she had not the support of the Lord she could not do this thing."

Governor Endicott was not so easily moved. When Catherine Scott indicated her willingness to die for her faith, the Governor replied, "And we shall be as ready to take away your lives, as ye shall be to lay them down." But the protest against the treatment of the Quakers continued to grow.

After William Brend had been so cruelly beaten that he seemed about to die, even Governor Endicott became so alarmed at the attitude of the people that he announced that the jailer would be prosecuted. The later execution of a woman, Mary Dyer, added to the discontent, and even the General Court began to weaken. Virtual abolition of the death penalty followed; there were problems in getting the constables to enforce laws which became even milder. By 1675 Quakers were meeting regularly without any disturbances in Boston.

This story illustrates what seems to happen in conflicts where the nonviolent campaigners succeed, and where the success is not due to coercion. In the beginning the Puritans rejected any common feeling which might exist between them and the Quakers; to them the campaigners must test it, and must analyze the situations in which it seems disproven. The suffering of the Jews was incalculable, but the ground composed of their action (and inaction) caused their suffering to be seen as non-human. Suffering so perceived does not have the power to "melt the hearts of the evil-doers." It may be noted that when the suffering of the Jews is perceived as human, even now, it begins to have a leavening influence, as in the Europe of today.

Identification by suffering in a context of good will, openness, and bravery, is the process which persuades and converts. Persuasion ends when I realize that "those whom I have exploited or violated are human beings like me," but conversion goes further than this. I am open to conversion when I agree to look again at the issue causing contention. This reexamination may take place through discussions and negotiations, or through silent supplication, as when the Untouchables stood for four more months on the empty Temple Road, when the barriers were taken down but the caste Hindus were still not converted to the idea of the Untouchables' right to the road.[2]

People change their attitudes most often when criticism of their attitude does not imply criticism of them. Separating the issue from the opponent, the "sin from the sinner" is difficult in any conflict situation; the nonviolent campaigners must take special pains to make the distinction clear. For example, in the course of the Gandhi-led South African Satyagraha the government was seriously troubled by a railroad strike which was not connected with the campaign for civil rights. As a chivalrous "don't hit a man when he's down" gesture, Gandhi called off the campaign until the strike was settled. This one act seems to have been of enormous significance in leading to a settlement satisfactory to the Satyagrahis.

The campaigners must show patience also, if they are seeking to convert the opponent. In the Vykom Temple Road Satyagraha the Brahman opponents expected the Untouchables to reenter the roadway as soon as the police cordon and barricade were removed. The campaigners' restraint threw them off balance, and this additional act of patience brought victory.

Notes

1. Note that what we are calling a mechanism does not refer to a goal, for a variety of goals may be won by the same mechanism. Neither do we refer to methods such as boycott, strike, vigil, sit-in, although the methods people choose probably affect the mechanism by which they win. Finally, we are not referring to results, for we are discussing here not only nonviolent action which yielded favorable results for the campaigners. The mechanism which we are considering is the answer to this question: what happened to the opponents in the course of the struggle?

2. The Vykom Temple Road Satyagraha took place from the spring of 1924 to the autumn of 1925 in Travancore State, India. Its object was to remove the prohibition upon the use of roadways passing the temple by Untouchables. A group of several hundred, many of them high caste Hindus, first made processions along the road, then took up positions opposite a police barricade set up when orthodox Hindus used violence against the satyagrahis. Gandhi persuaded the authorities to remove the barricade, but the satyagrahis refrained from using the road until the Brahman opponents were fully won over to their position. In the autumn of 1925 the Brahmans declared, "We cannot any longer resist the prayers that have been made to us, and we are ready to receive the Untouchables."

Chapter 3

Gandhi's Decentralist Vision:
A Perspective on Nonviolent Economics

David J. Toscano

Introduction

Any attempt to describe the social and political theories of Mohandas Karamchand Gandhi would do best to heed his own words. Writing for *Harijan*[1] in 1933, Gandhi said:

> I am not concerned with appearing to be inconsistent. In my search after truth, I have discarded many ideas and learnt many things. . . . When anybody finds any inconsistency between two writings of mine, if he still has faith in my sanity, he would do well to choose the later of the two on the same subject.[2]

These "inconsistencies" of which the Mahatma speaks are seemingly very apparent in many of his writings. His loudest critics suggest that these were the result of simplistic, idealistic thinking on Gandhi's part which could not be translated into the real world. Other analysts argue that inconsistencies were in keeping with Gandhi's enigmatic nature, which made it difficult for opponents, much less social scientists, to classify and categorize his thought.

If either of the above analyses are true, it would most probably be the latter. While Gandhi was not primarily a social and political philosopher, he was nonetheless a deep thinker who attempted to project his individual ethical code into the social sphere. As a social activist who dealt with a great number of alternatives (both

73

in terms of action strategies and visions of a new Indian society), he often seemed puzzling and enigmatic. However, this appearance was not the result of an inconsistent, fuzzy mind. Instead, it was the natural outgrowth of his personal ethical system and what he called his "experiments with truth," which entailed continuous reexamination and refinement of his social ideals.

As noted above, Gandhi was first, and primarily, a social activist.[3] However, his vision of an ideal society, *Sarvodaya*, included many strains of thought. At some times, Gandhi spoke like an anarchist, intent on the destruction of the state and its coercive power; at others, he appeared as a capitalist espousing the virtues of private property. His thoughts on machines and industrialization run the gamut from primitive communist concerns about the alienating tendencies of all modern technology to socialist ideas that technology and industrialization become problems only when a particular set of social relations (capitalism) control society. Whatever his perspective on a particular issue at any specific moment, his social thought was in a state of continual evolution consistent with Gandhian principles and means. His ideas and social philosophy emerged in the context of political struggle guided by the Gandhian technique of satyagraha, or "truth-force." Upon examination of Gandhian objectives, principles, and means, it will become apparent that the Mahatma's inconsistencies were, in fact, extremely consistent with his personal ethic, which entailed a continual reexamination of a person's position consistent with the search for truth.

The Reality vs. the Ideal

J. Bandyopadhyaya suggests that the only way to understand Gandhian social thought is to examine the dialectical interplay between real situations and the ideal solutions in Gandhi's mind.[4] The Mahatma was constantly confronted by the practical political difficulties associated with the struggle against injustice. These problems constituted real-life barriers to the implementation of the Gandhian vision. As a result, Gandhi was forced to adjust and refine his methods of obtaining his ideals in line with pragmatic political considerations. In this way, we can see Gandhian philosophy as an exercise in the application of the results of reflection on ethics to the problems of human organization and social development. For Gandhi, practical social, economic, and political programs evolved out of the interplay between the existing situation (real) and the principles of satyagraha (ideal). Hence, the dialectical process; political, economic, and social ends are constantly generated, challenged, and regenerated due to changing historical circumstances and in keeping with Gandhian principles and objectives.

Joan Bondurant describes three categories of Gandhian concepts which are important to an understanding of his social and political thought.[5] First, there are Gandhian *objectives*, such as *swaraj* (Indian independence) and *Sarvodaya* (ideal society), which were developed and refined over the course of Gandhi's life. Second, there are Gandhian *principles*, the most notable of which include: (1) nonviolence; (2) adherence to truth; and (3) dignity of labor. Finally, there are Gandhian *means*, which include satyagraha, *Bhoodan* (land-gift), and *Nai Tailim* (system of education). Of all these terms, satyagraha becomes the most important for us because it is through satyagraha as an end-creating technique of struggle that we can best understand Gandhi's social and political thought.

The term "satyagraha" was developed by Gandhi in the course of his struggle to secure rights for Indians living in South Africa in 1906. Before that time, people had labeled Gandhi's nonviolence "passive resistance," a term which the Mahatma felt did not reflect the nature of this powerful technique. Satyagraha, when broken into its roots, connotes both truth (satya) and firmness or force (agraha). Hence, the term "satyagraha," which Gandhi called "the Force which is born of Truth and Love or nonviolence."[6] Satyagraha was the technique by which Gandhi and his followers could cling to truth. This "clinging to truth" would inevitably take some form in social and political philosophy because Gandhi, like Marx, felt that the criteria of truth lies in the meeting of human needs. Gandhi went farther than Marx in one crucial respect: while Marx accepted a philosophy of history which defined the content of those needs (production) and indicated their satisfaction (communist society), Gandhi perceived the necessity of developing an approach, a tool, whereby substantial human needs could be met as the relative truth of a situation emerged in social struggle.

The most persistent theme which arises upon examination of

the concept of satyagraha is the notion that the technique is truth-creating; that is, it helps opponents in a struggle to discover a just resolution to their conflict. Gandhian means are "the end in process and the ideal in the making."[7] Therefore, in Gandhian thought, we find an emphasis, not upon absolutes and substance, but on relatives and process. This emphasis contrasts dramatically with more dogmatic approaches used by other groups seeking the overthrow of colonial regimes. Hence, a social and political thought which is seemingly inconsistent but instead is in fact continually evolving and refining itself consistent with "adherence to truth."

Gandhi believed that "we have always control over the means and never on the ends."[8] Furthermore, one is never capable of knowing the absolute truth in any situation. As a result of these two facts, Gandhi counseled the use of satyagraha, which excludes the use of "violence because man is not capable of knowing the absolute truth and therefore not competent to punish."[9] The use of satyagraha would bring forth an end consistent with the truth. "The means," said Gandhi, "may be likened to a seed, the end to a tree; and there is just the same inviolable connection between the means and the end as there is between the seed and the tree."[10]

It was during the course of struggle using the principles of satyagraha that Gandhi evolved a number of his visions of an ideal society. These visions were often extremely vague, perhaps owing to Gandhi's belief that the concrete details of any ideal vision would need to be worked out over a period of time by participants in the new society. Hence, his statement, "When society is deliberately constructed in accordance with the law of non-violence, its structure will be different from what it is today. But I cannot say in advance what the Government based wholly on non-violence will be like."[11] As an idealist, he attempted to live according to the Kantian prescription:

> To create an ideal community of rational beings, we need only act as if we already belonged to it; we must apply the perfect law in the "imperfect state."[12]

For Gandhi, this ideal community *(Sarvodaya)* was derived primarily from John Ruskin's *Unto This Last*. Gandhi felt Ruskin's ideas so important that he translated this work into the Indian dialect of Gujarati, entitling it *Sarvodaya*—The welfare of all. From this book, the Mahatma gained the following insights: (1) "That the good of the individual is contained in the good of all"; (2) "All work has similar value"; and (3) "That a life of labour, i.e., the life of the tiller of the soil and the handicraftsman, is the life worth living."[13] This concept of *Sarvodaya* formed the basis of Gandhian thought on political and economic decentralization. His emphasis on the individual, the dignity of work, and the importance of agricultural and handicraft, small-scale production would find their form in policies of rural economy, swadeshi, khadi, and panchayat raj.

As stated earlier, there was a continuous dialectical process between reality and the ideal in Gandhi's mind. It was always important for him to keep the ideal in mind when speaking of social policy. Nevertheless, Gandhi had a social scientist's sense that it is through social organization that people find themselves as individuals. There is, to use the terminology of symbolic interactionists, no "self" without a "society." Therefore, Gandhi's advice that individuals live in keeping with an ideal society did not go far enough; he had to move into the practical area of reconstructing social organizations so as to maximize the importance of the individual.

The India of Gandhi's time was marked by an imperialist relationship vis-a-vis Great Britain, concentration of political and economic power in the cities, and high unemployment, especially in the villages. Consequently, he emphasized swaraj (self-rule and independence), swadeshi (belonging to or made in one's own country), trusteeship, and decentralist political and economic organization so as to rebuild the villages of India. The Gandhian proposals represent a synthesis of anarchism, French syndicalism, and English guild socialism with the concept of satyagraha.

Proposals for a decentralized polity formed the core of guild socialism. English social thinkers who advocated this stance harkened back to the days of the medieval craft guild, with its emphasis on cooperative association. While the state would own the means of production in their proposed society, the guilds would regulate their use. In Gandhi's thought, this concern translated into a call for national trusteeship and control of certain institutions coupled with the demand for village economic and political democracy.

Gandhi was sympathetic to much of the anarchist vision as well.

Throughout his life, he shared Peter Kropotkin's deep distrust of the state, whether it be capitalist or socialist, as a hierarchical power structure which crushes local initiative. "True progress," said the anarchist Kropotkin, "lies in the direction of decentralisation, both territorial and functional . . . ."[14] We find this sentiment expressed throughout Gandhi's writings. Gandhi's acceptance of the anarchist vision, however, did not extend to the means by which to abolish the state. While certain anarchists like Max Stirner would use violence to abolish the state, Gandhi maintained his commitment to satyagraha.

Finally, Gandhi drew strength from French socialists who, while adopting the economic theory of socialism and the anarchists' critique of the state, also advanced a policy of syndicalism (nonpolitical direct action) aimed at building a society of self-governing industry. While their methods were often too drastic for Gandhi (the Mahatma, for example, did not approve of all strikes), the notions of direct action and decentralized self-governance would occupy his thought until his death. These three ideas influenced Indian nationalist thinking on the building of an Indian polity based on their tradition of village communities governing themselves and ordering their economic life on the basis of mutual aid and cooperation.

Self-sufficiency, coupled with respect for certain traditional institutions, was the essence of what Gandhi called "swadeshi." He described swadeshi as:

> that spirit in us which restricts us to the use and service of our immediate surroundings to the exclusion of the more remote . . . . In the domain of politics I should make use of the indigenous institutions and serve them by curing them of their proved defects. In that of economics I should use only things that are produced by my immediate neighbours and serve those industries by making them efficient and complete where they might be found wanting.[15]

Political Decentralization

In Gandhi's ideal state, the emphasis would be upon the individual, who would reach self-realization through cooperation with other individuals. Therefore, it stood to reason that government should be as close to individuals as possible. To attain this goal,

Gandhi worked to build a society based upon decentralized village industries and self-sufficient rural communities. In Gandhi's hopes, the movement for swaraj (self-rule) implied more than simply independence for India; it signified an extension of all-embracing self sufficiency down to the village level.

To some degree, attempts at organizing the rural masses into economically and politically self-reliant communities predates Gandhi. In fact, the swadeshi (home production) movement of 1905-06 had such a focus. But it was Gandhi who integrated the ideas of swadeshi with a critique of the state.

Gandhi found it almost impossible to justify the coercive power of centralized government. "The state," he said, "represents violence in a concentrated and organized form."[16] This explains, in part, his unwillingness, despite the requests of millions of Indians, to assume the presidency of the newly emerging nation. For him, "A society based on non-violence can only consist of groups settled in villages in which voluntary cooperation is the condition of dignified and peaceful existence."[17] Village living was the only possibility for "true freedom." Reliance upon the state would lead, said Gandhi, to a decline in self-discipline, social commitment, and the social obligation of one individual to another. Furthermore, the full power of the independence movement rested in the villages. Delegation of village authority to the national state after independence, thought Gandhi, might lead to paralysis of local struggles to end injustice. As we will see later, Gandhi's fear of this development led in part to his proposal of trusteeship to deal with the question of economic equality.

Similar to Emerson and Thoreau, Gandhi felt that the "ideally non-violent state will be ordered anarchy. That state will be the best governed which is governed the least."[18] In a 1942 issue of *Harijan*, Gandhi defined his concept of village swaraj (village self-rule) in greater detail. Each village would be self-contained, both politically and economically. Each would have its own theatre, waterworks, and school. Government would be conducted by the panchayat (village council of five people, both male and female). Satyagraha would be the means by which social order was maintained. Organization of village life in this way would ensure "perfect democracy based upon individual freedom."[19]

Gandhi's village republic idea was not totally new. For example, Kropotkin's *Mutual Aid* describes such villages in different countries in Europe before the industrial revolution. Like Kropotkin's communities, the economic bases of Gandhi's village governments would be cooperativisation and mutual aid. The panchayat would discourage caste differences and promote economic efficiency and self-reliance. Panchayat raj (rule of local units) did not mean that surrounding communities would be ignored. In Gandhi's scheme, "the rural republics gradually passed into larger political organizations on a federal basis rising layer upon layer from the lower rural stratifications on a broad basis of popular self-government."[20] In this way, Gandhi's nonviolent state, or "Ram Rajya" as he sometimes called it, would be a federation of self-governing, autonomous, village republics. The central authority would manage problems of common interest such as banking, health, education, but final decision-making power would rest in the panchayats.

Gandhi's practical proposals of decentralization and self-sufficiency made a good deal of sense to those who thought seriously about reversing the trends caused by colonialism in India. The India of Gandhi's time had become greatly dependent on foreign imports, to the detriment of its own economy. This was particularly true in the case of clothing. Before the British had entered India, the country had produced all of its own cloth in the millions of "cottages" scattered throughout the nation. "A hundred and fifty years ago," Gandhi stated, "we manufactured all our cloth. Our women spun fine yarns in their own cottages, and supplemented the earnings of their husbands."[21]

Colonization by Great Britain, coupled with the rise of the British textile industry, ended this self-sufficiency as it destroyed the cottage industries of India. In the process, Indian unemployment rose, economic development in the countryside was inhibited, and the subcontinent became more dependent on Great Britain for her survival. To reverse these trends, Gandhi advocated swadeshi (home production) in the form of khadi (handspun cloth). This movement to increase Indian production and use of her own products was designed to build up India's economy and independence, to help remedy some of the problems of unemployment, and to reduce economic dependence on all foreign countries.

To give the individual peasant greater control over his or her life entailed a decentralization of the power then concentrated in the cities of New Delhi, Calcutta, and Bombay. In addition, dispersal of power among the 700,000 villages of India would make the defense of the new nation much easier. "Centralisation," said Gandhi in 1939, "cannot be sustained and defended without adequate force . . . the palaces of the rich must have strong guards to protect them against dacoity. So must huge factories."[22] However, decentralization and democratization through village self-rule would not necessarily bring India the "true freedom" of which Gandhi frequently spoke. As Marx suggests in his analysis of the panchayat-based traditional society of India, villages were often contaminated by distinctions of caste and by slavery, and "subjugated man to external circumstances."[23] Therefore, true democracy, as I think Gandhi would have readily admitted, could not be brought about solely by a particular social and political organization such as panchayat raj. A means by which people could struggle for justice was needed as well. Gandhi felt satyagraha would fill that need.

Economic Decentralization

Critics often label Gandhi as a romantic idealist who would forsake modern civilization for the tranquility of village life. However, upon review of his writings it is difficult to come to such a conclusion. His emphasis on decentralization was not solely a return to the past, but was also based on a belief that it was the only way to solve the problems of India brought on by colonialism and the division of town and country. According to Gandhi, the capitalist path of development through modern production techniques accentuated the division between town and country, leaving mass unemployment in rural areas of the nation. Coupled with this capital-intensive development of industry was urbanization, which removed rural industries and skills from the villages and left further unemployment in its wake.

Gandhi said that unemployment in the countryside was a product of colonialism. When manufacturing was done outside the nation, or in the cities, it created what he called a "double slavery"—slavery under the foreign yolk and slavery to "our own inertia and sloth" brought about by loss of self-discipline and dignity as a result of unemployment. It was with these thoughts in mind that Gandhi advocated a policy of economic self-sufficiency in the villages, a "khadi mentality" as he called it.*

Gandhi was determined to reverse the process by which one-half dozen cities in India and Great Britain were living on the exploitation of the country villages. In 1941, he commented on the components of a khadi mentality. His idea entailed a determination to find all the necessities of life in India through the labor and intellect of the villagers. Every village would produce and use all its "necessaries" except for a certain percentage, which it would contribute to the requirements of the cities. In this new rural economy, cities would be clearing houses for village products. The urban centers would find a "natural place" in the economy which would be beneficial to both town and country. Agriculture would be the foundation of economic development. "You cannot build nonviolence on a factory civilisation," said Gandhi, "but it can be built on self-contained villages. . . . Rural economy as I have conceived it, eschews exploitation altogether, and exploitation is the essence of violence."[24] Again, we see practical proposals developing through the interaction of real political conditions (impacts of colonialism) and Gandhian principles (satyagraha and nonviolence).

It is important to note that the economic village units, like the political units, would be joined together, cooperating for the betterment of all. For Gandhi, self-sufficiency would be "overdone":

> Self-sufficiency does not mean narrowness. To be self-sufficient is not to be altogether self-contained. In no circumstances would we be able to produce all the things we need. So though our aim is complete self-sufficiency, we shall have to get from outside the village what we cannot produce in the village: we shall have to produce more of what we can in order thereby to obtain in exchange what we are unable to produce.[25]

The goal of self-sufficiency, therefore, was independence and self-improvement. From this base, the villages could cooperate among themselves as well as with urban areas.

The cities and the urban classes would have an important role

---

*As stated earlier, the word "khadi" means "hand-woven cloth." Gandhi encouraged people to make their own clothes so as to become more self-reliant and less dependent on the British. The "khadi mentality" extended this idea of self-reliance into other village industry as well.

to play in this decentralization. Gandhi hoped that the Congress would send "elites" into the countryside to help organize self-sufficient political and economic units. In addition, he hoped that village swaraj would aid in breaking down the differences between town and country. Feeling that a "division of labour there will necessarily be," but believing that it should not be "a division into intellectual labour to be confined to one class and bodily labour confined to another class," he suggested that city dwellers readjust their lives to be more in harmony with nature by making reparation to the countryside.[26] This is not to say that he wanted to depopulate the cities. Instead, it suggests that the urban class stop exploitation of the country and encourage manufacturing for use instead of for profit.

Trusteeship

While Gandhi hoped that the organization of villages into self-sufficient political units would bring about equality and justice, numerous critics, Marxists and socialists among them, felt that other action was necessary. These decentralist organizations, they said, could not speak to the injustices caused by caste differences. Furthermore, panchayat raj did not transfer the ownership of the means of production from capitalists and rich landowners to the workers and peasants. Without such a change, the socialists and Marxists argued, the fundamental cause of economic inequality would remain. They proposed that the state should seize and control private property after independence. Gandhi, with his misgivings about the centralizing power of the state, balked. Instead, he advanced the idea of trusteeship by which "the rich man will be left in the possession of his wealth, of which he will use what he reasonably requires for his personal needs and will act as a trustee for the remainder to be used for the society."[27]

Gandhi saw this as an alternative to the evils of both private and state ownership. He argued that the acquisition and ownership of property entails responsibility and therefore should be used for the good of the community. Since the generation of wealth is the result of labor and cooperative effort, the wealth producing power of capital must be held in trust for the good of the community.

Gandhi's conception of trusteeship evolved somewhat over time.

Throughout his life, he believed that "trusteeship provides a means of transforming the present capitalist order of society into an egalitarian one. It gives no quarter to capitalism, but gives the present owning class a chance of reforming itself . . . . It does not recognize any right of private ownership of property, except so far as it may be permitted by society for its own welfare."[28]

Originally, the state was to have no say in the matter; capitalists were to convert under pressure of the people who lived nearby. Gradually, however, Gandhi began to talk about "statutory trusteeship," by which the state would regulate the rate of commission given to an owner of property, commensurate with the service rendered to society. According to this formulation, trusteeship would be defined and regulated through statute, thereby turning capitalists into laborers who receive state regulated remuneration as "commission."

Gandhi seemingly had more misgivings about the centralist tendencies of the state than the exploitation caused by private ownership. Yet, if capitalists refused to voluntarily act as trustees, Gandhi agreed that the state would have to intervene and deny them their holdings through a "minimum exercise of violence."[29] Furthermore, Gandhi gradually became reconciled to the idea that the state could (and would) accumulate capital. Believing that private capital accumulation was impossible without exploitation and hence violence, Gandhi felt that in a nonviolent society, there was no room for private capital accumulation. In a nonviolent society based on "trusteeship," capital eventually would be accumulated by the state. That Gandhi saw this is clear:

> The accumulation of capital by private persons is impossible except through violent means, but accumulation by the state in a nonviolent society is not only possible, it is desireable and inevitable."[30]

How he squared this with his misgivings about the state is not exactly clear. Ganguli suggests that Gandhi was thinking in terms of "social capital formation" and introduced the concept of "social control" as part of his trusteeship theory as a result.[31]

In 1946, Gandhi had the occasion to counterpose this concept of "social control" as an alternative to nationalization of industry. In this formulation, trusteeship was not vested in the "capitalists" or the "state" but instead in all the laborers of an enterprise (both workers and owners) in a kind of profit sharing arrangement. Ganguli says that although workers' control and participation in management were socialist ideals which one can reconcile with Gandhi's philosophy, one should not think of social control as a substitution of workers' "real ownership" for the capitalists' "real ownership." Gandhi may, of course, have eventually moved in this direction. After all, he, like Marx, believed in the primacy of labor and on numerous occasions suggested that the means of production ought to be owned by those who used them. However, his writings on the subject of trusteeship are fraught with contradictions which were seemingly never resolved. This may have been the result of an overly idealistic belief that various class interests and conflicts could be reconciled to the benefit of society as a whole. His belief in the inherent goodness of the owners of capital, an assumption upon which his trusteeship theory rested, contrasted sharply with the actual social and economic situation in India during his lifetime. Given his constant reflection on social policies, however, he may have eventually reconciled these contradictions, and developed new proposals for remedying economic inequality.

The proper role of the state in the advancement of just and equal social relationships plagued Gandhi throughout his life. Gandhi knew that the ideal state, which would consist of a loose federation of self-sufficient villages, could not be brought into existence at a single stroke. And since he did not want private enterprise to develop to uncontrollable proportions and thus frustrate the ideal state altogether, he favored state ownership of certain "key industries." This was, to be sure, a concession made to the "real" by the "ideal" in Gandhi's mind but he thought it better to compromise in this regard for the sake of a long-range vision.

The Battle with Industrialization

The conflict between the decentralist vision and the problems of a newly emerging nation also had their impact on Gandhi's views regarding industrialization. Many westerners have come to view Gandhi as anti-industry. They imagine him sitting cross-legged in his loin cloth, merrily spinning away a hot Indian afternoon. Such an impression clearly misunderstands both Gandhi's thoughts on industrialization as well as the role of spinning in the independence movement. It is true that his *Hind Swaraj* (Indian Home Rule), first published in 1909, contained the most scathing attacks on machinery and western technology. Written with an extremely defensive, nationalist bias against the West, *Hind Swaraj* argued that the West must throw over modern civilization and that increases of comfort do not produce moral growth. If the East were to adopt Western methods, it would lead to a meeting of the two civilizations, but this gathering would be an "armed truce" owing to the Western indulgence in militarism.

This argument has often been viewed as an attack on machinery and technology. Gandhi was, however, laying stress not on machinery as such, but on the capitalist system with its motive-forces of greed, exploitation of labor, and labor-saving for the few. "My fundamental objection to machinery," he wrote, "rests on the fact that it is machinery that has enabled these nations to exploit others."[32] For Gandhi, the question revolved around how machinery fit into his ethical system and his plans for developing an ideal society. With this in mind, one can cite a number of reasons why Gandhi would oppose development of machinery in India. First, the development of machinery and mass-productive techniques supplanted jobs throughout India, especially in the villages. Since work is necessary both for moral growth and physical sustenance, technological developments which caused unemployment were seen by Gandhi as detrimental to the attempts at building *Sarvodaya*. "What I object to," he said, " is the craze for machinery. Men go on 'saving labour' till thousands are without work and thrown on the streets to die of starvation."[33] In addition, development of machinery would lead to further concentration of wealth in individuals and cities and therefore run contrary to Gandhi's decentralist vision. Mass production, he feared, would lead to overproduction and imperialist tendencies in India. Finally, the Mahatma felt that machines led to the growth of economic competition while he was attempting to build a society based on cooperation.[34]

In this light, it is again important to emphasize the spinning wheel as a symbol of the Gandhian movement against colonialism. The central effort during the years of the nationalist struggle for independence lay in the propagation of khadi, hand-spun by millions of Indians in a cooperative effort to build home industry.

Spinning, therefore, was not simply a symbol of Indian resistance technology, but also served economic functions through the actual supply of cloth and the development of self-sufficiency.

When reviewing Gandhi's writings carefully, it becomes apparent that he is more opposed to the introduction of mass-production techniques than to machinery per se. In his words, machinery was a "wooden thing and can be turned to a good purpose or bad."[35] Mary Anderson suggests that Gandhi evaluated the worth of machines on the basis of three criteria: (1) the degree to which they preserved labor; (2) the degree to which they could be used in small factories; and, (3) the degree to which they promoted or undermined self-sufficiency.[36] This suggests that the thrust of Gandhi's thought is not against machinery, but instead toward decentralization and technology's role in the process. Accordingly, Gandhi saw the Singer Sewing machine as a progressive invention and supported a rural electrification program.

Conclusion

From the above analysis, it should be strikingly clear that Gandhi's ideal system was decidedly decentralist. His vision of political institutions in the new society saw the panchayats as most important. Economic institutions would be decentralized by the promotion of khadi and other village industries. These organizational forms would form the basis of Sarvodaya. However, it must be reemphasized that Gandhi realized the limits of reformed and new institutions; progressive social organization could not insure equality and justice. The technique of struggle called satyagraha, therefore, was necessary to maintain the developing just and decentralist social order. Through this method, small groups would be empowered to protect their new-found equality and justice.

Gandhi's vision of a new society provided an inspiring picture (not a forecast based on quantitative inputs) of what social institutions would look like if his personal ethics were translated into reality. To be sure, many of his proposals took the form of "ideal types," of models by which other ideas could be judged. However, Gandhi felt that projection of an ideal was the only way to make progress in the real world. He believed, consistent with his adherence to satyagraha, that in the course of nonviolent struggle, the truth would emerge. As the truth became clear, new structures and ideals would develop to advance the cause of social justice. The words below should provide some insight into his reasoning in this area. When asked whether the ideal state would have government, Gandhi replied:

> Euclid's line is one without breadth, but no one so far has been able to draw it and never will. All the same, it is only by keeping the ideal line in mind that we made progress in Geometry. What is true here is true of every ideal.[37]

Notes

1. The *Harijan,* a news weekly, was founded by Gandhi in 1932. Gandhi used the term "Harijan," which means people of God, to describe India's caste of untouchables.
2. *Harijan,* 24 April 1933; quoted in B. N. Ganguli, *Gandhi's Social Philosophy,* New York: John Wiley & Sons, Inc., 1973, p. 307.
3. See, for example, Gene Sharp, *Gandhi Wields the Weapon of Moral Power: Three Case Histories,* Ahmedabad: Navajivan, 1960.
4. Jayantanuja Bandyapadhyaya, *Social and Political Thought of Gandhi* Bombay, New York and London: Allied Pub., 1969.
5. Joan Bondurant, *Conquest of Violence,* Berkeley: University of California, 1969.
6. *Ibid.,* p. 8.
7. Krishnalal Shridharani, *War Without Violence,* New York: Harcourt, Brace Javanovich, Inc., 1939.
8. Gopi Nath Dhawan, *The Political Philosophy of Mahatma Gandhi;* Bombay: The Popular Book Depot, 1946, p. 59.
9. Bondurant, op. cit., p. 16.
10. H. J. N. Horsburgh, *Nonviolence and Aggression,* London: Oxford University Press, 1969, p. 43.
11. *Harijan,* 11 February 1939; quoted in Ganguli, op. cit. p. 147.
12. Ganguli, op. cit., p. 145.
13. M. K. Gandhi, *An Autobiography,* Boston: Little, Brown & Co., 1957, p. 299.
14. Ganguli, op. cit., p. 166.
15. M. K. Gandi, *Speeches and Writings of Mahatma Gandhi,* 4th edition, Madras: Nateson, n.d. quoted in Bondurant, op. cit., pp. 106—107.
16. *Ibid.,* p. 170.
17. *Harijan,* 13 January 1940, pp. 410—11.

18. Ganguli, op. cit., p. 171.

19. *Harijan*, 26 July 1942, p. 238; in M. K. Gandhi, *Selected Works*, Shirman Narayan, (ed.), Ahmedabad, 1968, vol. VI, pp. 345—346.

20. Shanti Gupta, *The Economic Philosophy of Mahatma Gandhi*, Delhi, p. 161.

21. Louis Fischer, *Gandhi: His Life and Message for the World*, New York: New American Library, 1954, p. 83.

22. *Harijan*, 30 December 1939: quoted in Bandyopadhyaya, op. cit., p. 117.

23. Karl Marx, "British Rule in India," in Marx and Engels, *On Colonialism*, Moscow, p. 37: quoted in Bandyopadhyaya, p. 122.

24. *Harijan*, 4 November, 1939, p. 331.

25. M. K. Gandhi, *Selected Works*, VI, p. 348.

26. D. G. Tendulkar, *Mahatma*, Bombay: Jhaveri and Tendulkar, 1952, vol. III, p. 349.

27. *Harijan*, 25 August 1940, in Bandyapadhyaya, p. 132.

28. *Harijan*, 25 October 1952, p. 301

29. Ganguli, op. cit., p. 271.

30. *Ibid.*, p. 276.

31. *Ibid.*, p. 276.

32. Gandhi, *Selected Works*, VI, p. 377.

33. Ganguli, op. cit., p. 314.

34. For further reference on development issues in India, see N. K. Bose's "A Premature Metropolis" in *Scientific American*, Cities: Their Growth and Human Impact, San Francisco: Freeman, 1973, and G. Breese, *Urbanization in Developing Countries*, New York: Prentice Hall, 1966.

35. Gandhi, *Selected Works*, VI, p. 377.

36. Mary Anderson, "Gandhian Economics," unpublished paper, p. 8.

37. Gandhi, *Selected Works*, VI, p. 437.

Part II.

Social Change Movements in The United States

Radical-nonviolent action is a social phenomenon in which people seek to overcome domination and exploitation. Part II reviews cases of social movements that have appeared in the United States.

In this section on the United States, we begin with the personal experiences of David Dellinger as a nonviolent activist in jail. We see how he views the world with other prisoners in the routines of incarceration. We then examine the movements of far workers, nuclear power protestors, and civil rights demonstrators in the United States. In Chapter Five, Susan Abrams evaluates efforts of the United Farm Workers to secure decent working conditions for Chicano farmers. She concentrates on methods of nonviolent-direct action and their degree of success. In Chapter Six, Neil Katz and John Hunt then present a case history of a civil rights event in Albany, Georgia. They apply and investigate Gene Sharp's method for analyzing nonviolent dynamics. Finally, in Chapter Seven, Harvey Wasserman offers a picture of the newly emerging nonviolent battle against nuclear power within the U.S. and its implications for the international scene.

Chapter 4

Ten Days in Jail*

David Dellinger

> *The law, in its majestic equality, forbids the rich as well as the poor to sleep under bridges, to beg and to steal bread.*
>
> Anatole France

> *The best prison community is no more than an extreme totalitarian society, and the most it can produce is a good convict who is quite different than a good citizen. . . . Reformation of convicts must be attained chiefly outside any penal institution.*
> *Encyclopaedia Britannica,*
>
> Article on "Prison"

People generally laugh when I mention that I went from Yale to jail and that I got a more vital education from three years in jail

*Permission has been granted the author for the printing of this article originally published in *Revolutionary Nonviolence* (New York: Doubleday, 1971)

than from six years at Yale. The laugh always makes me a little
uneasy (even apart from the feebleness of the play on words)
because I am afraid it implies that far from being dead serious
I am merely indulging in a humorous exaggeration, since one
wouldn't really expect to learn more in prison than in a university.
A little reflection should convince most persons that one can learn
more about the nature of our society by sharing in a small way
the life of its victims than by interacting intellectually with its
privileged academicians. Be that as it may, I spent ten days in jail
recently and had my complacency jolted once again (nonconfor-
mists can be more complacent that we realize) and my imagination
quickened by this little refresher course in the realities that lie
behind the facade of our society.

I have never never forgotten my first experience of arrest and
imprisonment many years ago: how inexorably the transitions
took place from being treated as "saints ahead of our time" (a
comment by a member of the grand jury that indicted eight of
us for our refusal, as pacifists, to register for the draft); to mis-
guided and stubborn idealists (the attitude of the judge); to criminals with "no rights of any kind" who had better wise up if we
wanted to stay in one piece (as we were told by a guard five
minutes after being ushered out of the polite and superficially
civil-libertarian atmosphere of the courtroom into the prison world
into which no visitors are admitted and from which no uncen-
sored letters are released). If the details varied slightly this time,
the pattern was similar: only when we were safely out of sight of
judge and spectators were the realities of the prison system revealed to us.

My recent arrest grew out of a "vigil" outside the Central Intelligence Agency headquarters in Washington, D.C.** where ten
of us picketed, handed out leaflets, and began a two-week fast
(taking only water) in protest against the invasion of Cuba and to
help forestall future invasions. About a hundred persons joined
us for a brief supporting stint the first afternoon and nearly two
hundred and fifty were on hand the final day, but in between,
when the numbers were less, we soon found that some of the
police were not above a selective enforcement of the law. When
Bob Steed, of the *Catholic Worker*, sat down to rest a few hundred
feet from the vigil line on some concrete steps that led to a nearby

**C.I.A. headquarters have since been moved to Langley, Va.

Veteran's Hospital, one of the policemen hurried over and ordered him to move, under threat of arrest. When Bob pointed out that other people were sitting on the steps, the policeman retorted: "It doesn't matter. As long as you are connected with that project *you* can't sit here." Another time, when some us sat in a parked car for a few minutes we were told that we must drive away or be arrested for vagrancy. On this occasion the police failed to follow through on their threat, but the next day we were not so fortunate. After three days of fasting, seven of us decided to sit for a while on a narrow grass strip between the sidewalk and the wire fence that enclosed the C.I.A. buildings. We chose this spot not only because of its strategic location but also because we had seen passersby sit there without interference. No matter, we were ordered to move, and arrested when we refused to do so.

Those who engage in nonviolent demonstrations are not always allowed to decide for themselves whether or not the project will include civil disobedience. As the police become increasingly uncivil, the demonstrators are forced to become increasingly disobedient if they want the project to accomplish its objectives. On this occasion the object of the police was clearly to keep us as nearly invisible as possible. We were told that we could sit on the grass around the corner (where there were not so many passersby and where the relationship of our action to the C.I.A. would have been obscured) but we were arrested for sitting where we could engage in "free speech" most effectively. In court, the police admitted that we would not have been arrested for sitting around the corner and that we had been completely nonviolent, but we were convicted of disorderly conduct on the grounds that our demonstration *might have provoked other persons to violence against us*. The judge offered us a suspended sentence if we would promise not to repeat the action, but since our objective was not to preserve our own private liberty (we could have done this by staying home in the first place) but to protest public evils, we were unable to make such a deal. We chose instead to express our conviction that Americans must set aside their own personal convenience in order to act as counterweights to America's criminal foreign policy which, in Cuba, included not only economic boycott and indirect military aggression but having its spokesmen lie in their teeth about it at the United Nations.

To make clear the pattern of police dishonesty and abuse of

power, even outside the prisons (in prison democratic restraints on the officials are at a minimum), let me tell what happened the day we were released from jail. We informed the police of our intention to have a poster walk the following day, with several hundred persons marching from the C.I.A. headquarters through the streets of Washington, past the White House and to the site of a mass rally. Several officials, including the acting Chief of Police, told me that we could not do this because (1) parades are not allowed without a permit (on previous occasions I had learned that permits are not usually granted for *such* parades); (2) no one is allowed to parade past the White House; and (3) our route went past several foreign embassies and no one is allowed to carry a sign within five hundred feet of an embassy. The reasons sound plausible and on a number of previous occasions peace walkers have yielded because on the one hand they believed what they were told, and on the other hand they lacked a united conviction that the seriousness of the occasion justified the disregard of local ordinances and the risk of arrest. Nonetheless, I had also participated in poster walks and leaflet distributions, both in Washington and other cities, where the police had backed down when the demonstrators refused to be intimidated. I knew that earlier that very day the San Francisco-to-Moscow Peace Walkers had carried signs over part of the same route without a permit and that a thousand Quakers had been allowed to do the same, a few months earlier. After consultation with the rest of the planning committee I informed the police that we knew of these precedents and that in any case we felt that the immorality of the intervention in Cuba made it imperative for us to speak out publicly in this way, even if it meant another arrest. The police not only yielded but provided an impressive (if undesired) official escort for our "illegal" procession. Perhaps the noble old slogan "Eternal Vigilance Is the Price of Liberty" should be replaced by a more earthy, and paradoxical one, something like this: "Being ready to go to jail is the only way of remaining free."

Most convicts would rather serve time in an old-fashioned jail or pen than in a liberal "correctional" institution. The basic prerequisite for a decent life—freedom—is lacking in either case, but in the "reformed" institutions the prisoner finds that he is subjected to a kind of manipulation and psychological assault that the old-fashioned warden and keepers had no interest in. I remember a Christmas at the Danbury Federal Correctional Institution in Connecticut when the Christmas party consisted of an exhibition of dancing and singing by the warden's young children and their classmates. When the performance was over, the warden mounted the platform and made a speech in which he kept reminding the prisoners that if they hadn't broken the law they could have been with their wives and children on Christmas Eve, as he was. Perhaps only those who have been deprived for a lengthy period of the company of wives, children, and loved ones can appreciate how cruel this little sermon was and how it embittered rather than enlightened the men. Never did I receive a half-hour visit (we were allowed a total of one hour of visits a month) without having my parents or fiancee subjected to a prior interview with the warden or a social service worker in which they were treated to a lengthy analysis of my various character defects. Wives were often told, on the basis of "scientific" case-studies, that they should divorce their husbands, or stop visiting them, because they were "no good." Censorship of reading material, "to help rehabilitate the convict," was so extreme that at one time only one New York newspaper (the New York Times, which appealed to the warden but not to many of the inmates) was allowed to circulate and copies of it were distributed only after every news story that dealt with crime had been cut out. When a friend sent me a copy of The World's Great Letters, the censorship department passed it on to me only after having deleted a letter by Benjamin Franklin which was considered "salacious." Did they really think that the inmates would have learned more about the perverse glories of crime from the New York Times than from their fellow inmates with whom they were joined in the common, embittering experience of living in an "extreme totalitarian society"; and with whom they united in a thousand imaginative ways of "beating the system" (everything from stealing food and manufacturing a powerful prison brew to smuggling tobacco, at great personal risk, to men in the "hole")? Did they think that sexual abuse and insensitivity were more apt to result from reading a letter by Ben Franklin than from being locked up for years without contact with loved ones? If anyone had interrupted one of the jailhouse bull sessions on sex to read out loud the offending passages from Franklin he would have been hooted down for boring the audience.

The Washington, D.C. jail was an uneasy compromise between the old-fashioned jail in which confinement and the prevention of escape are almost the only concerns, and the modern paternalistic institution which tries, unrealistically, to combine confinement with rehabilitation. In the main, it succeeded in combining, in slightly modified form, the shortcomings of both types of institution and the virtues of neither. On the one hand, we were subject to classification interviews with social service workers whose sheltered, conformist lives had so limited their ability to grasp the realities of the system that it is hard to imagine their ever understanding a criminal or establishing any significant human contact with him—even if they had any interest in considering him as anything but a "case." (In the first information-gathering my name was somehow transcribed as David Dillings and a series of interviewers insisted that I must sign my name in this fashion if I did not want to go to the "hole." I suppose that in some future court appearance I shall be accused of having used an alias.) On the other hand, the daily routine was such as to encourage utter boredom, and physical and mental deterioration. We were awakened at 4:30 a.m. and spent the entire day sitting in the overcrowded chapel, without reading material, work, exercise, or diversion of any kind. The windows were even frosted to prevent looking outside. The only breaks were the three daily meals and the periodic "counts." In our case, we were continuing to fast, so benefited from the mealtimes only by having a brief respite from living in a dense crowd. There were 160 beds in my dormitory, arranged in doubledeckers so close together that if anyone lying in his bed (we were only allowed on the bed between 9:30 at night and 4:30 the next morning) stretched his arms out, he would touch the beds on both sides. I am told that the prisoners are allowed to go to the stockade for two hours on Sundays, but since it rained we watched television instead. As beautiful women and expensive status symbols were flashed on the screen, I looked at the men around me and thought that the crime of many of them was to have been hypnotized by the lures of our society and to have sought to attain them by methods which were outside the law (the ground rules of capitalist society) but not necessarily more antisocial than the accepted legal ones. In varying degrees they lacked the education, the contacts, the pigmentation, the patience, the inherited capital, or the hypocrisy to attain their goals by accepting methods of living off the labor of others—collecting rents, profits, dividends, interest or the excessive salaries of the professional and managerial classes; buying or hiring cheap and selling dear; excelling in the attractive packaging or psychologically effective advertising of an inferior product, etc. The man who pockets a cool million by speculating in slum-clearance housing or installing inadequate air-conditioning in fancy apartment houses becomes a public hero by setting up a scholarship fund or contributing to charity, but the man who sat beside me, his eyes glued to the TV screen, had "lost all his rights" because he had stolen some jewelry.

The question is does a person ever lose his rights as a human being? Both kinds of prison operate on the assumption that he does. As I entered the D.C. jail I was greeted with the words, so familiar to me from previous experiences: "You have no rights." (In liberal institutions the advances of modern penology are summed up in the fuller phrasing: "You have no rights, only privileges.") A "good convict" is one who acquiesces in this defamation of character until he finally explodes in resentful violence or becomes a shadow of a man who is made a trustee or is considered safe to release on parole. I have seen men put in the "hole" for "silent insolence," because the system cannot function without breaking the spirit of its victims, and the light of independence in a man's eye is more frightening to the authorities than occasional violations of administrative regulations.

As pacifists we revealed at least a few signs of inner-directedness and this caused immediate tensions with the authorities. We also tried to go out of our way to be sensitive to their human qualities, and the more contact we had with individual guards the more willing they were to overlook our minor transgressions, in apparent (if somewhat bewildered) appreciation for being treated, for a change, as fellow human beings. They were more used to opportunistic, subservience without personal respect than to foolhardy resistance combined with respect. Traditionally tough guards who had gotten to know us pretended not to notice our idiosyncratic violations of prison routine, but whenever we entered a strange part of the prison and encountered new guards we were in danger. On one occasion, when we had been escorted to a new area and were waiting to see what would happen (prisoners are seldom told where they are going or why), two of us were excoriated for looking out a partially open window. When I asked, as gently as I could, what harm there was in looking at the grass, the guard became nervous and felt the need to assert his authority. He ordered me to take off some paper buttonholes with which we managed to keep our shirts from being constantly unbuttoned because of the oversized buttonholes. His manner was so arbitrary (and the practice of wearing the buttonholes so well established) that I felt it necessary to explain that I was chilly, that the shirt would not stay buttoned otherwise, and then, in response he shouted, "You are in prison now; shut up and do as I say." To this I replied that even prisoners had the right to be treated civilly.

When, as a result, I was thrown into the "hole," the modern prison's equivalent of the medieval dungeon, I found that the approximately five-by-six foot damp strip cell, part of which was taken up by a toilet which could only be flushed from the outside, was already occupied by two other prisoners. There was no room for all of us to lie down at one time, but we managed by having two of us put our feet and legs up the wall while the third put his on the toilet. One of the prisoners was upbraiding the other for being a damn fool. "It don't make no difference that you're innocent," he said. "They don't want you to plead not guilty. You would've got off with thirty days. Now you'll get six months." "I know." said the other, "but it was a matter of principle with me."

The seasoned, guilty man had been in the "hole" a week, for having a fight. The principled "damn fool" had been taken to the barber shop earlier that day in anticipation of his appearance in court the following morning. He had an attractive pompadour hair style and had balked when told that he would have to have it cut another way. "Just don't give me no haircut at all," he had said, " 'cause when I appear in court I wants to be mine own self." But for this act of self-assertion he had been thrown in the "hole." It wouldn't have been right under any circumstances, but I couldn't help thinking that here was a man who apparently was innocent, and who, in any event, was supposed to be presumed innocent until proven guilty. Because he could not afford bail, however, he had already lost all his rights.

When I walked out of jail after my ten days were up, I couldn't tell whether I felt more elated at having my "freedom" or depressed at the thought of those whom I had left inside. I know, from previous experience, that I shall never forget some of them and that I shall never meet any finer persons out of jail than some of the friends I made inside. But I also know how easy it is to get caught up in other routines, and how hard it is to convince people that the only way to reform jails is to abolish them. For jails are necessary for the preservation of "law and order" in a society where there are rich and poor, overprivileged and underprivileged.

Chapter 5

The United Farm Workers Union

Susan Abrams

The fierce, bloody history of farm labor organizing in California contains the stuff from which melodramas are made and real-life hopes and dreams destroyed. From the first large-scale organizing efforts (by the Industrial Workers of the World) in 1905 through strikes involving perhaps 100,000 workers during the Depression years, the same pattern of vigilante terror against strikers—beatings, mass arrests, and jailed leaders—is repeated. The growers' enormous power over "rented slaves" was, in their own minds, apparently so tenuous that even the mildest demand for autonomy threatened their entire way of life. Yet the sporadic physical violence the growers resorted to was, in fact, only an intensification of the violence of everyday life for farmworkers so poor and demoralized that there remained among them little anger to arouse.

Bluntly stated, there were too many farmworkers in California, the nation's major produce region. Their numbers swelled by influxes of Asian immigrants, Mexicans in search of work, Dust-bowl refugees in Depression years, the farmworkers were well aware that rebellious employees could always be replaced by those who were more compliant and also willing to work for less money. Most recently, the growers had imported thousands of Mexican nationals, with government sanction, under the so-called Bracero program (1942-1964). Like the Mexicans working here illegally,

102

the "Braceros" realized that protest spelled immediate deportation.

Themselves the victims of racism in dusty towns whose restaurants sported a whites-only policy, each ethnic group of farmworkers was goaded to racial tension with competing groups by growers who had learned how to forestall organizing. Migrating from place to place as the different crops ripened, farmworkers were an organizer's nightmare. Even their temporary homes were owned by the growers, who could not only deny access to organizers, but evict workers at will. The power of individual growers, whose huge ranches bore little resemblance to the "family farm," was quickly augmented by the police and by state and local officials who refused to pass laws in the farmworkers' favor. Describing agriculture as the basis of the American economy, growers moved easily to the position that those who dared disrupt it through strikes were dangerous agitators. The public's fears of the ragtag, often non-white, migrants were roused to fever pitch by the local press, which was as eager to condemn their demands as it was loath to expose their wretched living conditions and question the causes of their misery.

Like black slaves before them, farmworkers were portrayed as simple souls, happy in their work under sunny skies, easily able to bend and stoop all day. The statistical exterior of their lives, even into the 1960s and 1970s, tells a rather different story—one of employer power and employee powerlessness so great that the status quo could have been accepted for nearly a century.

The nation's three million farmworkers, about 300,000 of them in California, have a life expectancy of 49 years; 800,000 children under 16 work in the fields; infant mortality is 125 percent higher than the national average and accidents 300 percent higher. Most farmworkers show symptoms of pesticide poisoning; few go beyond elementary school; and 90 percent of their housing is substandard. Farmworkers are hired out "in lots" to growers by labor contractors, who discriminate against women and older workers at will and reserve a generous part of each paycheck for themselves.

Unorganized and shunned by townspeople who fear an added burden on either their taxes or consciences, farmworkers have hardly been in a position to gain the influential allies in government who might curb the growers' power. Like reservation Indians, farmworkers have long been removed from most Americans' lives, including those of potential supporters.

Unemployment compensation, disability insurance, social security, not to speak of such amenities as toilets and clean drinking water on the job, have been as little known to farmworkers (except in Hawaii, whose labor history is unique), as they are assumed by other workers. The National Labor Relations Act (NLRA) of 1935 specifically excluded farmworkers from its provisions for union elections, collective bargaining, and investigation into charges of unfair labor practices. Before the Taft-Hartley (1947) and Landrum-Griffin (1959) amendments restricted its pro-union stance, the NLRA did allow millions of American workers to organize. Without even the flimsiest mechanism for negotiations, farmworkers have had to resort to the poor substitute of strikes to force their demands upon the growers' attention.

Organizers were often outsiders who, although frequently exhibiting great courage, were remote from farmworkers' lives and came with "hidden agendas" whose rhetoric only fed local redbaiting. With a focus on strikes and lack of grassroots leadership, the "unions" collapsed when the organizers left. There were some gains, to be sure—a pay raise here and there, some outside support—but never enough to change the power balance. The usually temporary reforms were imposed from without or agreed to by growers as token gestures to disuade from further organizing. The AFL-CIO and its predecessors the AFL and CIO were conspicuous by their lack of interest in organizing farm labor, whose differences from industrial workers they never quite understood. Said Paul Scharrenberg, at one time the AFL's secretary-treasurer in California, "Only fanatics are willing to live in shacks or tents and get their heads broken in the interests of migratory labor."[1]

What was there, then, to inspire confidence in yet another organizing effort, as Cesar Chavez began his cautious travels in 1962, sounding out the hopes and fears of California farmworkers? Could the almighty growers be dragged, prodded or cajoled into the modern age, induced to grant their workforce the basic rights and dignities which most other American workers had long since taken for granted? Could it be done by people so vulnerable that it seemed almost cruel to ask them to risk anything? Could anger, once aroused, be channeled into the patient, creative, and unfamiliar tactics of nonviolence rather than erupt into the violence which would spell the movement's quick demise? Had earlier organizers been at fault or were their failures due entirely to the enormous power, used without scruple, against them?

Chavez, himself a former farmworker, had tremendous faith in farmworkers' own potential, in the power of people, once aroused, to do for themselves what needed to be done. When his colleagues' resistance to union-building became clear, Chavez gave up his job as director of the Community Services Organization (CSO) and, with scant savings, moved his large family to Delano. He soon attracted two other capable CSO staff members: Gilbert Padilla and Dolores Huerta, later UFW vice-president and top negotiator, and the only prominent woman labor official in the nation. In retrospect, their organizing tactics contrast so sharply with those of earlier activists that one is tempted to view them all as deliberate attempts to overcome past failures. They also anticipate the UFW's nonviolent methods, yet some tactics were surely born of necessity or of practical temperaments. One is, after all, more likely to learn of techniques which succeed.

Chavez and his co-workers were, like most farmworkers, Chicanos, not "anglo" outsiders. They took the time to sound out people's ideas, to argue, and to convince them not only that joining the Farm Workers Association (FWA) could be beneficial but that the growers were not invincible, that economics, not Fate, had them in its grip. Talking to workers in the fields, in their homes, in grocery stores, they set up house meetings, whose participants themselves then set up further meetings.

The CSO experience with poor Chicanos, as well as contacts made in ten years of activism, proved invaluable in one-to-one organizing, in providing social services (e.g. as interpreters in court, as welfare payment advocates), in applying pressure on elected officials. A worker who experienced a direct benefit gave his or her loyalty to the fledgling organization, whose staff worked as hard as did farmworkers, giving up their private life entirely and exhausting themselves racing between housemeetings up and down the countryside. "After all, if you're outraged at conditions, then you can't possibly be free or happy until you devote all your time to changing them and do nothing but that,"[2] as Chavez later put it. His sense of inevitability was greater than many other dedicated activists. Aware that farmworkers identified unions with strikes and violence, Chavez conceived and presented the FWA (later NFWA) as a cooperative venture with a social service orientation, including a credit union, health care, and death benefits. This was not just a ploy to gain converts. Chavez, in contrast to earlier organizers, envisioned strikes and union contracts as five or ten years in the future and possible only on the basis of a well-functioning organization. His "union" would, in exchange for the dues which farmworkers paid only with considerable sacrifice, provide desperately needed services, compensating for employer and local government negligence. It would grow out of and be defined by farmworkers' needs rather than political ideology. Sacrifice, hard work, and, eventually, numbers, must make up for the power and wealth of the growers. Chavez insisted that no outside funds be accepted: "Even when there are no strings attached, you are still compromised because you feel you have to produce immediate results." The movement "might get too far ahead of the people it belongs to."[3] Furthermore, for the farmworkers' budding self-confidence, it was essential that they be dependent on no one else.

The patient, grassroots organizing might have continued for many years, had the NFWA not been propelled, somewhat against its will, into joining the 1965 strike against Delano grape growers begun by the Agricultural Workers Organizing Committee (a Filipino affiliate of the AFL-CIO). The meeting at which the strike vote was to be taken was, by design, held on Mexican Independence Day. Chavez exhorted the workers to a nonviolent stance, while also appealing to the Mexican revolutionary tradition. The strange amalgam was well-devised. Farmworkers' familiarity with sacrifice, their deeply felt religious feelings, and even burgeoning Chicano pride were later enlisted in the service of nonviolent action. Suffering, as one worker put it, became "suffering for a purpose." Nonviolence as a philosophy was made more viable and acceptable through its blending with obviously compatible religious elements. The long-submissive workers were roused to nonviolent action far removed from their former passivity. It was, first of all, an agreed-upon tactic, deliberately assumed and, secondly, of a militant, often provocative nature. Masses, familiar songs, and even boisterous theater became a regular part of meetings and sometimes picket lines. These activities not only aided morale, but also helped the farmworkers adapt to unaccustomed and often dangerous activities.

The early picket lines included veterans of the Civil Rights struggles in the South, who were familiar with nonviolent tactics. Stretched along a dusty road, waving red banners with a black Aztec eagle (the union's symbol), shouting "*Huelga!*" (strike), the picketers tried to convince workers to leave the fields and join them. Chavez has described the picket line as "the best labor school we could ever have."[4] There people learned to articulate their demands, stand up for themselves, and make their commitment visible.

> The picket line is where a man makes his commitment, and it is irrevocable; the longer he's on the picket line, the stronger the commitment. A lot of workers make their commitment where nobody sees them; they just leave the job and they don't come back. But you get a guy who in front of the boss, in front of all the other guys, throws down his tools and marches right out to the picket line, that is an exceptional guy, and that's the kind we have out on the strike . . . the picket line is a beautiful thing, because it does something to a human being. People associate strikes with violence, and we've removed the violence . . .[5]

Unfortunately, the growers were unchanged by picket line confrontations and hadn't removed the violence. Given a chance by the NFWA to meet for negotiations before the strikes began, they refused even to consider the possibility of dialogue with people they viewed as inferior, whose "insolence" must have amazed them as much as it outraged them. As the movement and its support grew, the growers came to realize that they faced far more than strikes, that to accede to farmworkers' demands meant to give up the comfortably anachronistic control which they, nearly alone among American employers, still exercised.

> Almost to the saturation point, growers had absorbed the propaganda of their own lobby, which for generations had boosted the notion that agriculture is entitled to special immunities from the effects of bad weather, competition, and even labor problems.[6]

As grower Jack Pandol told one reporter, "But all Chavez is trying to do is replace my power structure with his."[7] The concept of shared power, of mutually beneficial work arrangements, was not so much threatening as foreign under these circumstances. The farmworkers' approach could indeed seem revolutionary and thus "communist-inspired" where anything short of total control upset too many cherished notions of one's proper place in the world. Yet, this union, unlike some of its predecessors, did not push its demands or goals beyond a shift in power to its radical restructuring, as embodied, for example, in land reform.

The growers were men used to having their way and they responded swiftly and predictably. Picketers were beaten up, sprayed with pesticides, threatened by attack dogs, and nearly run over by fast cars, often under the eyes of the police. Town officials tried to close down union offices out of sudden concern with fire code violations. Police stationed themselves day and night outside strikers' homes. It was, as John Gregory Dunne points out in his chronicle of the strike, all curiously out of date, more akin to the 1930s with "embattled growers, untouched by labor's consolidation over the past three decades" and "a town . . . mobilized to combat the Red Menace."[8]

There were incidents of retaliation by strikers; it's hard to know how many. However, there were fewer incidences than one might either expect or regard as justified, considering not only the insults to picketers' dignity and threats to their lives, but also the years of misery which preceded the strike. Strikers' harassment of strikebreakers probably included some physical violence, such as smashing windows, but usually it consisted of what Chavez later referred to as "hounding and educating them." Strikers might hold "a pray-in or a sing-in in front of their homes, or we would put two or three pickets with 'A Scab Lives Here' sign to parade up and down the street for a while."[9] Strikebreakers were satirized in skits performed by *El Teatro Campesino* (farmworkers' theater). As Ronald Taylor notes, the skits "brought the bigness of agribusiness down to a ludicrous scale . . . [and] gave the workers a vent for their anger; they could laugh and cheer and see themselves as something more than helpless *peons*,"[10] while learning some of the broader issues involved.

There was a great deal to do besides train the new groups of workers in nonviolence and overcome their fear of the police ("If they're not afraid, then they can keep a lot of things cool, but the moment they're uncertain, then anything can happen," as Chavez put it). There was little money for food, for the gas needed to drive to the picket lines. There was scarce time to plan strategy when one had to react quickly to a barrage of grower-police strategems.

Some of the strikebreakers were probably encouraged to slow down their pace or otherwise cut into the growers' profits a bit. Strikers themselves learned how to "cooperate" less and less with their harassers. For example, police insisting on photographing and identifying each picketer at first easily had their way, but later had to spend hours processing just a few slow-talking subjects. Strikers maintained picket lines around the clock, requiring police presence in three shifts, in order to make harassment expensive.

But picket lines alone, no matter how nonviolent or otherwise unusual, were not enough for victory in the 1960s any more than they had been 30 or 60 years earlier. The reasons were both concrete and overwhelming: there were too many strikebreakers available; the violence continued unabated; local judges were only too willing to grant injunctions restricting picketing; and there was no money to pay strikers.

The growers had destroyed every earlier organizing effort because local power was in their own or allies' hands. Thus, in order to assume some of that power themselves, the farmworkers needed, as an intermediate step, a source of power beyond Delano or even California. The tactic was to be a nationwide call to boycott grapes that would enlist the widest possible range of support. Through justified appeals to morality and through a deliberate focus on the obvious David-Goliath aspects of the struggle, the farmworkers could gain economic leverage over the growers. If attempts to stop the harvest of grapes couldn't work, an attempt to stop the sale of grapes might. It was something new, something different and, again, required enormous work and organization. It also required faith in the public's ability to care about the existence of people they had never seen. Although moral outrage could be mobilized, moral pressure couldn't be brought in the abstract. A concrete tool was needed. The four-year grape boycott (1966-1970), the first national boycott on behalf of labor ever to succeed in the United States, was not won on moral grounds, as clear as they were, but because grape growers lost a lot of money. Refusing to see the conflict in moral terms, the growers took refuge in economic arguments (e.g., that paying higher wages would bankrupt them and/or cost consumers more). While it was easy to demolish such false arguments intellectually, what "did the growers in" were, ironically, the real economic facts of life.

The reality of economic power had to be dealt with by both sides. Nonviolent tactics, some learned from Gandhi or the Civil Rights Movement, others fashioned for the occasion, were needed which would not only propel *La Causa* to national attention, but keep it there, amid the bustle and fadishness of news items, the immediacy of each individual's personal cares. I'll consider some of those tactics later.

From a place few had ever heard of, Delano became the symbolic and national focus of struggles for social justice. As other observers have pointed out, the growers would have been far better off if they hadn't destroyed the picketing efforts and thus led the farmworkers to develop the boycott.[12]

Viewed on less explicit practical terms, an economic boycott can be an organizing tool of some emotional satisfaction, a way of adding support to support and also of sharing responsibility widely. As Chavez, mindful of precedents, put it: "Gandhi has taught that the boycott is the most nearly perfect instrument of non-violent change, allowing masses of people to participate actively in a cause."[13] The "most nearly perfect" instrument was also the most practical, probably the only practical one. Yet it was hardly an "inevitable" choice, as the story of pre-Chavez organizing bears out.

The political climate was becoming rather more receptive to the farmworkers' demands. The Civil Rights, anti-war, and student movements had sharpened public awareness of poverty and injustice, as well as shaped activists who could be enlisted in a cause which seemed akin to their own. Television documentaries on migrant labor conditions had reached millions; Senate subcommittee hearings on the subject (March, 1966) were held in California, with Senator Robert Kennedy and the Catholic bishops in the state coming out on the farmworkers' side.

There were so many appealing issues to latch on to (some of them more emphasized during the grape, lettuce, and Gallo wine boycotts of the 1970s, but included here) and thus many possible constituencies for attentive organizers to mobilize. Some of the issues were: social justice for the poor (who picked the food we eat, yet are themselves malnourished, in the world's richest nation); equal opportunity for minority group members; the right of workers to organize; the obscene power of giant corporations; damage to the environment (by growers' misuse of dangerous chemicals); the potential power of consumers to influence food policy; and, of course, the power of nonviolent direct action.

The union's commitment to nonviolence helped enormously throughout its history to gain public support, especially from the religious and middle-class liberal sectors—for many good reasons and a few bad ones. If I fasten on some of the latter here, it's not to denigrate the many people of good will who were drawn to *La Causa*, but to suggest a few political or emotional complexities.

Brown-skinned Chicanos with sometimes beautiful Indian faces, spiritedly singing in Spanish, have an exotic appeal for people outside the southwestern states. The union's soft-spoken, apparently saintly, and charismatic leader, Cesar Chavez, became a media favorite. The nonviolent "oppressed" were less frightening than those whose anger exploded into ghetto riots. The "simple Mexican peasants" were sufficiently remote and thus easy to romanticize (a tendency Chavez worked to deflate among volunteers in Delano). To say that a nonviolent stance can be linked to concepts of "the meek and downtrodden," the poor who "are always with us," the grateful recipients of church charity, is not to fault either a nonviolent stance or the farmworkers' union. Boycotting grapes soothes the conscience while involving no risk. One can, obviously, support the United Farm Workers Union without absorbing, to the point of activism or at least outraged awareness, the facts of American economic and political life. It's easier to feel pity for the poor than to understand that the systems that make this misery possible must be changed.

There are various ways, not mutually exclusive, or explaining the possibly amazing combination of supporters which the UFW attracted—students, labor leaders, radical activists, Catholic bishops, minority group members, suburban liberals, and hippies. These supporters kept working together into the 1970s, after other multiracial alliances had dissolved and other movements had been torn apart by factionalism. The conditions of farmworkers' lives were so appalling that they often aroused both sympathy and anger where one was given a chance to explain them. Writers Meister and Loftis touch on a significant point in their comment that "the supporters saw the strike as a demand for equal opportunity, free of the ideological motivation that would have divided them."[14]

People can see in a movement what they want to see, provided its political fabric is either amorphous or multifaceted. Accepting the inevitable, activists should probably be grateful for support on whatever political level possible, while hinting, here and there, at a more comprehensive analysis. The UFW is a unique and strange creature, now labor union, now social protest movement, with civil rights, ethnic pride, and religious elements thrown in for good measure. It contained something to antagonize nearly every potential constituency, yet, in fact, ended up with enough appeal to hang on to most. The union/movement contrast is messy. For some who support the UFW for its "third world appeal" or for its religious aspects, "union" is a bad word, summoning up either slick bureaucrats out of touch with the rank-and-file, a sell-out to the establishment or "lower class" laborers—grubby, if earnest. On the other hand, trade unionists, most especially the AFL-CIO hierarchy and, ironically, even the growers, would have much preferred a more conventional union without ethnic/religious "trappings," red flags and shouts of "Viva la huelga!," and a non-violent stance with disconcerting tactics foreign to industrial organizing. Al Green, director of the AFL-CIO affiliate, AWOC, viewed his organization as engaged in "an honest-to-God trade union fight, not a civil rights demonstration. . . ." The [Chavez-led] NFWA is administered by ministers. We [AWOC] will continue in our own *union* way."[15] AWOC and NFWA did eventually merge in August, 1966 after an unhappy one-year alliance, forming the United Farm Workers Organizing Committee, AFL-CIO. It became a full-fledged union affiliate (the UFW) in 1972.

Whole-hearted AFL-CIO support, never forthcoming, could have made a great difference to the farmworkers. While director George Meany and other AFL-CIO officials were noticably ill-at-ease with the UFW's style and often disappointed in its seeming lack of concrete successes (measured in number of members and contracts), one wonders if they weren't also at times embarrassed by the tiny union's ability to organize farmworkers. That was something which the huge, powerful, and monied union-conglomerate had failed to do.

As the grape strike and boycott continued, some supporters joined the Delano picket lines, distributed food to striking farmworkers, or helped with the paperwork. A small core of what were to become long-time "regulars" took major responsibilities: Dolores Huerta and Gilbert Padilla, Richard and Manuel Chavez

(Cesar's brother and cousin), attorney Jerry Cohen, Leroy Chatfield, the Rev. Chris Hartmire and Jim Drake, Larry Itliong from AWOC, Nick and Virginia Rodriguez Jones, Marshall Ganz (a veteran of the Civil Rights Movement) and others. From students on vacation to members of the Migrant Ministry, a close and invaluable long-time ally, there was plenty for everyone to do.

> Chavez conceded matter-of-factly that he and those around him might indeed be described as "fanatics." Most of them worked day and night for no more than $5 a week, food, and a floor to sleep on, and under NFWA orders "to be servants" as Chavez put it, "with their only objective to help farmworkers have a union." Chavez felt that was the only way it could be done; that "the only ones who make things change are fanatics." He couldn't "ask people to sacrifice if I won't sacrifice myself," and neither could the volunteers. "If you don't live the same kind of life as the poor people you are trying to help," asked one volunteer, "why should they trust you?"[16]

Some supporters sent money or goods: $5000 a month from the United Auto Workers Union; the proceeds of benefit folk concerts, cocktail parties, church collections and bake sales; turkeys at Thanksgiving and Christmas stockings filled with toys for farmworker children. Cars and trucks came day after day, piled with donated canned goods, hundreds of eggs a week pledged by one union, with drug samples sent by doctors.

Nationwide the boycott was a wonderfully flexible tool. The once innocuous grape, now hated, inspired ingenuity! One could simply not buy grapes (hardly a staple of anyone's diet) or convince one's friends not to buy and one's grocer not to stock. One could wear a "Boycott Grapes" button, arrange fund-raising events, or write letters supporting the boycott to newspaper editors. There were leaflets to distribute and allies to seek at church meetings and in union halls. Convincing the managers of restaurants and college cafeterias not to use grapes was a challenge. Boycott staff members (farmworkers and organizers from California as well as local people) were joined by hundreds of volunteers in dozens of cities who maintained picket lines in front of stores selling grapes, rallied at produce terminals at 6:00 am, and got big-city mayors to issue proclamations of support for the UFW. There was something compatible to every life-style and amount of free time. Taken together, it was exhausting and exhilarating. It also worked.

Meanwhile in California, in the tradition of good social change organizing, the union was active on many fronts, e.g., trying to prod Congress into including farmworkers under the National Labor Relations Act or filing lawsuits against growers and their allies. Union members also engaged in nonviolent direct action, as has been the case all through its history. Several examples are instructive here and will have to serve for many. They make clear either how one could use difficult circumstances to advantage or, as long-time UFW observer Ronald Taylor points out, how an event could both stimulate national interests (through skillful use of the media), and be an effective organizing tool among the farmworkers themselves.

After a sheriff ordered pickets to stop using the word *huelga*, organizers collected farmworkers, clergy, and other supporters willing to go to jail (44 in all) and announced to the sheriff that they would disobey the injunction on October 20. In an incident not without its comic aspects, the sheriff, plus deputies and paddy wagon, picketers, and reporters "set out from the NFWA head-quarters in one of the strangest farm labor strike caravans of all time."[17] It took almost an hour of driving around until they found workers in the fields! Pickets shouted *Huelga!*, lined up for arrest, and went to jail while cameras clicked and the sheriff made a fool of himself. While most confrontations were neither engineered nor pleasant, some could, as here, be used "to provoke issues that could be exploited by boycotters in the metropolitan areas."[18] The indispensable *national* press, as Taylor notes,[19] was not under the agribusiness thumb.

After pickets were sprayed with pesticides at the Schenley (wine-grape) ranch, a small group of farmworkers and supporters left Delano for a 300 mile, 25 day march to Sacramento, the state capital, to bring their case before Governor Pat Brown. The style was ceremonial; the banner of the Virgin of Guadalupe, Mexican patron saint of the poor, was borne high in a pilgrimage combining penance and protest. Stopping in thirty settlements along the way, the marchers were fed and housed by farmworkers who joined them for daily masses and meetings. There they learned both of events in Delano and of ways in which they, perhaps timid yet, might themselves take action. And all this in a religious and cultural mode familiar to them. Rallying in Sacramento on Easter Sunday (April 10, 1966), 8-10,000 supporters celebrated the news that the Schenley Company, also under boycott pressure, had agreed to sign the union's first contract, even if the governor had decided to spend the day vacationing at singer Frank Sinatra's estate. The march may well, as Chavez noted years later, have helped its participants train for "the long, long struggle" and added to their self-confidence and courage through its slow, but concrete progression.[20] It also, through media coverage, awakened new supporters and reinvigorated old ones. For the union, Delano-based and immersed in the strike and boycott, the march was a way of reactivating interest among those it unwillingly had neglected after having had to abandon its plan of slow, steady organizing.[21]

On February 19, 1968 Chavez announced to farmworkers gathered in the meeting hall that he had been fasting for five days out of concern and dismay that they were being tempted to violence. As Chavez later told Jacques Levy, "I thought that I had to bring the movement to a halt, do something that would force them and me to deal with the whole question of violence and ourselves. We had to stop long enough to take account of what we were doing."[22] The farmworkers were demoralized after more than two years on strike. Some feared that nonviolent tactics would never bring them to their goals and perhaps also marked them as cowards. Some harkened back to the Mexican revolutionary tradition, others spoke of the violent labor strikes of years past and the more recent Ghetto riots.

Declaring that the movement was not worth the taking of a single life—either farmworker or grower—Chavez told his audience that violence was not only no proof of masculinity, but the easy way out, a refusal to exert the energy and imagination which nonviolence required. The Civil Rights Movement was example enough that resorting to violence would only bring more violence down upon the poor. The union was responsible to those whose dreams it had nourished.

During the rest of Chavez's 25 day fast, hundreds of farmworkers from across the state camped outside his room, waited to speak with him, and attended daily masses. Family and friends urged Chavez to end the fast (which did, in fact, severely damage his health). With Chavez the center, the motivating force of the union, his death might well mean its demise. Some non-Catholic staff and supporters, already uncomfortable with the union's religious overtones, were embarrassed by this most dramatic Christian/Gandhian event. Others expressed discomfort that Chavez was being played up as a saint, that religion was being exploited, or that the whole thing was being manipulated for the benefit of the press.

Thousands of farmworkers and supporters rallied to mark the public end to the fast. Mass was celebrated, with Senator Robert Kennedy breaking bread with Chavez. Martin Luther King, Jr. (whom Chavez never met personally, but whose ideas and spirit influenced him over many years) sent a telegram praising Chavez's "courage in fasting as your personal sacrifice for justice through nonviolence. Your past and present commitment is eloquent testimony to the constructive power of nonviolent action and the destructive impotence of violent reprisal." King's closing words, "The plight of your people and ours is so grave that we all desperately need the inspiring example and effective leadership you have given,"[23] are, in retrospect, sadly ironic in light of King's death less than a month later. Chavez was to become his successor as the nation's most visible and important advocate of nonviolence.

In a prepared speech that others had to read for him, Chavez himself concluded with these words:

> When we are really honest with ourselves, we must admit that our lives are all that really belongs to us. So it is how we use our lives that determines what kind of men we are. It is my deepest belief that only by giving our lives do we find life. I am convinced that the truest act of courage, the strongest act of manliness, is to sacrifice ourselves in a totally nonviolent struggle for justice. To be a man is to suffer for others. God help us to be men.[24]

Reading this some years after the event, one is struck, to be sure, by its simple eloquence and thoughtfulness. Yet what a curious combination this is, with its welcomed rejection of traditional "macho" assertiveness, while still leaving no place for the courage of women.

The fast was a success. In Chavez's words, "The good effects were way beyond my dreams. The work schedule began to pick up, dedication increased, and the whole question of using violence ended immediately."[25] The nightly masses were also an in-

tense experience for many farmworkers and an effective way of
bringing them together both physically and emotionally. As both
journalists and intimates have pointed out, the fast made obvious,
to the growers as well as to the farmworkers, the seriousness with
which Chavez took nonviolence.[26] While played up in the media,
the nonviolent stance had not been adopted for media consumption.

Yet the fast, the first of several that Chavez undertook, raises
several ticklish questions for nonviolent activists. "For the issue
[of nonviolence]," Nicolaus Mills writes, "is not a matter of debate
or of formal democratic procedures. Indeed, the whole point of
Chavez's fasts is to make nonviolence beyond question as far as
the UFW is concerned."[27] In earlier union and CSO days, Chavez
had threatened to resign unless his Chicano colleagues did something about their racism toward blacks and Filipinos. But not all
people would condemn violence as absolutely as racism or necessarily applaud each specific nonviolent tactic. It is difficult to
determine the degree of philosophical as well as tactical commitment to nonviolence among the UFW leadership apart from
Chavez. While others seem to match him in degree of dedication,
hard work, and so on, Chavez's unique efforts, such as the fast,
may make union democracy impossible. To continue Mills' provocative comments, "Within the UFW, opposing Chavez is a matter of conscience, not merely votes, and given the sacrificial style
of leadership he has exercised, opposition is almost fated to peter
out. For it invariably calls into question not just the issue at hand
but Chavez's Gandhi-like moral stature within the UFW."[28] The
degree to which the union is identified with Chavez and his insistence on overseeing even the smallest administrative details
compound the leadership problem.

On July 29, 1970 California grape growers, smarting under
boycott pressure, signed contracts with the UFW. Dolores Huerta's
remarks at the time are perhaps the most fitting: "What's happened here is a miracle. But it didn't come about by magic."[29]

Contracts not only promised higher wages, but grower-contri-
butions to health and social service plans, restrictions on the use
of pesticides, as well as other safety clauses. But the major provision in this absurdly new power-sharing arrangement was the
establishment of hiring halls, from which UFW members would
dispatch workers to nearby ranches as needed. Gone were the

hated labor contractors who procured batches of workers at a handy profit to themselves. Hiring on the basis of seniority, without discrimination against women workers, had arrived. Ultimate power over the workforce shifted from employer to union. Ranch committees would administer the hiring hall, investigate grievances, and deal directly with the growers. The decentralized union structure would encourage rank-and-file leadership, build self-confidence, and ensure that the workers themselves maintained control over their work lives.

It was a heady victory but there was little time to celebrate. Just the day before, nearly all California lettuce growers had announced the signing of contracts with the Teamsters Union. Eager to head off a UFW organizing drive, they had hit upon an ingenious alternative. If they would eventually be forced to recognize a union, why not a union which was as loath to share power with workers and look out for their needs as the growers were! To refurbish an old phrase, if the Teamsters hadn't existed, the growers might have tried to invent them.

The Teamsters were the antithesis of the UFW in every respect. Thrown out of the AFL-CIO in 1957 for its corrupt practices, the nation's largest union nurtured a "tough-guy" image, as well as Mafia ties and widespread pension fund fraud. Its officials' affluent lifestyle, slick, efficient manner, and conservative politics put the growers more at ease than the ragtag UFW ever could. They also exhibited a goodly share of contempt for the workers. But then that is what the so-called "sweetheart contracts" are about, negotiated between employer and company-preferred union without input from the workers. The labor contractor and child labor were back in; grievance procedures, safety clauses, even toilets in the fields, and the slightest hint of democracy were out. Seven thousand lettuce pickers sympathetic to the UFW went out on strike. Violence flared again, and the lettuce boycott was on.

Eager to protect its cannery workers and truckers from disruption in harvests (or future UFW unionization), with one set of officials trying to increase its power through an upsurge in membership, the Teamsters had been fooling around in agriculture since the early 1960s.

Reeling under the blow, the UFW didn't have time to nurse its wounds. However, part of its strength lay in its ability to spring back, to readjust, to develop new tactics. While orchestrating a new boycott, it also had to set up the mechanism for administering grape contracts. Chaos reigned for a good while, hardly adding to the growers' enthusiasm for the union.

But there were many new assaults to deal with, as agribusiness wasn't about to content itself with a single weapon. In the words of UFW intimate Jacques Levy, "By 1971, the time had come to stamp out the farm workers' union. Its opponents understood, as few others did, La Causa's potential and its power."[30] Agribusiness sympathizers introduced legislation in at least seven states to restrict strikes and boycotts and otherwise cripple unionization efforts, which they feared would soon spread from California. For example, in Arizona the UFW organized a campaign, ultimately unsuccessful, to recall Governor Williams, who had refused to veto the bill there. In Oregon, supporters held a four-day prayer vigil on the state capitol steps to force a veto from Governor McCall, who was also besieged by telegrams from across the country, threatening a boycott of Oregon lumber. It worked. As UFW attorney Jerry Cohen described it, "It was really a perfect example of how the boycott machine and a few really organized people could be mobilized. All the ingredients were there. It was just a question of guiding it a little bit, and not being afraid to raise a little hell."[31] In California, Proposition 22, a grower-sponsored initiative to curb farm labor, was defeated on November 7, 1972 by a vote of 58 percent to 42 percent after an intense UFW campaign and it put an end to such legislative attempts nationwide.

But again, a UFW success was also a UFW defeat, in that it engendered yet another grower assault. When the UFW grape contracts expired in 1973, the growers suddenly discovered that, like the lettuce pickers, their workers preferred the Teamsters.

The UFW "was a revolutionary movement that is perpetrating a fraud on the American public,"[32] so Teamster president Frank Fitzsimmons had declared to the American Farm Bureau Federation, meeting in national convention on December 12, 1972. He cozily sought a mutually beneficial relationship. The Teamster initiative was probably aided, possibly engineered, by the Nixon administration, newly reelected with strong Teamster support. In 1971 and 1972, Charles Colson, Nixon advisor and later Teamster laywer, had notified the Labor and Justice Departments that they were not to enter the UFW-Teamster battle unless it was to harm the UFW.

The loss of the grape contracts was a stunning blow, the Teamsters had renegotiated their unexpired lettuce contracts shortly before. It also gave the lie to idealistic notions that the growers had changed, had learned to respect the tiny union which had proven its mettle in the 1960s. The second grape strike began April 16, 1973. It raged for exactly four months, until two UFW members were murdered and the picket lines called off. Over 3000 farmworkers and supporters from across the country were arrested on picketlines after defying court injunctions, many in acts of massive civil disobedience. Hundreds were beaten up by police or Teamster "goon squads," paid $67.50 a day per man. By jailing them, the police only increased the workers' commitment to the union. The level of physical violence and of every sort of intimidation was enormous. It is a great tribute to the UFW that it was able to maintain its commitment to nonviolence even with as many as 10,000 picketers, many of them new to the struggle.

The second grape boycott was harder. The Teamsters provided the growers with a handy facade to hide behind, supposed proof that their workers, given a real choice, would disgard the UFW. Slick grower advertising campaigns lured a naive public and ill-informed media to focus on a phony "jurisdictional dispute" between two unions, whereas, in truth, the growers had remained the real obstacle to UFW progress. Grocers were exhorted not to interfere with shoppers' "freedom of choice" by banning grapes. Thirteen million dollars was not too much for the Gallo Wine Company, the world's largest, to spend in one year on public relations when, after six years with a UFW contract, it too brought in the Teamsters.

Some people were tired of boycotts ("Wasn't that over years ago?"), tired of a union which, it seemed, couldn't quite make it. Segments of the liberal press, which had helped catapult the UFW to national attention, were tired too. Prophecies of doom, as in the *New York Times Magazine* cover story for September 15, 1974 ("Is Chavez Beaten?" by Winthrop Griffin), can, obviously, become self-fulfilling. However, social change activists need also beware when the press, oversimplifying matters, touts their successes! This happened sporadically in the 1970s with media claims that the UFW had emerged victorious and consequently led the unwary to think the boycotts were over.

Yet, somehow, enough people still cared. Boycott staff and supporters held all-night vigils, were beaten by hired thugs while picketing, and debated Gallo vice-presidents on TV. They formed "human billboards" along highways, holding signs which reminded motorists of the boycott, maintained sit-in's at chainstore headquarters, and put on New Year's Eve benefits. Boycott and ranch picket lines encouraged each other. Like the farmworkers, supporters quickly learned to articulate their position and, in the face of violence, both prove and reinforce their commitment. The National Council of Catholic Bishops and other religious groups affirmed their support; so too, with more vigor than heretofore, did the AFL-CIO. Pope Paul VI received Chavez and European labor unions vowed to stop grape shipments.

Although down to just a few contracts, the UFW, significantly, still maintained its clinics and social service centers, even established a retirement village for Filipino farmworkers. Contracts or none, the UFW was committed to meeting the workers' needs, which hadn't evaporated when the Teamsters took over. Constructive programs, as well as protest actions, continued, to the extent that the union could raise funds for them.

With the growers hurt by the boycotts and the Teamster local embroiled in a power struggle, Jerry Brown's election as governor of California in 1974, after eight years of the reactionary Ronald Reagan, provided the needed breakthrough. Under pressure from Brown, all parties agreed to the Agricultural Labor Relations Act (ALRA), which went into effect August 28, 1975 and provided for secret ballot elections. The growers still had tricks up their sleeves—they intimidated workers to the point where many elections were a fraud, often refused to negotiate contracts when the UFW had won elections, and pressured the state legislature to cut off funds to implement the ALRA. Yet the UFW had still managed to win the majority of workers. Its struggle had finally been given the legitimacy of law, although the mechanism was flawed and open to abuse.

As of Mid-1977 the UFW continues, embattled, but apparently victorious, having signed, on March 10, 1977 a jurisdictional pact with the Teamsters, leaving farmworkers organizing to the UFW. Yet mindful of the growers' power and their ability to hone new weapons whenever threatened, one's optimism is tinged with caution.

Even if all opposition were to melt magically away, the UFW still has enormous tasks ahead in organizing and providing social services for the unorganized mass of California farmworkers, not to mention those in other states. It will need to confront many problems, some already acknowledged, from increased mechanization in the fields to a union leadership's growing distance from the workers. Chavez and his colleagues have their dreams still. They include dealing with the nonfarm issues farmworkers face such as racial discrimination in the schools and eventually, on to the problems of poor people, both urban and rural, across our country. A "Poor Peoples' Union" someday? Perhaps no more unrealistic a dream than a farmworkers' union seemed 15 years ago. ·

The UFW has been often eulogized by advocates of nonviolence, Cesar Chavez revered for his selflessness, and the UFW boycotts taken as a model for successful organizing. Nevertheless, the student of nonviolence comes up against several thorny problems. Most available statements on nonviolence are by Chavez himself. But what is the commitment of other long-time staff to nonviolence as a philosophy, as a tactic? What of the farmworkers themselves? The boycott staff? Chavez's remarks are sometimes idealized, often hard for observers to translate into concrete examples. UFW chroniclers usually neglect the day-to-day realities of the boycott staff, which is most supporters' only contact with the union. For the sake of completeness, of deflating myths which hamper social change efforts, and of my own pragmatic temperament, I conclude with a brief look at two issues: the often difficult relations between UFW staff and supporters and some anti-utopian, visibly effective aspects of Chavez's own nonviolent commitment.

The UFW problems that one is more likely to see mentioned are its administrative inefficiencies at the ranches or Chavez's tendency to dominate decision-making. Staff members' tendency to antagonize the supporters so crucial to its success is, I suggest, a significant, if disappointing, aspect of the union's campaign. It also points up more general problems of organizing for nonviolent social change.

Energetic and intense, the UFW staff traditionally harness

enough hard work to their bold initiatives to get things done. Yet hard work is not of necessity good work. And the moral right- eousness which adheres to one's cause or one's pride in sacrifice to it are not viable substitutes for either careful planning or sen- sitivity in personal relations. Singleminded concentration on a goal does often bring results. One recalls Chavez's remark that "the only ones who make things change are fanatics." Committed staff people do elicit enormous amounts of work from those they contact as well as themselves. Yet, having sacrificed their own private lives, living as well as working with UFW colleagues, staff members often forget that supporters have private lives, jobs, and other political interests. Driven to the point of exhaustion and always short of money, the staff, understandably, feels harassed, but, in turn, plays upon others' guilt feelings: the outside world, not to speak of supporters, owe them everything. Competent and sensitive potential staff members often shy away from that final commitment, unwilling to sacrifice not only their private lives, but their decision-making power to an undemocratic structure. The staff/volunteer dichotomy of other movement groups is ex- aggerated here. The staff members, while sometimes less mature and less experienced politically than volunteers, treat them with condescension on the basis of their own more visible commitment. Yet what supporter, in this or other groups, wants to be merely a "body" at a picket line or demonstration, used but not listened to?

Constructive criticism is not only not solicited, but viewed as a betrayal of *La Causa*. Some staff members are too young to have had prior experience with other movement groups or arrogantly dismiss them as of little consequence. Yet how much might they learn from the women's movement about the personal dynamics of political life and from the peace movement about the depth and breadth of a nonviolent commitment which goes far beyond the simple dictum "Thou Shalt Not Hit."

One might protest that the UFW staff has so much to do just in dealing with their own and the farmworkers' simple survival needs that they can't worry about the subtleties of supporters' feelings. And yet a truly nonviolent movement must concern itself with such subtleties if it is to be worthy of its name. Supporters may, as with the UFW, continue their work despite the staff, simply because the farmworkers themselves lay such strong claim to their concern; one tries to ignore the intermediaries. To be sure, movement groups can breezily offend supporters and exhaust staff, only to go on, when lucky, to ever new batches. Whether they should is still another question.

Social change movements face such enormous external obstacles that they cannot afford the luxury of burning people out or of incompetence and naivete beyond a certain, unavoidable level. Anti-elitism is all to the good where it implies skill-sharing and the fostering of self-confidence and democratic structures. But the belief that all people are equally skilled, or at least trainable, that enthusiasm can make up for experience, is ultimately destructive. To take a harsh line: people can be allowed to make their own mistakes only up to a certain point and that point must involve learning from one's mistakes and, where possible, having a rescue in the wings.

The UFW has often neglected training of both its staff and volunteers, dispatching them to this and that chore without careful scrutiny. For example, what leaflets or what responses would be most effective to shoppers? Thus one finds, over and over, inflammatory rhetoric, responses which are little tuned to the current situation, belligerence.

Of course there are crises—the UFW has had to live from one to the other for years—and one often must react quickly without much regard to well-laid plans or long-term strategy. But there's been too much exaggeration of crises ("If the UFW ever needed your help, it needs it now!"), with supporters unable to determine if, indeed, this day or this week is really the time to give up all else. The other side to this is exaggerated optimism, the belief that victory is soon at hand. While some people may need a belief in quick victories to keep going, it's demoralizing when promised victories don't materialize and people feel that they've been lied to.

A good cause and a steady flow of issues to stimulate action are beginning points for political campaigns, but are not sufficient in themselves to sustain support or respect.

Having expressed these scruples, one can point to many visibly effective organizing principles, some of them simply the more attractive side of those just dealt with. A young volunteer once asked Chavez why the UFW alone had been able to organize farmworkers. "There is not secret," Chavez smiled, "we just try harder."[33] To hard work and sacrifice, patience is added. "Time is our greatest ally," Chavez has commented, "time is for the poor what money is for the rich."[34] And what a pivotal sentence that is, for if the UFW has proven anything, it is that there are substitutes for money and powerful allies. Among these substitutes are the boycott, an insistence that strategy be rooted in the farmworkers' own needs rather than any "outside agendas," the ability to "keep the pressure on" one's adversaries without letup. Another vital substitute is ongoing organization, unglamorous in the extreme, which doesn't just exist from demonstration to demonstration, but includes public events among its myriad of daily affairs. There is a kind of lively perseverance, a high-spirited earnestness, the ability to be refreshed by a few songs together, by a rally with more participants than expected, and a shared Mexican meal.

While nonviolence is not merely a tactic for Chavez, to be disgarded when the going gets tough, it is very firmly grounded in a decidedly unsentimental awareness of strategy and human vulnerability. As Jan Addams remarks, Chavez "brought to nonviolence a new understanding of the necessity for the hard work of solid organization and a determination to make his efforts a victory for farmworkers, rather than merely a witness for justice."[35] The UFW's nonviolent strategy is born out of practical necessity, the knowledge that it leaves more options open as well as upholds the sanctity of life. And, as Chavez has stressed over and over, "nonviolence is really *tough*. You don't practice nonviolence by attending conferences—you practice it on the picket lines."[36] A longer, provocative statement by Chavez is worth quoting here for the way it shrinks to size the value of discussing nonviolent principles in a vacuum:

> We're not nonviolent because we want to save our souls. We're nonviolent because we want to get some social justice for the workers. If all you're interested in is going around being nonviolent and so concerned about saving yourself, at some point the whole thing breaks down—you say to yourself, Well, let *them* be violent, as long as *I'm* nonviolent. Or you begin to think it's okay to lose the battle as long as you remain nonviolent. The idea is that you have to *win* and be nonviolent. That's extremely important! You've got to be nonviolent—and you've got to win with nonviolence! What do the poor care about strange philosophies of nonviolence if it doesn't mean bread for them?[37]

In the case of the UFW, it has meant bread for them and new hope and the enormous ground covered from their initial crippling fear and belief in the invincibility of their powerful masters. The farmworkers whom the UFW has touched cannot revert to their former selves, a life without expectations or a lack of awareness of how power is wielded—and also won.

Notes

1. Dick Meister and Anne Loftis, *A Long Time Coming. The Struggle to Unionize America's Farm Workers*, New York: Norton, 1977, p. 39.
2. Jacques E. Levy, *Cesar Chavez, Autobiography of La Causa*, New York: Macmillan, 1975, p. 5.
3. Cesar Chavez, "The Organizer's Tale," *Ramparts*, 1971, reprinted in Renato Rosaldo, Gustav L. Seligmann, and Robert A. Calvert, *Chicano: The beginnings of bronze power*, New York: Winston Press, 1974, p. 60.
4. Meister and Loftis, op. cit., p. 136.
5. Ronald B. Taylor, *Chavez and the Farm Workers. A Study in the Acquisition and Use of Power*, Boston: Beacon Press Paperback, 1975, p. 136.
6. John Gregory Dunne, *Delano*, revised and updated edition, New York: Farrar, Straus & Giroux, 1971, p. 100.
7. Ibid., p. 106.
8. Ibid., p. 7.
9. Levy, op. cit., p. 192.
10. Taylor, op. cit., p. 144.
11. Levy, op. cit., p. 190.
12. Peter Matthiessen, *Sal Si Puedes. Cesar Chavez and the New American Revolution*, New York: Delta Paperback, 1969, p. 95; Meister and Loftis, op. cit., p. 134.
13. Meister and Loftis, op. cit., p. 140.
14. Ibid., p. 134.
15. Taylor, op. cit., p. 153.
16. Meister and Loftis, op. cit., p. 137.
17. Taylor, op. cit., p. 142.
18. Ibid., p. 211.
19. Ibid., p. 209.
20. Levy, op. cit., p. 207.

21. Taylor, op. cit., p. 169.

22. Levy, op. cit., p. 272.

23. Joan London and Henry Anderson, *So Shall Ye Reap. The Story of Cesar Chavez and the Farm Workers' Movement*, New York: Apollo Edition, 1971, p. 184.

24. Matthiessen, op. cit., pp. 195—196.

25. Levy, op. cit., p. 275.

26. Matthiessen, op. cit., p. 184; Fred Ross, quoted in Levy, pp. 277—278.

27. Nicolaus Mills, "Unique Union, Special Problem," (review of Ronald B. Taylor, *Chavez and the Farm Workers*), *Dissent*, XXIII, 1, Winter, 1976, p. 99.

28. Ibid.,

29. Meister and Loftis, op. cit., p. 164.

30. Levy, op. cit., p. 441.

31. Ibid., p. 452.

32. Meister and Loftis, op. cit., p. 184.

33. Bill Daniel, "Hard Work, Good Times," *Fellowship*, XLII, 10, October, 1976, p. 26.

34. Wayne C. Hartmire Jr., *National Farm Workers Ministry*, Some comments on the New York Times article, October 8, 1974; unpublished.

35. Jan Addams, "The United Farm Workers Union," in Robert Cooney and Helen Michalowski, (eds.), *The Power of the People. Active Nonviolence in the U.S.*, Culver City, CA: Peace Press, Inc., 1977, p. 178.

36. Jim Forest, "Nonviolence on the line—an interview with Cesar Chavez," *WIN*, IX, 25, September 6, 1973, p. 6.

37. Addams, op. cit., p. 179.

Chapter 6

Nonviolent Struggle in Albany, Georgia

Neil H. Katz and
John P. Hunt

Introduction

During the winter of 1963—1964, a small group of peacewalkers from the Committee for Nonviolent Action (CNVA)[1] waged a major civil liberties struggle in Albany, Georgia. The city authorities had established a reputation as hard-line foes of integration and civil liberties. Seeking change, the CNVA peacewalkers achieved significant gains through a variety of nonviolent action tactics—civil disobedience, noncooperation in jail and court, long-term fasting, support vigils, and skillful negotiations. As a major development in both the civil rights and peace movements, the history of the Albany struggle holds an interest of its own. As an example of a successful use of nonviolent struggle to create change, the Albany case contains additional importance.

The study of nonviolent action has begun to receive substantial scholarly attention. In his seminal work, *The Politics of Nonviolent Action*,[2] Gene Sharp draws on history, political science, and sociology in proposing a theoretical structure to explain the dynamics and processes of nonviolent action. Sharp's book, a monumental breakthrough in the scholarly literature on nonviolent action, suggests the need for further research to refine and to clarify the methods and operations of this struggle technique. Detailed examination through the case study method provides a basis for this next stage of inquiry.

The following study will proceed by presenting first a thorough description of the Albany struggle. Then, in order to discern more about nonviolent action and to build upon existing research, the authors will examine the Albany events in terms of the theoretical outline offered in Gene Sharp's *The Politics of Nonviolent Action*. Finally, the authors will summarize their findings and discuss some ways their research and similar case studies might refine existing theoretical perspectives.

The descriptive part of this study is based on the point of view of the nonviolent action grievance group. We have done this for two reasons: (1) we are interested in analyzing the factors through which a nonviolent action group achieves change; and (2) the available sources were CNVA documents, some published reports, and city newspapers.[3] Within these limitations, we have tried to be as objective and critical as possible in both our description and analysis.

The Albany Struggle

Concern over civil rights and the United States' policy toward Cuba motivated members of the Committee for Nonviolent Action (CNVA) during 1963 to initiate plans for a Quebec-Washington-Guantanamo Walk for Peace. Although its organizers desired to focus primarily on foreign policy, the walk also embraced the struggle for racial equality. Demonstration actions were planned at every military base which the walkers would pass. The walk team itself would be integrated and refuse to follow policies of racial segregation. On May 26, 1963, a CNVA walk contingent left Quebec City, Canada. After the peacewalkers demonstrated at Griffin Air Force Base in Rome, New York on July 3, the walk team faced no major difficulties until late October when it reached Georgia. Here, a series of confrontations highlighted the walkers' stand on civil rights. Walkers met with violence and arrests in Lawrenceville, Griffin, and Macon, but it was not until they reached Albany that a major confrontation ensued.[4]

Albany, 176 miles south of Atlanta, had long practiced a policy of racial discrimination. Although 42 percent of its population in 1963 were black, whites controlled all positions of social, economic, and political power. In 1961, this power structure had successfully confronted and defeated a major integration effort led by the Student Nonviolent Coordinating Committee (SNCC). At the same time, a coalition of local Negro groups joined to form the Albany Movement. This body employed the demonstration and sit-in tactics with which Negroes in other areas had successfully reduced official segregation.

However, Albany authorities, led by Police Chief Laurie Pritchett, took a hard-line stance against integration. They made mass arrests and refused to negotiate with, or otherwise recognize the Negroes' leaders. Chief Pritchett explained his position to reporters: "We can't tolerate the NAACP or the SNCC or any other nigger organization to take over this town with mass demonstrations."[5] During the 1961 struggle, Albany police arrested over 700 demonstrators, including Dr. Martin Luther King, Jr. Pledging his police force to nonviolence, Pritchett won propaganda support and claimed that he fought and defeated King with the civil rights leader's own tactics. With King's withdrawal, Albany became the symbol of hard-core segregationist resistance to the mass demonstration technique.[6]

In December, 1963, before CNVA's arrival in Albany, an advance walk team approached Chief Pritchett to negotiate the terms of their entry. The walkers desired to march through the downtown streets of Albany and demonstrate their support for disarmament and racial equality. Citing pre-Christmas crowds and traffic congestion, Pritchett refused to allow the team to march through the downtown shopping area. The walkers protested that throughout the march, officials of other cities had granted them such access. Albany authorities, however, held to their position that the walkers not march north of Oglethorpe Avenue, the dividing line between the Negro and white sections of the city. The walkers decided to noncooperate with this ruling.

On December 23, Albany police arrested thirteen members of the walk team and one local supporter as they entered Albany and turned into the main shopping area north of Oglethorpe. After their arrests, the walkers continued to noncooperate with Albany's authorities. Twelve of the fourteen did not willingly go with arresting officers and forced the police to carry them to the paddy wagon on stretchers. Jailed to await trial, all fourteen disavowed bail, ignored jail regulations, and stopped eating. Eight would not walk to the courtroom on the date of their trial. Once in the courtroom, the walkers refused to sit in a segregated manner.

At trial on January 8, the fourteen walkers, convicted on charges of parading without a permit, congregating on sidewalks, and refusing to obey the lawful summons of policemen, were sentenced to 25 days in jail or were fined $102. Two walkers paid their fines and were released. Eleven of the others remained in jail and continued to fast. Several more walk supporters were later arrested and found guilty on similar charges. Then, on January 14, 1964, the city, by suspending their sentences and placing them on 30 days probation, released all of the imprisoned walkers. In this first series of arrests, Albany authorities imprisoned 22 pacifists. Nine fasted 24 days, three spent time in the hospital, two fasters received intravenous feedings, and doctors administered vitamin injections to each of the long-term fasters.

Upon their release from jail, the walkers refused to leave the city. Seeking compromise, they proposed eight alternative walk routes, some of which did not even include Main Street, their initial objective. They also offered a choice of five different dates and any hour between 10:00 a.m. and 4:00 p.m. Pritchett and City Manager Stephen R. Roos found all the proposed routes unsatisfactory "from the point of view of traffic control, the sentiment of the people, and other reasons."[7] Some Albany citizens considered this rejection of compromise dishonorable and overly rigid.[8]

The walkers refused to yield. When they again attempted to march into the forbidden areas on January 27, Albany police arrested seventeen walkers. Four days later, seven nonviolent activists were arrested at a disarmament demonstration at nearby Turner Air Force Base. During this second jailing, unhealthy jail conditions and weakness from long-term fasting took their toll on the walkers' stamina. Several could neither move nor walk without tremendous effort. However, because of their commitment to the struggle, most of the arrested walkers continued their fast and noncooperation with jail authorities.

In response to the peacewalkers' actions, Albany city officials employed a variety of violent and nonviolent weapons. In jail, walkers were often denied soap, towels, writing material, sanitary napkins, and eyeglasses. They were also placed in cramped, squalid jail cells. For example, authorities places the male walkers in the "hole," a 10 ft. × 12 ft. prison cell where seventeen men shared six beds with filthy mattresses which never dried out because the rain came in through cracks under the floor. Also, officials read menus to the fasting walkers, threatened cessation of medical attention, isolated walk leader Brad Lyttle in a separate cell, threatened transfers to jails noted for their brutal treatment of civil rights agitators, and used secret tape recorders at "private" walk-team meetings.[9]

In addition to these problems the walkers faced in jail, the Albany authorities frequently violated proper court procedures. Often Chief Pritchett seemed to control the trials himself; he took over many of the prerogatives of the judge even to the point of introducing the court's decision. During trials, whispered conferences took place between the judge, the city attorney, and the chief of police. Sentences were often typed up in advance. In one trial, the judge denied every objection made by the Negro attorney representing the walkers and sustained all those made by the city attorney.[10]

To counter these acts of repression and intimidation exercised by the Albany authorities, CNVA members outside of jail pursued several types of action. Throughout the struggle a small group fasted and kept a vigil on the steps of city hall. Walk supporters made frequent inquiries to city and jail authorities about the status of the jailed activists. CNVA as a national organization fulfilled a crucial supportive and facilitative role. A. J. Muste and Dave Dellinger, two of the more well-known and influential CNVA members, held numerous negotiating sessions with Albany authorities. CNVA maintained an office in Atlanta to coordinate walk publicity and mail information to influential Georgians. The national office in New York City organized support demonstrations in several cities throughout the United States.

In addition to this support from their own group, several third party actions began to benefit the walkers, especially as the struggle continued. During February, the city's major daily newspaper, the *Albany Herald*, began to publish more news stories about the walk and printed letters to the editor supporting both sides of the conflict. Also, the *Atlanta Constitution*, the *Atlanta Journal*, the *New York Times* and the *Chicago Tribune* covered the Albany events.[11] In addition, the walkers received supportive letters from persons and groups in Toronto, Montreal, London, New York, Philadelphia, and elsewhere. Norman Thomas, Norman Cousins, and New York Congressmen Ryan and Lindsay sent telegrams supporting the walkers to city officials.[12]

At this stage, the struggle also began to attract other forms of national and international attention. English walk member John Papworth's arrest and subsequent beating by drunks in his jail cell led to debate concerning the Albany conflict in the British House of Commons. Also, members of the British radical pacifist action Committee of 100 picketed outside the United States Embassy in London and cabled protests over Papworth's treatment to Albany Mayor Jimmy Davis and United States President Lyndon Johnson. The *London Times* sent inquiries. Similar international protest followed the arrest in Albany of three Canadians, one for being "idle and loitering." The *Toronto Telegram* telephoned Albany to express their indignation over these arrests and sent a telegram to the United States Department of State requesting a probe into the situation. In addition, the Albany conflict was mentioned twice in the Canadian Parliament.[13]

Two United States government agencies put pressure on Albany officials to find a more creative solution to the conflict. The United States Department of Justice sent a representative from their Atlanta office to look over the situation. The State Department, after receiving reports from England and Canada, telephoned Mayor Davis. In addition, several civil liberties lawyers became involved. One travelled to Albany from New York to launch a suit against the city for unconstitutional actions. Ten students from the Florida State University Student Citizens for Peace Committee arrived in Albany to aid the jailed walkers. Support demonstrations for the walkers were held in cities in New England, Minnesota, New York, California, and Quebec. These actions buttressed the faith and energy of the peacewalkers and enabled them to continue the struggle until an agreement was reached.[14]

Also, by mid-February, there had developed considerable pressure within Albany itself for the city authorities to negotiate in good faith with the walkers. Some white Albanians expressed distress at the financial burden of keeping in jail and intravenously feeding fasting walkers and showed concern that Albany's business potential and reputation might suffer. The Albany Movement, heretofore sympathetic but relatively inactive, published strong supportive letters in Albany's newspapers and scheduled a voter registration demonstration for February 22. In the wake of these developments, jailed walkers decided on February 15 to continue their fast for one more week. Events soon moved toward resolution of the struggle.

During the week after February 15, a group of three Quakers from the American Friends Service Committee (AFSC)—James Bristol, Cal Geiger, and Carl Zeitlow—worked with walk leaders, a group of influential white ministers,[15] and Albany city officials to establish a compromise agreement. In their talks with the ministers and city officials, the AFSC negotiators discovered a loophole that created an opening for compromise. In the eyes of the city, six or more people constituted a parade. Therefore, the main CNVA walk team agreed to march along the parade route prescribed to them prior to the initial arrests. However, during the walk an integrated team of five, wearing picket signs, would deviate from the main route for a four block loop to walk and hand out leaflets in the disputed downtown section. Also, CNVA would give up plans to again picket at Turner Air Force Base. Walkers who had been arrested but not tried would sign pleas of *nolo contendere* to city charges. Others would get their 30-day terms reduced by three days. All would be released on February 22, two days before the compromise walk on February 24.[16]

Both sides accepted the compromise, and on February 22, the walkers were released. Forty-one convictions had been handed down since December 23. Some of the walkers were in the 27th day of their second hunger strike. For most of them, only an 11 day interval had elapsed between the second fast and the first. Several of these walkers had fasted for as many as 51 days. After leaving jail the walkers retired to Koinonia farm outside the city for a much needed recuperative period. On February 24, the five walkers first entered the forbidden streets of Albany. A third jailing was barely averted when Chief Pritchett, after some disagreement, allowed the peacewalkers to distribute leaflets on the north side of the street. The walkers, however, successfully completed their march and left Albany feeling that they had made a significant breakthrough in the struggle for nonviolence and racial equality.[17]

Discussion and Analysis

The political basis for nonviolent action, according to Gene Sharp, rests on the postulate that "political power disintegrates when people withdraw their obedience and support."[18] In discussing his theory of power, Sharp lists six sources of power (authority, human resources, skills and knowledge, intangible factors, material resources, and sanctions) and seven reasons for obedience (habit, fear of sanctions, moral obligation, self-interest, psychological identification with the ruler, zones of indifference, and absence of self-confidence among subjects).[19] He describes power as an interactive phenomenon, any explanation of which must be based on an understanding of the interplay of its three component parts: the ruler (or leader), the subject (or follower), and the situation.[20] Then, in setting forth his theory that nonviolent action can redirect power by striking at its sources and undermining popular obedience, Sharp distinguishes three broad categories of action through which nonviolent struggle operates.

Protest and persuasion involve "symbolic actions intended to help persuade the opponent or someone else, or to express the group's disapproval and dissent." Noncooperation describes acts characterized by "withdrawal or the withholding of social, economic, or political cooperation." Nonviolent intervention occurs "where the nonviolent group acts largely by direct intervention." In such cases the action group "clearly takes the initiative by such means as sit-ins, nonviolent obstruction, nonviolent invasion and parallel government."[21]

These methods of action can lead to change in three ways—conversion, accommodation, and nonviolent coercion. Conversion involves a change of heart on the part of the opponent such that he/she willingly supports the changes desired by the nonviolent actionists. In accommodation, the opponent has not altered in belief or ability to continue the struggle, but has concluded that it is best to grant some or all of the demands at this time. Nonviolent coercion occurs when the opponent has lost the ability to continue the struggle and has unwillingly surrendered his/her position.

At the Albany struggle's outset, the subject group exercised almost no control over the sources of power in the city. The CNVA team were outsiders, and the Negro community, although potentially a source of power and authority, initially had little direct access to the decision making controls of the city. Chief of Police, Laurie Pritchett, representing the governing elite of Albany, wielded power through political cunning and the ability to command obedience. The white power structure obtained obedience primarily through habit, fear of sanctions, and lack of self-confidence among the black population. These factors had been reinforced by the resounding defeat of King's civil rights forces in 1961 and the subsequent intimidation of local Negro leaders.

Chief Pritchett felt his success in keeping control was at least partially attributable to his ability "to take a hard stand against desegregation in public, make a commitment, abandoning which would mean loss of face, and not backdown."[22] This meant that in Albany there would be no demonstrations north of Oglethorpe Avenue, the dividing line between the white and Negro sections. Pritchett successfully held this position during the 1961 struggle and had enforced it ever since.

In face of the 1963 walk, Chief Pritchett publicly stated that traffic congestion during the Christmas shopping season was his reason for holding to the north of Oglethorpe ruling. However, according to walk leader Bradford Lyttle, "almost certainly, the real and unexpressed reason was that if the walkers, a racially integrated group, were permitted to demonstrate downtown, the same right, heretofore grimly and desperately denied, would have to be granted to Albany's Negroes, to the Albany Movement."[23] Pritchett added credibility to this belief when he told the walkers, "If I let you, there'd be others."[24]

CNVA's original plans for action in Albany were to engage in the protest and persuasion tactics which had characterized their passage through other cities during the march. They sought to carry signs and distribute leaflets calling for peace and racial justice. However, faced with Chief Pritchett's north of Oglethorpe stand banning such action in the main downtown shopping area, the walkers chose to confront the issue by following their preferred walk route. This refusal to comply with Pritchett's ruling had thus transformed the mode of their original plans for protest and persuasion to one of noncooperation. After Pritchett's forces arrested them, the walkers pursued further noncooperation both in jail and in court and, through the use of their fast, began nonviolent intervention.

The walkers' fast, or hunger strike, became their main nonviolent weapon. Although Lyttle called the fast a "silent prayer to work to soften the adversaries' hearts and let the march continue",[25] the walkers' use of the fast involved more than protest and persuasion. Their public willingness to slowly starve for their human rights not only created misgivings of conscience among their opponents, but also interfered with the authorities' ability to repress them. Furthermore, it developed interest in the walk. In addition, the fast placed a financial burden on the city of Albany. Since city officials were unwilling to let the walkers become seriously ill or perish in their jail, they hospitalized them, gave them frequent vitamin injections, and administered costly intravenous feedings. As one peacewalker put it, "We (the peacewalkers) tax their minds, their muscles, their pocketbooks."[26]

The character of events during this first stage of struggle closely conforms to the outline Sharp presents. According to Sharp, "the launching of nonviolent struggle will almost always sharpen the conflict, cause the conflicting groups to become more sharply delineated, and stimulate previously uncommitted people to take sides."[27] Nonviolent action forces a response from the opponent. "(When) . . . unwilling or unable to grant the actionists' demands," the opponent will respond with repression.[28] Repression involves the enforcement of sanctions. Effective nonviolent action will meet repression with solidarity and defiance.

In Albany, having determined that an injustice existed, the nonviolent action group chose to initiate struggle. Parties to the conflict quickly became polarized. City officials, the law enforcement apparatus, and many white citizens of Albany all rallied to the support of Chief Pritchett in his opposition to the peacewalkers. On the other side, the peacewalkers, although small in number, became more resolute in their stance and began to solicit sympathy from the until then dormant Albany Movement. These initial developments were followed by an escalation of tactics on both sides.

The second stage of action includes the continued fasting and noncooperation of the walkers and the increased severity of the authorities' repression. Polarization, which had set in at the initiation of struggle, also persisted during this second stage. However, the walkers, aided by actions from their supporters, maintained and renewed their solidarity. At this point the walkers' fast and their insistence on their moral and constitutional right to demonstrate north of Oglethorpe began to strike at several key points in the authorities' power position. The fast placed a financial and moral burden on the city officials. The refusal to abide by the north of Oglethorpe stand forced the city to deal with the issues of civil rights, civil liberties, and the future role of the Albany Negro community. The walkers' concentration on issues of wide appeal also helped bring about third party involvement. From these conditions the walkers' nonviolent actions began to produce effects which Gene Sharp calls political jiu-jitsu.

Jiu-jitsu refers to a method whereby the opponent's strength reacts against itself and ultimately becomes a source of defeat. During nonviolent struggle, Sharp claims that "by combining nonviolent discipline with solidarity and persistence in struggle, the nonviolent actionists cause the violence of the opponent's repression to be exposed in the worst possible light."[29] The resulting political jiu-jitsu can produce several specific effects: the opponent may appear despicable; the general population may become alienated and may join the resistance; persons divorced from the conflict may show support for the victims of repression; public opinion may lead to political and economic pressures; and, finally, the opponent's own agents and troops may begin to doubt the justice of his policies.[30]

Despite Pritchett's public stance of meeting nonviolence with nonviolence, many of these jiu-jitsu dynamics and consequences occurred in the Albany struggle. The peacewalkers met the city's initial use of repression with solidarity and defiance. As the struggle continued, acts of secrecy and intimidation increased on the part of the city. The walkers maintained their resistance, however, and political jiu-jitsu did take effect causing substantial change to occur. The Albany Movement's activity was most important, but the emerging national and international pressures also contributed to giving the walkers additional leverage in settling the conflict. In addition, splits occurred among the Albany authorities own group. After initially giving Chief Pritchett their total support, Mayor Davis and City Manager Roos began to favor a compromise stand. The City Council's voting patterns became increasingly divisive on the walk issue.[31]

Nonviolent action had thus been effective and had operated in much the manner Sharp's analysis suggests. Through their use of nonviolent struggle the walkers had diminished the authorities' control of power in Albany. However, although the city's use of sanctions initially solidified the walkers and crystalized third party support for the nonviolent actionists, it also increasingly taxed the walkers' spiritual and physical strength. These conditions encouraged each side to accept a compromise solution.

The compromise allowed both parties to save face and exact some victory. Pritchett officially explained the compromise to the press by saying the "Walk did not constitute a parade but was considered by the city as picketing" and (we) do not arrest pickets unless they pose a threat to peace or unless they violate a city ordinance or state law."[32] Also, the city claimed success when the walkers agreed to forego a second demonstration at Turner Air Force Base and to plead *nolo contendere*, reversing their stand on noncooperation.

The walkers also achieved significant gains. They had broken the city's stand on integrated demonstrations. Lyttle, stating that "the power of such a system lies largely in the myth of invincibility it can generate around itself," concluded that, "although (we) didn't win the right to demonstrate anywhere we wished . . . (the victory) was complete in that (we) succeeded in cracking the system of police oppression."[33] Important events that transpired immediately after the compromise was agreed upon lend credibility to Lyttle's contention. On February 22, a few hours after the CNVA walkers were released from jail, the Albany Movement held its largest and most effective political action since the aborted 1961 demonstrations. According to an eyewitness account by A. J. Muste, "In groups of four or five, 50 Negroes picketed in front of city hall and city jail, in front of county office and county jail, fully prepared to be jailed again and possibly brutalized as in the past. This time, not one was arrested or physically attacked."[34]

Accommodation comes closest to describing the change mechanism which led to the compromise in Albany. The walkers, outwardly committed to seeking conversion, found at the outset of the struggle that change would probably not occur through such means. As Lyttle explained, in this conflict situation "the issues were generated by more than misunderstanding but flow from fear of at least one side that its power, privilege and prestige may be lost."[35] Also, the walkers' confined time frame for action, their limited numeric, economic and political strength, their status as non-community members, and their restricted ability to use repressive sanctions curbed their chances to coerce the Albany authorities. By mid-February, the walkers felt the strain of their long-term struggle. Differences of opinion developed on whether to continue their jail-in and fasting.[36]

Moreover, by this time city officials knew that they could neither convert the walkers nor defeat them without alienating substantial and influential third parties. Support for Pritchett's hardline stance had dwindled. Because of these factors, both the Albany authorities and the walkers welcomed a compromise agreement to end the campaign. Both sides sought to end the conflict not because they agreed with their opponent or because they could no longer continue their struggle, but because the compromise agreement allowed them to discontinue a new unpleasant situation with some measure of honor and success.

Summary

The wealth of relevant variables in this study demonstrates the difficulty in identifying particular cause-effect sequences and in objectively measuring their relative impact in a complex, sustained struggle campaign. However, factors that contributed to the resolution in Albany can loosely be grouped under four general classifications—economic, political, social-psychological, and strategical.

Economic

Increasing public knowledge of the economic cost to the city of maintaining the walkers in jail caused decay in the extent of citizen support for continued repression of the walkers. According to Mayor Davis, the walkers' care cost the city approximately $500 a day. The total expense of about $25,000 for the walkers' nearly two months in jail was a substantial sum for a city of 60,000 to incur. Also, the pressures of indirect economic loss were considerable. According to the walkers, several business people expressed fear that Albany's reputation as a stable community attractive to new business would suffer.[37]

Political

Political factors played an important role in forcing the compromise. As the struggle continued, more people, both inside and outside Albany, urged the Mayor and the City Council to negotiate. For example, several letters in the Albany and Atlanta papers referred to Albany's stance as "inflexible" and it was widely felt that the punishment was disproportionate to the "crime."[38] The statements of federal government officials and of international and national groups placed considerable pressure on Albany officials to resolve the crisis in a jointly determined, peaceful manner.

Social-psychological

As a result of the walk teams' persistence and resolve in their nonviolent resistance and the ensuing support for them of third parties, some dissension did occur among the opponent groups' own supporters. For example, the Mayor eventually decided to follow City Manager Roos' plea for compromise instead of Pritchett's insistence on a hard-line position.[39] According to the walkers, similar attitudinal and behavioral changes took place among Albany's Negroes, the white ministers, the personnel at Turner Air Force Base, the doctor in charge of the walkers' care in prison, and even, to some extent, in the attitude of Laurie Pritchett.

Another important factor in this nonviolent struggle was the constant primacy of human interaction. Throughout the Albany struggle, all parties to the conflict continued to meet and discuss the issues. Although coercive elements clearly were paramount in forcing a settlement, the main protagonists did gain some understanding, empathy and respect for one another. These factors contributed to the movement toward accommodation and compromise. Walkers spoke of their increasing human ties with Chief Pritchett and the people of Albany. Pritchett reciprocated with deeds such as sending the jailed walkers a postcard from his vacation trip and extending wishes to "take care of yourself." Because nonviolent struggle was used in place of passivity or violent struggle, feelings of respect and kinship among the combatants increased while feelings of contempt decreased. These bonds led two peacewalkers to remain in Albany after the immediate struggle had ended to facilitate better community racial understanding.[40]

Strategical

The development of the Albany conflict supports Sharp's contention that the grievance group must select appropriate struggle issues. The peacewalkers' main issue, which they defined as first amendment rights, was one with which many people could identify and sympathize. The walkers sought to repeat in Albany only their usual types of sign-carrying and leafletting, which had been done in hundreds of towns in many states and foreign countries. In the walkers' moderate proposal, there was no attempt to force racial integration or to depart from legal norms.

Thought and planning also went into the walkers' choice of tactics. The fast, appropriately, received emphasis as the main method of action. This particular tactic uniquely combined the use of moral strength (respect for the walkers' commitment) to convert, and the use of fear (of the walkers' death or physical impairment) to coerce. As Lyttle correctly stated, "Fasting forced the issue and prevented the city from imprisoning us indefinitely."[41] But because of the moral element of fasting, the walkers succeeded in coercing without alienating potential supporters. Importantly, the walkers could implement their tactics with a small group of committed members. Thus, the walkers more correctly assessed their own strength and that of their opponents that did the Albany authorities.

Conclusion

In his analysis of the Quebec-Washington-Guantanamo Walk, CNVA member Dave Dellinger wrote that "the first lesson of Albany is that nonviolence has the power to win tangible victories against seemingly overwhelming odds, if its practicioners are prepared to make almost limitless sacrifice."[42] However, despite Dellinger's claim, the success of Albany cannot be attributed to any one factor such as the steadfastness of the walkers. As demonstrated in this paper, the tactics that the walkers used were varied—civil disobedience, refusal to pay bond, long-term fasting, support demonstrations, economic coercion, publicity, mailings, and skillful negotiations. Each factor contributed in different ways to the walkers' victory. Not only a resolute will, but strength and effective strategy made success possible in this nonviolent struggle.

This paper illustrates the interconnectedness of factors that contributed to the resolution of the Albany conflict. Acts of protest and persuasion, noncooperation, and nonviolent intervention were used. Polarization and repression preceded and influenced the political jiu-jitsu effects. Throughout the course of the struggle, interaction continually occurred among the various parties. The walkers' shift in emphasis from protest and persuasion to intervention tactics motivated changed responses from the city authorities. As the political jiu-jitsu effects began to take hold, support for the party initially holding power began to diminish and polarization and repression levels declined. Although at different times elements of conversion, accommodation, and coercion took place, change occurred mainly through a process of accommodation.

Although in substantial agreement with his analysis, this study fails to support some aspects of Sharp's discussion. By his selection of historical cases to illustrate general propositions, Sharp implies two causal phenomena that the Albany case does not sustain. First, Sharp mainly focusses on instances in which the opponent meets the grievance groups' nonviolent action with acts of violent repression. In these cases, the political jiu-jitsu effects are usually clear and dramatic. The reader might conclude the successful nonviolence, operating mainly through political jiu-jitsu, is heavily dependent upon the use of violent repression by the opponent. Second, Sharp's examples imply that the grievance groups use of nonviolent action affects a change in the opponent's stance by means of conversion, accommodation, or coercion. One might get the impression that only the opponent willingly or unwillingly undergoes change because of pressure applied by the grievance group.

Neither of these causal phenomena took place in the Albany struggle. Because of Police Chief Pritchett's familiarity with nonviolence, his agents rarely used overt physical violence against the walkers. Also, as the struggle developed, the grievance group, like its opponents, changed its attitude and demands. Both sides pursued a strategy to persuade or force their opponent to change its mind or behavior. Each side adjusted their strategy in response to their opponent's tactics until the process of accommodation allowed for a compromise to take place. More attention needs to be given to cases like this in which the nonviolent action group faces an opponent who minimizes the use of overt physical violence.

In sum, this study indicates that historical case research can serve to extend essential knowledge regarding nonviolent struggle. Case studies can fulfill several purposes—to give a more complete description of the actual campaign development, to indicate the interconnectedness and relative importance of factors which lead to crisis and its resolution, and to help provide a clearer indication of how to operationalize and weigh relevant factors of nonviolent action in order to set the stage for a conceptually valid quantitative analysis. The authors, therefore, suggest that descriptive case and analytical studies are a worthwhile addition, and, perhaps, necessary prerequisite, to other social scientific studies of nonviolent action. In combination with these other methods, case study research can provide a basis from which a more systematic analysis of nonviolent struggle will become possible.

Notes

1. The national Committee for Nonviolent Action (CNVA) was an informal organization of radical pacifists who arranged direct action projects on peace and justice issues. Begun in 1957, the national CNVA merged into the War Resisters League in 1967.

2. Gene Sharp, *The Politics of Nonviolent Action*, Boston: Porter Sargent, 1973.

3. The authors examined the *Albany Herald*, the *Atlanta Constitution*, and the *Atlanta Journal* for the dates December, 1963-March, 1964. The authors called Albany Newspapermen and wrote personal letters to the major Albany officials involved in the 1963—1964 struggle to seek their help in researching this paper. None of the letters has been answered.

4. See Dave Dellinger, "An Integrated Peace Walk Through Georgia," in Dave Dellinger, *Revolutionary Nonviolence*, New York: Doubleday and Company, 1971, pp. 284—299.

5. Howard Zinn, *SNCC: The New Abolitionists*, Boston: Beacon Press, 1964, p. 130.

6. See Zinn, *SNCC*, pp. 127—128 and Brad Lyttle, "Special Report—The Peacewalkers' Struggle in Albany, Georgia," Brad Lyttle's files, Box 1, Albany kits, CNVA Manuscript Collection, Swarthmore College Peace Collection (hereafter cited as CNVA MSS).

7. "News Release," January 27, 1964, Albany, Georgia, Brad Lyttle Manuscript Collection, Swarthmore College Peace Collection (hereafter cited as Brad Lyttle MSS), Box 1.

8. Letters expressing this opinion were printed in the Albany newspapers.

9. See Barbara Deming, *Prison Notes*, New York: Grossman, 1964, and Brad Lyttle to Erica Enzer and Ralph Degia, February 1, 1964, Quebec-Washington-Guantanamo Walk, Albany, Georgia, A. J. Muste Manuscript Collection, Swarthmore College Peace Collection (hereafter cited as A. J. Muste MSS), Box 23. Deming's book provides an excellent personal account of the Albany struggle. Her observations greatly aided us.

10. Ralph Degia, "Cuba Walkers Win Major Concession From Georgia Officials," *Liberation*, Vol. IX, March, 1964, p. 5; "Why Are the Peacewalkers in Jail? A Fact Sheet on the Quebec-Washington-Guantanamo Walk for Peace in Albany, Georgia," Quebec-Washington-Guantanamo Walk, CNVA MSS, Box 2; Lyttle, "The Peacewalkers' Struggle."

11. There was a significant difference in coverage of the Albany events among the three Georgia newspapers we examined. While the *Albany Herald* and the *Atlanta Constitution* printed spotty, and often misleading, news stories concerning the peacewalkers' actions, the *Atlanta Journal* gave fairly comprehensive and accurate coverage to the events.

12. Deming, *Prison Notes*, p. 160.

13. "Arrest of Peace Marchers Protested—Canadians Ask U.S. Probe," *Miami Herald* (February 21, 1964), Albany, Georgia, Brad Lyttle MSS, Box 2; "Press Release," February 24, 1964, Albany, Georgia, Brad Lyttle MSS, Box 1; Deming, *Prison Notes*, p. 160; Rowland G. Moscow, "Free At Last, Free At Last," *Sanity*, Vol. I, No. 11, March, 1964, Albany, Georgia, Brad Lyttle MSS, Box 1.

14. "26 Now In Albany Jail," February 5, 1964, Albany, Georgia, Brad Lyttle MSS, Box 1; Moscow, "Free At Last, Free At Last"; Deming, *Prison Notes*, p. 160.

15. One of these ministers, a Rev. Wilson, wielded tremendous influence as Mayor Davis and several of the City Commissioners were members of his congregation.

16. Deming, *Prison Notes*, pp. 132—142; "News Release," February 24, 1964, Albany, Georgia, Brad Lyttle MSS, Box 1; "CNVA in Albany," Albany, Georgia, Brad Lyttle MSS, Box 1.
17. "News Release," February 24, 1964; Deming, *Prison Notes*, pp. 174—176.
18. Sharp, *Politics*, p. 63.
19. Sharp, *Politics*, pp. 11—12, 19—23.
20. Sharp, *Politics*, p. 18.
21. Sharp, *Politics*, pp. 68—9.
22. Brad Lyttle to Erica Enzer and Ralph Degia.
23. Lyttle, "The Peacewalkers Struggle."
24. Deming, *Prison Notes*, p. 31.
25. "News Release," December 23, 1963, Albany, Georgia, Brad Lyttle MSS, Box 1.
26. Deming, *Prison Notes*, p. 70.
27. Sharp, *Politics*, p. 524.
28. Sharp, *Politics*, p. 536.
29. Sharp, *Politics*, p. 657.
30. Sharp, *Politics*, p. 113.
31. Deming, *Prison Notes*, pp. 130—153.
32. "Walkers Walk Off From City," Albany *Herald*, February 24, p. 9.
33. Brad Lyttle to Jim Bristol, May 1, 1964, Albany, Georgia, Brad Lyttle MSS, Box 1, p. 7.
34. A. J. Muste to 'Dear Friend,' March 13, 1964, Quebec-Washington-Guantanamo Walk, Albany, Georgia, A. J. Muste MSS, Box 23, SCPC; Deming, *Prison Notes*, p. 178.
35. Brad Lyttle to Jim Bristol, p. 6.
36. Deming, *Prison Notes*, pp. 140—160.
37. Brad Lyttle to Jim Bristol, p. 5; Deming, *Prison Notes*, p. 70.
38. General review of letters to the editor, Albany *Herald*, Atlanta *Constitution*, and Atlanta *Journal*, January-February, 1964.
39. Deming, *Prison Notes*, p. 130.
40. Deming, *Prison Notes*, pp. 170—180; Edith Snyder, "Review of Albany Project," June to October, 1964, Albany Project, CNVA MSS, Box 2, SCPC.
41. Brad Lyttle to Jim Bristol, p. 5.
42. Dellinger, *Revolutionary Nonviolence*, p. 300.

Chapter 7

The Nonviolent Movement Versus Nuclear Power*

Harvey Wasserman

New England Struggle

Seabrook, New Hampshire, is a small town on the Atlantic Coast about an hour's drive north of Boston. Its low coastal plains are filled with gorgeous, deep-green marshes that play host to magnificent white seabirds. On July 9, 1976, the Public Service Company (PSC) of New Hampshire began leveling the town dump on the edge of the Seabrook salt marsh to prepare the site for construction of a nuclear power plant.

Though the town is small (population: 5700) and conservative, the twin 1150-megawatt reactors, lately estimated to cost at least $2.5 billion are not welcome. Despite promises of jobs, tax and business benefits, Seabrookers don't want the plant. For many, one stumbling block is the massive influx of workers into their small, quiet town; for others, it's the environmental damage and the threat of radiation; for still others, it seems to be just plain down-home New England cussedness and an age-old desire—now become a demand—to be let live in peace.

Thus the people of Seabrook had already voted against the nuclear project. The PSC bulldozers were a declaration of war

*Acknowledgement is made to *The Progressive* (Madison, Wisconsin), September, 1977 issue and *New Age*, Vol. II, No. 5, for this article, which appeared, in part, in each magazine.

against thousands of New England seacoast residents who had strong apprehensions about the plant, the thermal pollution it would spew into the Atlantic, and the hazards of radiation leakage, catastrophic accident, and disposal of nuclear wastes.

Within days after the coming of the bulldozers, an umbrella coalition—the Clamshell Alliance—began planning a series of actions at the Seabrook site that would usher in a new age of political activism in the 1970s and pose a formidable threat to the electric industry's program of nuclear construction.

More than a dozen grass-roots anti-nuclear groups had been in operation around New England by the time construction at Seabrook began. Indeed, with seven active reactors in the region, one under construction, and eight more proposed, the anti-nuclear movement here had already become something of a subculture. Groups in Maine were fighting proposed construction at Sears Island; people in Boston and Plymouth were trying to block a second reactor planned for Plymouth; a network of organizations in Connecticut was moving against three active plants and one under construction in that state; the town meeting of Charlestown, Rhode Island, had voted against the twin reactors planned there, and activists in southern Vermont were focusing on the notoriously inefficient and dangerous Yankee plant at Vernon.

Strong resistance had also been building for more than three years against twin reactors planned for the town of Montague in western Massachusetts. In 1974, the Pioneer Valley anti-nuclear forces had won 47.5 percent of the vote in a referendum against the Montague plant, and had carried 33 percent in favor of shutting down the Vermont Yankee plant as well as a smaller reactor at Rowe, Massachusetts. In the same balloting, Wendell, Massachusetts became the first town in America to vote to dismantle active commercial nuclear power plants.

With its long winters and scarce fossil reserves, New England has long been the region where the nuclear industry felt it could make its best case for atomic energy. But the resistance has been fiercest here, partly because of regional traditions of political activism and partly because the anti-nuclear forces decided early in the game to base their strategy on community organizing.

Seabrook represented the first new nuclear construction in New England in three years. With six reactors on the drawing boards and at least one other (Pilgrim II at Plymouth) nearing the con-

struction phase, it was clearly time to move. Through several
weeks of meetings in the summer of 1976, representatives of New
England grassroots organizations hammered out a new strategy.

The Clamshell Alliance would employ mass civil disobedience.
The actions, however, would be occupations, not demonstrations.
Following the model set by nuclear opponents at Wyhl, West Germany, we opted for a long-range program that would aim at
taking the Seabrook site and holding it.

The tactic of mass occupation, although untried in the United
States, seemed to be our last resort. Nobody was winning any
legal interventions, and there was no prospect of governmental
action. We were not merely protesting nuclear construction—we
were trying to stop it. Our actions would not be for show. If we
failed, it would be because we lacked numbers, not intent, and
next time we would be back with more people.

As an umbrella coalition, the Clamshell Alliance would help
coordinate and focus the energies of the grassroots groups without imposing a rigid structure. All Clamshell meetings would operate on consensus rather than majority vote. There would be
task-oriented committees, but no officers. The Alliance office
would be a switchboard, resource, and convening center, but decision making would remain firmly in the hands of the local
groups.

The Alliance adopted a plan for training people in the tactics
of nonviolence. In "affinity groups" of eight to twenty people, the
occupiers were fully instructed in the legal ramifications of what
they were about to do. There was discussion of the nuclear issue
in general and of the Seabrook situation in particular. The groups
reviewed the plan of action and related it to historic applications
of the nonviolent technique. Finally, they "role played" the exercise they were about to undertake.

This last element proved immensely helpful. The prospective
occupiers acted out various parts in the coming drama—in turn
playing police, media, medics, support people, and occupiers.
The game allowed us to see the coming action from every perspective. It also added a dimension many of us had missed during
the antiwar demonstrations of the 1960s and early 1970s: putting
ourselves in the position of the police and forcing ourselves to
assess their attitudes.

The affinity groups became functioning units providing the

background and personal support that turned the occupation "army" into an organized community. Each affinity group had a spokesperson who would represent it at decision-making huddles along the march route, on the site, and in prison. Each group had its medical and media people and at least one person who would avoid arrest and serve as outside liaison through protracted occupations or incarcerations.

The nonviolence training was evident even in the first occupation on August 1, 1976. Eighteen occupiers—all from New Hampshire—walked along a mile of railroad track to become the first Americans to take part in mass civil disobedience at a nuclear reactor construction site. All had participated in a training session, though many of them knew each other well enough to act as an affinity group long before an occupation was ever contemplated.

On August 22, 1976, more than 1500 Clamshell members rallied near the site and 180, representing all six New England states, occupied the PSC property. This time the training and affinity structure were crucially important—not only in keeping our community together, but in reducing tensions with the state police. We told the police everything we planned to do and gave them no reason to mistrust our word.

Because of the tight group structure, any disrupters on our side could be quickly identified and isolated. Later we learned that the state police had also done role-play training. Everyone had a reasonably good idea of what was about to happen. There was an air of good feeling and self-assurance among both the police and occupiers that made the event seem more like a ballet than a traditional political confrontation.

The lack of rancor made it easier to keep the focus on the issue. August 22 became our peaceful "shot heard round the world" and it made New England aware of nuclear power as nothing else—short of a melt-down or a still larger occupation—could have.

Riding high on the tide of our first major success, the Clamshell scheduled a third occupation for October 23. But by mid-September we had serious second thoughts about Clamshell's real strength and its mass appeal. There would be more to building a movement than merely getting busted at Seabrook.

The scheduled occupation was converted into an alternative

energy fair and mass bike ride that drew 3,000 people to Hampton Beach State Park on a cold, windy October weekend. We used the fair to highlight our commitment to natural energy. We also announced a new occupation date—April 30, 1977—and settled in for a winter of serious organizing.

Through the fall the Alliance had functioned as an informal meeting to coordinate the rallies and actions. Our problems had been simple logistics—where to stage speeches, now to train occupiers, how to publicize it all, and, of course, how to make the necessary support arrangements.

By October, the realities of building a durable movement had become more clear. We would have to strengthen the local groups, solidify our community outreach programs, and start a campaign to reach working people.

Our main instrument was the committee system, which performed the nitty-gritty tasks and absorbed new people who were willing to work. A resource committee became responsible for producing and distributing literature, speakers, films and general information. A farm-labor committee worked on getting a foothold in the union and agricultural communities, and produced fliers on the jobs issue as well as a leaflet to distribute to the National Guard in anticipation of a larger action. Legal, media, and finance committees went to work. Recently we have added a concert committee and an alternative energy committee to promote our growing emphasis on conservation and solar power. New committees are added, and old ones dissolved, as our needs change.

A coordinating committee composed of representatives from both the local groups and the other committees serves as a clearing house for decisions on how and when to have centralized actions, but no important decisions can be made without going back to the locals for consensus, any major decision thus takes at least two weeks—usually more—and can require hours of discussion involving any Clamshell member willing to participate. Two major Clamwide congresses have also been convened to give final solidarity to upcoming actions.

If the group consensus system seems cumbersome and slow, it has also proved to be a key factor in the organization's high morale. The Alliance has continually moved toward decentralization, and dialogue is constant. Anyone can take part in our meetings—a perpetual Clamshell phenomenon aptly described by one National Guardsman as a "tribal ritual."

But another thing the Quakers taught the Alliance was to conduct meetings in a stern but gentle manner aimed at eliminating repetition and accomplishing real work. Indeed, participatory democracy as practiced by the Clamshell Alliance has always danced that thin line between process and paralysis. The system is vulnerable to nitpicking and petty bickering, and without basic trust—and a sense of humor—the process would grind to a halt. But we are fighting corporate power, not imitating it, and good-natured compromise has been part of the Clamshell mystique from the very start.

As the Clamshell members dispersed for the winter, the grass-roots campaign on the New Hampshire seacoast gained momentum. The foundations had been laid in the early 1970s, when Aristotle Onassis had tried to build a huge oil refinery at Durham. The town had voted no, and despite the best efforts of Governor Meldrim Thomson, the plant had been defeated.

Along with their rock-ribbed conservatism, New Hampshirites have a strong tradition of home rule. There is a deep attachment to local roots and a stubborn Yankee insistence on the idea that what the community says, goes. New Hampshirites don't like outsiders forcing unwanted projects down their throats, and a nuclear power plant is no exception.

As construction of the plant became more imminent, some of the organizations that had fought Onassis shifted to the nuclear issue. The company's arrogance on some local matters helped to move the people of Seabrook into the opposition. Through the winter of 1976-1977, organizers worked in surrounding towns with meetings, slide shows, and leaflets aimed at demonstrating that atomic reactors would do nothing for the clamming, fishing, and tourism on which the seacoast residents depend for their livelihood.

As work proceeded at the site, it also became clear that most of the labor force was being imported from out of state, giving the lie to the company's promise that the project would produce local jobs. The projected cost of the plant soared, and seacoast residents began to doubt that the reactors would lower their electric rates. In fact, when the PSC asked for a series of rate increases, the opposite seemed to be the case.

Last spring—town meeting time—Seabrook again voted against

the plant, this time to ban the transportation and storage of radioactive materials within the town. Eight neighboring towns soon joined in outright opposition or in support of Seabrook's vote.

As the Alliance began gearing up for its third occupation, local supporters played an essential role. Of all the problems leading up to the action, none was as difficult as finding staging areas for the large numbers of occupiers. In most cases, people would have to camp the night before the occupation. We would also need communications centers, support structures, and parking areas convenient to the site.

It had been one thing for local residents to vote against the plant; it was quite another to put their personal property on the line in support of civil disobedience.

The Alliance, however, got not only its staging areas, but also a barnload of donated food, and, on the day of the occupation, a host of cheering local residents who waved anti-nuclear signs along with American flags to usher the occupiers into the site.

The occupiers themselves presented the Alliance's second major problem. One trainer had prepared the eighteen August 1 occupiers; three or four AFSC veterans were available to deal with the 180 of August 22. But as April 30 approached, there simply weren't enough experienced group instructors around, so a training committee was set up to prepare around thirty more. The program soon expanded to include long sessions of free conversation on people's feelings and fears about the coming action, as well as assessments of the affinity group structure and what people expected of it. Some trainers began injecting a "provocateur" into the role play whose identity was known only to them.

The system did have its weaknesses, however, and the main one was the Decision-Making Body (DMB, soon known as "dumb"), an intricate structure meant to serve as the representative congress of the occupation. The DMB proved too cumbersome to make decisions quickly or meaningfully under the strained conditions at the site. Its total breakdown was relieved only by the mass arrests that cleared the area.

When the arrests began, we also encountered problems stemming from the disruption of the affinity groups. The police had their own interest in the structure, and purposely arrested people in a pattern designed to break up the groups.

But as time in the armories wore on, new affinity groups and new decision-making structures evolved. We are now considering training groups, and then deliberately breaking them up into new groups, as part of contingency planning for the next occupation.

Compared to our own basic logistic problems, the external resistance proved to be relatively minor. Just before August 22, the PSC had obtained a blanket injunction which was later used to level contempt charges against ten of the occupiers. As the April 30 action approached, the injunction was still in effect.

Meanwhile, the *Manchester Union-Leader*, William Loeb's powerful right-wing newspaper, spent the week predicting violence and bloodshed. And Governor Thomson charged that the Clamshell was a front for "communists" and "terrorists." We reiterated our commitment to peace and pushed ahead with our plans. By April 29, both Governor Thomson and the *Union-Leader* had muted their tones. At the same time, a court challenge to the injunction resulted in limiting its effect to a small section at the site where work was actually in progress, where equipment was stored, and where we had not intended to go anyway.

This lifting of the restrictions was not strictly magic. Thomson had indeed wanted us kept off the site, but Colonel Paul Doyon, chief of the New Hampshire state police, had other ideas. He had handled the August 22 arrests, was convinced of our nonviolent intent, and apparently decided it would be easier and safer to allow us onto the site and arrest us there, rather than risk chaos on the approach route and in the surrounding area.

On Saturday, April 30, an eerie calm prevailed as more than 2000 people marched onto the nuclear site without a trace of resistance. Police from five states were on hand, but they went a long way toward facilitating the march and making sure no one got hurt. Once again there was an unusual sense of community between occupiers and police, and once again it made it possible for us to keep the spotlight on the reasons for our action. It also vastly strengthened the Clamshell consensus on the importance of nonviolence.

For many Alliance members, nonviolence is sine qua non, a deeply held religious commitment inseparable from their specific opposition to nuclear power. Nukes are, after all, engines of violence to both people and the planet, and that is the basic reason we oppose them. The nonviolent technique helped us draw the line between nuclear power as a technology of destruction and solar energy as one of peace.

As a tactic, peaceful resistance at Seabrook has also raised some important questions about traditional political behavior. So far, the method had disarmed our opponents and brought out the best in ourselves. The nonviolent tone has lessened tensions at meetings, provided an air of calm throughout the organizing procedures, and made it possible to achieve trust among several thousand diverse people. It has also forced several hundred armed police and a violence-prone governor in an extremely conservative state to learn some novel lessons in human nature.

However, most important of all, the commitment to nonviolence has allowed us to attract a broad spectrum of people to both the nuclear issue and the prospect of personal participation in civil disobedience. Our unequivocal commitment to peace has opened neighborhood doors that might otherwise have been slammed shut.

With the help of nonviolence, we have witnessed the rise of a strong grass-roots opposition in one of America's most conservative areas. In this growing struggle to stop nuclear reactors, we have found a coherence and a solidarity that have been missing from this country for too many years.

International Struggle

Similar things might be said of the situation at Kashiwazake, a small town on the Sea of Japan, currently slated—in at least some people's minds—for as many as eight nuclear reactors. In the late 1960s the townspeople actually welcomed the project. Caught in an economic downswing, with many old fishermen desperate for some sort of relief, Kashiwazaki formally invited Tokyo Electric to build at least one reactor in their town as soon as possible. The project would bring jobs, compensation for the fishermen who would sell their fishing rights to the company, and even a boost in business, thanks to all the traffic of workmen and the like. To make things even rosier, the company assured local farmers that radiation from the plant would aid the growth of rice; it also told local cultivators of ornamental carp that the radiation would add attractive coloring to their fish.

But something happened in Kasiwazaki around 1971. Radical students began "infiltrating" from Tokyo to spread the word about the dark side of nuclear power. The jobs would be temporary, they said, and most would go to outsiders with special skills. The plant would give the town economy a temporary boom, and then burst it permanently when the job was done.

Also, the radiation wasn't really all that healthy, nor were the dealings of Tokyo Electric known to be all that pure. Kashiwazaki happens to be in Niigata Prefecture, home district of former Prime Minister Kakuei Tanaka, who was sentenced to a prison term. At the time of Tokyo Electric's original negotiations, Tanaka was still the most powerful man in Japan, and a great favorite among his former neighbors.

But later in the game an investigative reporter found that a company related to Tanaka had purchased land at the reactor site, presumably for a "resort," before the construction plan was announced. By the time Tokyo Electric's plans became public, the acreage had jumped in price twenty-five times over. When Tanaka's connections with the lucky company found their way into print, another item was added to the long list of "unfortunate errors" that would eventually land him in prison.

The land scandal cooled a few Kashiwazakians to the reactor, but what put many more over the line was some business about an earthquake fault. Much of Japan is seismographically unstable, and it was generally suspected that Kashiwazaki was no exception. To quiet public fear, Tokyo Electric issued a report stating that the most recent significant earth movements had occurred three-hundred thousand years ago, and therefore there was nothing to worry about.

Nuclear opponents, however, rather easily unearthed a geological report done by an oil company in the 1920s that showed Tokyo Electric to be exaggerating by a factor of at least ten. In Japan, such "white lies" are taken as personal insults, and very soon the project became considerably less than welcome. As of a recent count, 30 percent of the population was dead set against it and another 50 percent harbored "serious doubts." Understandably, the company has been hesitant to move into such a clime. The core of the opposition is among the local peasantry—farmers and fisherpeople—with the leadership roles often being played by tough, vibrant women over fifty, red-cheeked and strong-bodied from years of back-breaking work in the paddies and carp-ponds.

It was farm people who helped overrun the planned nuclear power site in Whyl, in southwestern Germany. The site is in the middle of a lush grape-growing area, on the Rhine, and a major fear among the militant farmers was that steam evaporating out the cooling towers might destroy the local weather patterns and thus their crops.

On February 22, 1974, a coalition of farmers, townspeople, and environmentalists from Germany, France, and Switzerland staged one of the largest nonviolent confrontations in the history of Europe. Inspired in part by a victory against a chemical plant slated for a site further up the Rhine, more than twenty thousand protestors gathered to occupy the Whyl site. To gain access, they had to break through ten rows of barbed wire fencing, and, in a series of nonviolent maneuvers, they were able to surround as many as three thousand police, who ended up having to request safe passage out of the area.

A main point of contention was that the plant would produce at least six times the amount of electricity that was needed in the area, and was obviously intended to serve the needs of heavy industry rather than those of the local population. The project was pushed persistently by the state government, two of whose top ministers are also directors of the Kernkraftwerk Sued Company, which intended to build the plant.

Since the occupation, however, a German court has cancelled the Wyhl project. Meanwhile, powerful anti-nuclear movements have grown up all over Europe.

Can This Really Be The End?

The movement to stop nuclear power is making rapid strides in Japan and the industrialized West. The issue has received tremendous media exposure, and the slow-but-sure graduation from dialogue to demonstration is just one of many signs that the campaign is moving rapidly towards a position of real mass strength.

At the same time, the nuclear industry seems to be suffering from problems that transcend the political. Nuclear construction costs are soaring everywhere at a rate that is hard to pinpoint but can safely be described as "astronomical." Basic material costs are going up at a rate of at least 10 percent a year, and perhaps double that. The price of raw uranium is also doubling yearly, and the cost of enriched uranium is heading clean out of sight, to the point where it may become altogether unavailable in the

near future. Westinghouse has defaulted on uranium supply contracts to some twenty domestic utilities, and the prospects for
building the necessary enrichment facilities in the near future are
dim, to say the least.

In the meantime, labor costs are also soaring, and with a consistent track record of two, three, and four-year overruns in construction time, the potential inflation is literally out of control.

Add to that the extremely poor economic performance of those
plants that have been completed—poor enough, in fact, to make
many conservative economists doubt whether nuclear power can
ever pay—and you have what might be termed a "delicate" economic outlook.

In such a situation, the implications of physical obstruction are
greatly magnified. The fact is that the nuclear industry was shaken
to its core by the energy crisis. Despite the obvious questions
raised about the future viability of oil, the rising costs of energy
forced a drop in consumption that also threw into question the
real future needs for nuclear-generated electricity. The accompanying tight money and soaring material costs wound a very
tight noose around the nuclear neck. In 1975 only eleven new
reactors were put on order in the U.S., only three in 1976, and
four in 1977. For this dramatic drop, the anti-nuclear movement
can take much credit.

Third World View

The task of the various national antinuclear movements does
not, however, stop at their countries' borders. If a combination
of economic factors and rising political opposition is driving the
nuclear industry to the wall at home, it is also driving it to the
Third World overseas, to a multibillion-dollar export trade that
turns the nuclear power question into a truly global affair.

By and large, the governments of the Third World have been
sold on a Western model of development. With large cities, large
industries, and large exports, many Third World rulers feel they
can pull themselves out of powerlessness and into their rightful
stand alongside the industrial nations. Such blueprints require a
great deal of power, of course, and that is where nuclear gener-
ators come in.

Actually, there are a few other things to account for. For one thing, most Third World nuclear customers are neocolonial dictatorships, ruled by corrupt cliques of generals and businessmen. For them, a nuclear power plant has the added attraction of plutonium waste that can be used for making nuclear bombs—not to mention a perhaps more basic incentive, the fact that any multimillion-dollar project is guaranteed to line the pockets of those on the inside. In the more corrupt countries, it doesn't really matter whether the project is finished or even started—what counts is the cash flow, and for that it's hard to beat a 600-megawatt nuclear station, which these days costs a minimum of $1 billion.

These are the concerns clearly at work in the Philippines, which is fast committing itself to a nuclear future. Indonesia would certainly like to follow suit, but it is already in debt to the tune of $10 billion dollars because of graft and executive extravagance in its national oil combine, Pertamina. Indeed, an Indonesian friend of ours, when told about the stringent safety requirements for nuclear construction, recoiled in horror. From 25 to 50 percent of the cash is guaranteed to disappear into official pockets, she explained; walls that need to be three feet thick would be lucky to make it to eighteen inches.

A tragic example of the possible consequences of such construction practices can already be seen in Thailand, at the Bang Ken reactor just north of Bangkok. Completed in the early 1960s under the Atoms for Peace Program, the reactor leaked radiation into both the atmosphere and public waterways for more than a decade before the facts were made public. The whole problem might have gone totally ignored had the Thai Left not overthrown the military dictatorship of Thanom Kittikachorn in the fall of 1973. Within a year Thai students exercised their newly won freedom by publishing *Top Secret: The Leaking of the Atomic Reactor at Bang Ken*. Based on material leaked from the reactor staff and on reports from the International Atomic Energy Agency (IAEA), the United Nations monitoring team, the book leveled charges of incompetence at government officials responsible for operating the plant. Documentation showed that radioactive gases were being emitted into the atmosphere, directly contributing to the high level of radioactivity in a heavily populated district nearby. It also showed that dangerous contamination had been dumped into the Bang Ken klang (canal) used to water padi(rice) land. This canal ultimately fed into the Chao Phrya River, which flows right through Bangkok. The students further charged that the reactor had shut itself down numerous times because of worn-out parts that could not be replaced since the original builders of the plant had left the reactor field.

Top Secret created a furor in Bangkok and may have been instrumental in bringing operations at Bang Ken to at least a temporary halt. The reactor is now closed, but its life is not necessarily over. It is being upgraded to 2 megawatts, and its fuel system is being altered. Meanwhile, the Thai Energy Generating Authority (EGAT) is pushing hard for the installation of at least one 600-megawatt commercial reactor. Whether they get it will depend almost totally on the political climate in Thailand; if the current swing to the Right stops short of dictatorship, an antinuclear movement of considerable weight is almost sure to develop.

Post-Thanom Thailand enjoys a freedom of information and a flow of opinion unique in the neocolonial Third World. But unfortunately the type of leakages experienced at Bang Ken may be, in fact, only a small taste of what is to come when plants as much as six hundred times larger begin sprouting up everywhere.

At the twin 200-megawatt reactors at Tarapur, north of Bombay, workmen have been observed handling radioactive wastes with bamboo poles, and the plant leaks radiation so badly that workers are rotated at an extremely rapid rate to avoid excessive exposure. Two Tarapur workmen are already known to have died of cancer—almost undoubtedly the result of radiation overdose—and how many other victims there have been so far is anybody's guess.

India's nuclear commitment is peanuts compared to that of the other Third World giants. Iran is said to be planning as many as thirty-six reactors (roughly one for every million people), and Brazil, Argentina, and South Africa are also thinking in terms of a nuclear future. South Korea is well along in its nuclear development; and a large quantity of plutonium—the magic ingredient for making atomic bombs—has already "disappeared" in Taiwan.

Fears of just such a development have finally prompted some public awareness of nuclear generator proliferation, and a whole slew of strongly worded international agreements have been designed to prevent the conversion of plant wastes into bombs.

But the idea of controlling such a widespread empire of radioactivity is out of the question. The sole international police force at present is the International Atomic Energy Agency (IAEA), a poorly-funded United Nations organization with a staff of forty inspectors and a very dubious political legacy. Like the U.S.'s old Atomic Energy Commission (AEC), the IAEA has devoted much of its energy to pushing, as well as regulating, international nuclear power. In at least one instance—involving Malaysia—we found that IAEA had recommended establishing a national atomic energy board that would both control and promote nuclear power, a conflict of interest that people in the U.S. have fought long and hard to eliminate.

The IAEA's funding comes largely from the nations selling nuclear plants, and its access to the countries buying them is at best tenuous. Under the circumstances, the idea that the IAEA could effectively police several hundred reactors across the planet is patently absurd. For the time being, at least, "nuclear reactor proliferation" means proliferation of nuclear weapons and radioactivity.

Atomic Economics

The nuclear plants also mean long-term indebtedness of the worst sort for the Third World. Demanding hundreds of millions of dollars of international loans, the construction of nuclear facilities also commits a country to a Western, industrialized, export-oriented economy. Regimes set on building 600-megawatt reactors are not going to be interested in decentralized, village-based development. They will have to begin thinking in terms of foreign exchange, which means a centralized population, centralized industry, and heavy exports, with all the pollution, exploitation, and misery that these conditions entail.

Meanwhile, the nuclear industry will have gotten the subsidies it desperately needs. At their worst, loans and aid for Third World reactors can be seen as a direct form of subsidization for the nuclear industry—with money passing from industrialized sources, briefly through the hands of Third World rulers, and then directly back to General Electric, Westinghouse, and the like. The nuclear vendors are then all set to build their reactors free of troublesome environmentalist interference and political opposition—a much more profitable proposition than at home.

It is a vicious cycle that will be extremely difficult to break.

France, West Germany, Canada, and the United States (acting in partnership with Japan) are all heavily committed to the nuclear export trade. We are now party to the spectacle of Japan serving as go-between for the sale of American reactors to Russia; ships carrying lethal plutonium wastes from Japan to Britain for treatment, then back again; the American nuclear physicist Dr. Edward Teller telling Indonesia to contract for twenty reactors in exchange for virtually all its oil; Iran, South Africa, and Brazil building regional empires potentially based on substantial nuclear stockpiles.

The full implications of the world nuclear trade are only slowly beginning to dawn on us. With media campaigning and rhetoric giving way to physical confrontation on the domestic scene, it is becoming painfully clear that humanity has never faced an issue with such permanent and all-pervasive conclusions hanging in the balance.

The challenge is truly amazing. The task that confronts us is bringing a halt to a trillion-dollar industry in the separate nations of the industrial world, then following that feat with the dissolution of one of the most immensely lucrative export trades the world has ever known. Whether it "can be done" depends upon a working international network of nonviolent activists at all levels of society, and it will demand the rapid maturation of a truly global ecological consciousness.

Part III.

International Social Change Movements

Part III looks at cases of radical-nonviolent action that have appeared abroad. Here we see how social change movements assume an international significance. In Chapter Eight, we look at the work of Danilo Dolci who helped create a frontier beyond the Mafia ridden politics of Sicily. In Chapter Nine, Charles Walker tells of the influence of the civil rights movement in East Africa and the Zambian government for independence. In Chapter Ten, Paul Wehr reports on his studies of nonviolent conflict in Norway and Czechoslovakia in resistance to the Nazi regime.

These examples of nonviolent action have repercussions that extend into the realm of political policy among nations. They also point toward new models for nonviolent action research in the future.

Chapter 8

Danilo Dolci: A Nonviolent Reformer in Sicily

Joseph Amato

In the late 1960s and early 1970s Danilo Dolci, a nonviolent, social reformer in Western Sicily, won a good deal of attention in this country. The attention came from the educated and liberal circles, usually associated with the university, and occasionally, the more progressive elements of trade unions. That is, in the main, it came from those who supported Civil Rights and the anti-War movements, those who identified themselves with the causes of the Fellowship of Reconciliation, the Catholic Worker, or other ideals surely tied to the American left. Of course, support for Dolci was strong from Italo-Americans who belonged to these same progressive circles.

The sources of Dolci's ample welcome in this country were several: An international reputation preceeded Dolci's visits to the United States. In select quarters of Europe, and elsewhere, he was known as "the Gandhi of Sicily;" from the 1950s on various individuals and committees composed of eminent writers and scholars throughout Italy and Western Europe had given their money and names to Dolci's cause. Dolci's prominence was also established by having won several prestigious prizes for his work in Sicily, including the Lenin Peace Prize. His successive nomination for the Nobel Peace Prize in the 1960s and early 1970s further strengthened his reputation. The excellent work done by The American Friends of Danilo Dolci, under the direction of author Jerre Mangione and sociologist Alfred McClung Lee, helped make Dolci's lecture tours to the United States a success. Mangione's service to Dolci was of inestimable value. After serving as Dolci's aide in Sicily in 1965, Mangione authored a major work on Dolci, *A Passion for Sicilians*, (1968), and was the crucial individual in the rejuvenation of the American Friends of Dolci.

There were also other reasons why Dolci was quick to win a following. There was his personal magnetism—although Dolci didn't speak English, by gesture, tone and sparkle of eye, this heavy set man, of light complexion, seemed to radiate the grace and intelligence, power, and authority, to do all that was associated with his protests and reforms. There was too a romance in a man from Sicily—a man who talked about such basics as the need for water for crops, fishermen and their torn nets, children without beds or bread; such adventures as attacking the omnipresent Mafia at home and its connections reaching to Rome and perhaps the Vatican itself; such sublimities as changing the fatalistic heart of the Sicilian. In practice and theory he seemed to be doing several appealing things.

He spoke of the poor of the underdeveloped world, who during the Vietnam War filled Americans with guilt. He did not propose violent revolution—which some found religiously offensive, others futile; but he suggested more appealingly an ideology which made democracy and nonviolence the fundamentals of revolution. In effect he was updating Gandhi, so that he could compete with Mao and Che. Here, in Dolci's teachings, was a poetic pragmatism, and yet a conception of risk, sacrifice, and moral service which accorded well with the aspirations of so many in his audience who cherished freedom; sensed, as much as ever, the need for profound reform; and found neither value nor possibilities in violent revolution.

For the Americans of Italian descent in Dolci's audience there were yet additional reasons that made him attractive. There was an ethnic pride in finding a man who was intelligent, spoke Italian, and won the interest of large numbers of people. They were flattered when he was compared to Martin Luther King, Cesar Chavez, and other important figures. Unlike Christopher Columbus, Leonardo da Vinci, Dante, and so many other "illustrious Italians," Dolci happened to be alive, not just a person of "history and art," but a man hard at work for people who, seemed to them, by conditions and misery, to be very much like their own grandparents. Dolci in some way, could be understood to be righting the wrongs their ancestors had suffered—there in Sicily or elsewhere in Southern Italy. For the more literate Italo-Americans, Dolci offered a direct route to attacking *la miseria* of the whole *Mezzogiorno*, described so vividly by Verga in *La Malavolgia*, Silone in *Fontemara* and *Vino e pane*, and Carlo Levi in *Christo si é fermato a Eboli*. Dolci offered a direct and moral approach to the complex world of the *Mezzogiorno* in specific and the underdeveloped world in general. His nonviolent strategy was a constructive, yet alluring, poetry in action; it invited support and study by certain select Italo-Americans as well as others. I was among those attracted to Dolci in the early 1970s. I raised a modest sum of money on his behalf, arranged for a visit to our college, wrote some favorable articles, and made two short trips to Sicily, the second I will mention in conclusion to this study.[1]

Life and Deeds

In the minds of many Sicily is a land of violence. For some it is "the Africa of Europe"—a dangerous and dark territory inhabited by a savage people. For others it is the epitome of the Italian South—where all the misery that afflicts the world of Naples and below is concentrated.[2] The historian himself can lend his craft to furthering the stereotype of a violent Sicily. He need only forget that Sicily was the land Plato chose for his Republic, that its poets sang of love before Dante, that its politicians helped create liberal Italy; and he need only recount how Sicily's history has been truly in great part but the story of violent successions of war, conquest and domination of Mediterranean powers since the times of the Phoenecians and Greeks. And even those who have little knowledge of the past to serve their violent portrait of Sicily can with little effort conjure a vision of Sicily that puts cynicism in every Sicilian heart, cunning in every Sicilian face, and the *Mafia* in every Sicilian situation. Thus, if only for the sake of contrast, the nonviolent, social reformer, Danilo Dolci is fascinating. He has spent the past 25 years of his life experimenting with and achieving nonviolent social change in Western Sicily.

Dolci's deeds have covered the whole spectrum of nonviolent action. They have involved him in the issuing of manifestos, the circulating of petitions, the organizing of demonstrations and the conducting of mass fasts. They have included the use of clandestine radio, strikes, sit-ins, and court cases. In turn, his long-range strategies to transform Western Sicily have led him to organize various types of cooperatives, conduct inquiries into the Mafia and inspire research on such diverse subjects as agriculture, health care, folk art, reforestation, Sicilian society, and politics. Dolci belongs to that small group of people whose very lives shape our consideration of the potential.

Dolci was born in 1924 into a middle class family in the town of Sesna, near Trieste. His early years, spent in a stable household, were occupied with the study of music and poetry, an extensive reading of world literature which included the religious classics of Christianity, Mohammedanism, Hinduism, Buddhism, Taoism and Confusianism as well as the writings of such authors as Dante, Shakespeare, Goethe, Schiller, Ibsen and, of special importance, Plato.[3]

The first visible signs of the young Dolci's commitment to nonviolence occurred in the midst of the Second World War. While "he had," in his words "never even heard the phrase 'conscientious objector,' " he already "felt strongly that it was wrong to kill people and was determined never to do so."[4] His specific revulsion to the Nazi regime led him intermittently in the year 1943 to tear up all the Nazi posters he came across in Milan. Later in that same year, he was arrested for reasons unknown to him while en route from Milan to Rome. By feigning that he was a politically disinterested artist, he won his release and passed the remainder of the war, like the hero of Silone's *Bread and Wine*, a fugitive from the law who found shelter with an Italian peasant family.

At the end of the War, Dolci returned to Milan in order to resume his studies in architecture. In 1949, months short of completing his degree and on the threshold of a promising career, Dolci abandoned his studies. Finding it impossible to reconcile himself to the thought that the greater part of his life's work would serve the rich, he went to Nomadelphia, a communal village for war orphans established and run by the remarkable Catholic priest, Don Zeno Saltini. While there, Dolci learned two essential principles: From Don Zeno's example he discovered how much good can be accomplished by the efforts of one person; from his own work with the children Dolci realized how much good can be achieved when people cooperate in improving their own conditions.

In 1952, at the age of twenty eight, Dolci made another crucial decision that led him towards becoming the Dolci we now know. He set out on his own for Sicily. Dolci had already shown his independence of mind by breaking off an engagement which probably would have led to a conventional middle class marriage and by refusing to bear arms during his obligatory period of service in the Italian army. Now, desiring to be the master of his own actions and no longer wishing to be associated directly with the institutional church, he was ready to test himself. Intent on serving the poor, Dolci returned to the small, impoverished fishing village of Trappeto on the Gulf of Castellamare, where his father was once stationmaster when he was young.

With little more than vivid memories of miseries once witnessed, Dolci arrived in Trappeto. Even though Dolci had probably read literary accounts of conditions in the Italian South, he was scarcely prepared to encounter the conditions of this legendary and violent territory to which he had come. Here, slightly to the west of Trappeto, is where Garibaldi and his Red Shirts had, less than a 100 years before, fought that first and bloody battle for a new Italy in which until very recently, the bulk of the peasants had little interest and knowledge and next to no trust. Here, even closer to the east, was the land of that famous peasant bandit Giuliano, who by cunning and bravery, through a mixture of Robin Hoodism, modern guerilla tactics, and political intrigue, had kept the Italian police at bay for seven years until 1950.[5] In this area the Mafia's rule was strongest in all of Sicily.[6] The signs of the social destruction caused by the Second World War and the post-war period were everywhere present.

Dolci's first experiences were shocking. All around him he discovered a violent order of life. He found houses without beds and water, children without schools and clothes, men without work or means to find it and a land and sea in the service of only the rich and powerful. Dolci's first responses were those of traditional charity. He tended to the poor and sick, borrowed and begged money, and established a small hospitality center in Trappeto.

One experience proved most shocking of all. Concentrated within it for Dolci was much of the suffering he had witnessed since his arrival. He saw a child die in her mother's arms as a result of malnutrition. Dolci's response was a life-or-death fast: Either the Italian government would fulfill its obligations to the people of this region or he would starve himself to death. "Rather than see another child die," Dolci declared, "I would prefer to die myself . . . if I cannot arouse people's love by living, I will arouse their remorse by dying."[7] "On the eighth day of his fast, having already suffered a stroke, Dolci, after consulting with the people, accepted the authority's belated offer to begin a local program of public works.

Whether Dolci's fast conformed to Gandhi's principles that a fast should be used for self-discipline and not used as a coercive weapon, is questionable. The results of the fast for Dolci's life, however, are not questionable. By risking his life, Dolci profoundly committed himself to the cause of the poor, and he convinced a few of the villagers of the sincerity of this commitment. In some small way, he had established a beachhead in the region.

As Dolci grappled with the problems of the poor of Western Sicily, he found himself at war with hosts of enemies. Counted among them were hunger, disease, illiteracy, unemployment, soil erosion, as well as multi-form varieties of Mafia violence, political corruption, and above all else, a culture that with the forces of centuries taught the inevitability of misery. He brought to his battles against them a whole range of nonviolent actions such as manifestos, demonstrations, sit-ins, strikes, and fasts. The most famous of all his early actions was a "reverse strike." In 1955, Dolci effected this reverse strike by leading a group of unemployed workers to repair a road without pay in direct opposition to police orders. He used the demonstration itself, as well as the court case which arose out of it, to publicize and test the citizen's right to work as guaranteed by the Italian Constitution.[8]

Dolci and his friends developed the strike in accord with the established principles of nonviolent action. First, they chose a significant problem, unemployment. Second, they developed their action in reference to the truth that men need work both to survive and to have dignity. Third, they structured their tactics as much as possible to avoid confusion over what was being done, acting only after clarifying discussion with the participants as well as the authorities. As is almost inevitable in any significant action, profound misunderstandings did arise: tools were mistaken for weapons and words for threats. Fortunately, no blood was shed. And the protesters succeeded in making it clear, the day of the strike and later in court, that work was needed and wanted. Yet, as they had expected, they were sentenced for trespassing, resisting arrest and other more minor charges. Similar to the effects of the Montgomery Bus Boycott on Martin Luther King and his allies, the reverse strike brought Dolci and his friends to a new level of consciousness. In 1955, thanks to the prize money he won from the Lenin Peace Award and additional funds furnished by Friends of Danilo Dolci groups which sprang up in England, Sweden and elsewhere in Western Europe, Dolci founded a center for long-range social change (*Centro di studi e iniziative*) at Partinico, a city of approximately 30,000 located a few miles inland from the village of Trappeto. In establishing the Center, Dolci was trying to embody what he had so far learned from action and what he conceived as ideal for the future. On the one hand, he was assenting to a new insight which his newly found friend and mentor, the influential Italian Quaker, Aldo Capitini, was clarifying for him: democracy and social justice can be realized through an open and nonviolent revolution.[9] On the other hand, Dolci was asserting that individual and small group nonviolent tactics in themselves were not sufficient to attain a thorough social transformation.[10]

The Center was intended by Dolci to be at the hub of his campaign in Western Sicily. Although it was never consistently staffed by more than a handful of amateurs, the purposes assigned to it were bold. It was to initiate long-range efforts to educate Sicilians to the methods of democratic action; to begin scientific studies to find more productive forms of livelihood; to undertake inquiries into the realities of Mafia power, under the special direction of Dolci's close friend from Milan, Franco Alasia; to promote various types of cooperatives; to make appeals to international experts in regional development to aid their cause. These efforts, in turn, convinced Dolci and his supporters that the problems and the possibilities of Western Sicily were in microcosm those of underdeveloped countries throughout the world.

Dolci's writings on Sicily and underdevelopment, written in collaboration with others, played an integral role in the Center's goals. The first major work, *The Outlaws of Partinico*, (1955), is a mosaic of interviews with the poor of Sicily as well as documents

pertaining to the reverse strike; its theme the plight of starving
and desperate people who encounter a state and police, which
are among their and the law's worst enemies.[11] In the second and
most famous work, *Report from Palermo*, (1956), the people are
allowed to speak for themselves through interviews; and again
what is shown, is the established disorder that rules all levels of
their lives.[12] In *Waste*, (1960)—a word which Dolci understands
as a form of violence—itemized are the human as well as natural
wastes that undermine the lives and potentials of Sicilians from
birth to death.[13] In *Chi Gioca Solo* (1967)—the title of which is
taken ironically from the first words of a Sicilian proverb which
runs "He who plays alone never loses!"—exposed are the roots
of a cynical fatalism which nurtures the Mafia by its distrust of
public authority and stops most Sicilians from even hoping for a
better society.[14] In a *New World in the Making*, (1964), Dolci reflects
on what he observed on his trips to such developing nations as
Russia, Yugoslavia, Senegal and Ghana. There he sets down the
basic principles of his nonviolent, democratic federalism, which,
as will be seen later, rests on three basic concepts: man as the
focal point of awareness and discovery; the group as a developing
and self-defining reality; and democratic planning of development at all levels of society.[15] In their entirety, these writings are
integral to the Center's attempt to discover what Sicily is and to
transform Sicily into what it might become.

Likewise inseparable from Dolci and the Center's work are a
series of efforts, during the last 15 years, to institute democratic
control of Western Sicily's water supply, to end illegal fishing in
the Gulf of Castellamare and to force a revision of building standards so that the inevitability of earthquakes does not mean—as it
did in 1968—the inevitability of immense destruction of life and
property. Their successes, according to one of the Center's newsletter (titled "A note on the Center," 1971), include: establishing
complete use of the water of the Jato and Carboj rivers; starting
and planning the use of the dam on the Bellice River for the
Roccamena area; introducing wine cooperatives at Menfi, Sciacca
and Partinico, and housing, building and irrigation cooperatives
elsewhere; sponsoring seminars in art and music, as well as starting a shop for the sale of local handicraft work. Additional note-
worthy successes that are claimed include: moral support and
scientific help to the earthquake victims of the Bellice Valley, and

the training of numerous local leaders in occupations and crafts.

There are two other significant accomplishments for which Dolci and the Center claim credit. First, Dolci and his friend Franco Alasia have conducted a 20-year campaign against the Mafia which has resulted generally in Sicilians being far more willing to openly denounce Mafia control of their lives. Specifically this campaign, begun in the middle 1960s, led to the downfall of a Christian Democratic minister and two undersecretaries who were in collusion with local mafiosi. Second, and perhaps most significant of all, has been an effort which covered 15 years and involved forcing the Italian state to build the Jato Dam.

Begun in the mid-1950s, the Jato campaign involved all of Dolci's enemies and all of his nonviolent tactics. It required investigating the agricultural, economic, and social implications of the dam; educating the people to the importance of such a dam and pressuring the state to begin and complete the dam despite serious Mafia and political resistance to it. Additionally, it meant mediating labor-management quarrels that developed during the building of the dam, as well as assuring democratic control of the waters that the dam would supply upon its completion. This success can be measured materially in terms of a substantial number of new tillable acres, the economic advantages of a longer growing season and the more varied crops. And, though less easy to measure, the dam meant for some—and this is the key to Dolci's philosophy of social change—tangible proof that the oldest peasant wisdom of fatalism did not always hold; people could work together for their mutual improvement.

What perspective should shape our judgment of Dolci's work in Sicily is debatable. A historian of Sicily need not be accused of cynicism if he were to suggest that Dolci's successes are infinitesimally minute when measured against the overall negative demographic, economic, social, and political trends which have continued adversely to affect Western Sicily during the past century and a half. Nor need one embrace the cynical aestheticism of Lampedusa, to suggest that Dolci has come nowhere near understanding the depth and diversity of Sicily, its people and history. Nor would it be justified to accuse a contemporary commentator on Sicily of heartless realism, if he were to suggest that Dolci's work is of little import when measured against the immense and abiding tasks that the national *Cassa per il Mezzo-*

giorno (The Fund for the South) has sought to carry out during the past two decades of its existence throughout the entire Italian South.[16] Numbered among the most significant yet evasive of these tasks—tasks at which the amply endowed *Cassa* has come nowhere near accomplishing—are: establishing large industry in various regions of the *Mezzogiorno* bringing into existence, by size and technology, truly workable and profitable farms, and developing a society, education, culture, and infrastructure which could lead the *Mezzogiorno* on the path of progressive and democratic growth.

More direct and personal criticisms of Dolci have been leveled by some of those once associated with him at the Center. They have criticized him for what they believe to be his frequent inconsistent, egotistic, and anti-democratic behavior;[17] his willingness to exploit his writings and people for funds;[18] and in the last decade, his growing, near singular and exclusive preoccupation with the academic design and the material building of a grade school.[19] Even some of Dolci's longest and firmest supporters sadly concede that the heroic period of research and action has definitely come to an end. And if a date for this be chosen, it would be 1970 when plans for the school—which Dolci insists on calling the Centro Educativo—were officially made public.[20]

Regardless of how much one shares these negative judgments, one conclusion nevertheless remains: Dolci has proven that one person can make a difference in the lives of many and that nonviolence is not without a role in awakening some of the minds and energies of a region. In his pursuit of social justice, he has created one measure of the promise of nonviolent action.

Thought and Hope

In his essays as well as his poetry, Dolci struggles with the tension that exists between the violent world that is and the peaceful world that could be. Violence today is of such a scale in the world, Dolci predicts, that mankind now chooses between a radically new and different future or no future at all. "We are," in his words, "living in a world of men condemned to death by all of us."[21]

For Dolci violence cannot be reduced to physical violence or the threat of it. Instead it must be understood in relation to that totality of ideas and forces that impede mankind, individually and collectively, from becoming what it can become. Violence is found, to choose a few different examples, in any distorted idea which lowers man's measure of himself, a disease that could be cured but is not cured, the waste of a river's water, an individual's failure to say yes to what he wants and no to what he does not want. Violence, in Dolci's view, cannot be defined simply, as Hannah Arendt suggests in her work *On Violence*, as actions committed without authority; nor can violence be defined solely, as many proponents of nonviolence would have it, as actions committed against the human spirit and person.[22] Instead, Dolci on the one hand understands violence in the Aristotelean and Thomistic sense, as all resistance against a thing reaching its full nature; and, on the other hand, Dolci, like Mazzini, conceives violence to be all those realities, actions, situations that impede peoples from realizing fully the potential good inherent within them.[23] In effect, for Dolci, violence is associated with all those forces, situations, ideas, and attitudes which, actively and passively, prevent people from reaching their fullest individual and social potential.

From this point of view, Dolci perceives despair as a form of violence. "If to despair is something more than to cry out, if it is to lose hope—to lose sight of the relationship between cause and effect, to lose the vision of the whole, or never know it, to lose all belief in chances for a better life—then we may say that the world is truly a desperate place." And from this point, Dolci proceeds to argue that "there will never be true peace . . . so long as the world knows hunger, poverty, ignorance, exploitation, unemployment and social systems which hinder man's fulfillment."[24] Morality itself, wrote Dolci, "must be equated with fulfillment both of the individual as well as the collectivity. The ultimate unity of mankind must be the basis for any system of ethics."[25] Everything that is antithetical to this unity is judged by Dolci to be immoral and a source of violence.

Upon this basis, Dolci's conception of nonviolent action is understandable. He relates the first and the final obligations of nonviolent action to building a new world. Nonviolent action cannot be conceptually reduced, as it so often is, to such passive notions as keeping purity of conscience or nonresistance to evil. Nor can it in practice be reduced to a set of tactics which, while seeking to minimize injury and hate, fight only particular social evils. For even though Dolci does not discount such traditional forms of nonviolent action as petitions, manifestos, and conscientious objection (which in his words is *"the primary instrument for mankind's salvation"*[26]), he nevertheless conceives nonviolence as inseparable from the revolutionary transformation of the present violent order.

Dolci's hope for a nonviolent revolution is profoundly utopian. It is tied to his belief in *"una pianificazione aperta, veramente rivoluzionaria"*—an open and truly revolutionary planning which will answer for all humanity those fundamental questions of "how we are, how we want to be, what we want to do, and how we want to do it."[27] The dimensions of this planning are universal. They "fulfill man's perennial needs to visualize humanity as unity and life as unified"; will take into account the varied economic, political and cultural conditions of peoples, and will ultimately result in a "planning with and not for humanity."[28] The planning will be regional in origin. It can only be initiated by the democratic and nonviolent interaction of specific peoples in terms of their shared problems and hopes. The planning will be international in consequence insofar as it rejects the primacy of nation-states in its conception and realization.

The consistent antistatism of Dolci's thought accounts for his rejection of both American and Soviet models of modernization. He judges American capitalism and Soviet centralism, to be inimical to people's nature and potential, and a threat to people's survival. As would be expected Dolci's ties are with the peoples of the Third World, and it is in relation to the problems of underdevelopment that his nonviolent and federalist conception of planning has its full meaning.

Dolci's commitment to progress through nonviolence in the Third World brings to mind Gandhi. Not only has Dolci undergone Gandhi's influence but he has come to embrace the most essential tenets and principles of Gandhi's thought.[29] For Dolci, as for Gandhi, the religious, in the broad sense of the word, dominates the political; all action must elevate rather than degrade the human person; truth and sacrifice, rather than force and coercion. These important similarities do not, nevertheless, mean the absence of basic differences between them: Whereas Gandhi did not develop his vision in reference to the possibilities of modern technology, Dolci does. While Gandhi assumed there was a permanent substratum to Indian culture and the Indian village,

Dolci essentially asserts that all peoples, even those of the most remote parts of the earth, must begin to prepare for a radically different future. In essence, Dolci perceives, as Gandhi did not, the irreversible and universal impulse toward modernization operative throughout the world. Consequently, Dolci who is far more our contemporary than Gandhi, explicitly joined his philosophy of nonviolence to the pressing task of society building.

Peace to Dolci means a new order. He insists repeatedly, as he did for instance at the Anti-Nuclear Arms Convention of 1962, that the problem of peace involves more than the relations of super powers.[30] Peace depends on the creation and the organization of new social forces, groups which until now have not had power. They alone finally can stop "the parasitical and violent action of the old structures."[31]

Dolci calls for the creation of new microcosms of democracy throughout the world. Inspired by the revolutionary theories of guerrilla warfare, he considers these microcosms as the cells of and the means to a new world order.[32] From the point of view of revolutionary tactics, Dolci believes them crucial for two reasons. They can direct attacks against the older structure at the precise points where success is most possible, and (here Dolci makes explicit reference to both Gandhi and Che Guevara) they can increase and multiply these attacks throughout the world in such a manner as to make it less possible for the older order to respond to them. Furthermore, these microcosms of democracy are essential to his revolutionary strategy, first because they teach democratic rights and processes; second, out of their struggle for self-definition will come plans and models for a new order. These democratic microcosms are, in Dolci's dream, both the vanguards and laboratories of a new world.[33]

Dolci charges the proponents of nonviolence with the most comprehensive and heroic obligations. At one point in his writings, he says that a strategy sufficient to effect a nonviolent transformation demands the following ten abilities:

1. achieving the development of consciousness and self-analysis on the part of concerned populations
2. promoting participation of the weak, alienated, and rejected
3. interrelating new, open and democratic groups which value everyone

4. developing in everyone the profound values which can sustain the nonviolent model

5. causing the population to undertake precise acts to denounce the existing violent structures

6. inventing continuously the most effective forms of nonviolent pressures

7. creating new groups

8. promoting organic and democratic planning for each zone and region

9. effecting the essential dialectics between consciousness and personal assumption of responsibility

10. contributing to the formation of necessary centers for world consolidation

These steps are for Dolci the essentials of a nonviolent revolution.[34]

At the heart of Dolci's nonviolent, democratic revolution is the call for a new mankind, a mankind which declares that "things can change" and that men can work together for a better future. What Dolci wants today for a beginning is a dialogue in word and act, in which the most personal feelings and the most universal aspirations, the most specific analyses and the most global problems, together form an integral part of one's self-discovery and self-definition. What Dolci wants is a new culture which will have at its center "a new moral intuition that identifies injustice with the violence which impedes, directly and indirectly, the development of persons, groups, and societies," and "justice with social change, nonviolent revolution . . . a new organic planning, . . . and 'the destruction, wherever necessary, of unacceptable contradictions."[35] For Dolci the beginning and end of this revolution require nothing other than, to use his daring phrase, "the invention of the future."[36]

Surely from one point of view, Dolci can be understood to be revoicing the radically utopian aspirations of such 19th Century romantic democrats and anarchists and socialists as Michelet, Proudhon, Mazzini, and Kropotkin. His belief that one can remake oneself seems to reiterate credos from that epoch in European history that lay between the French Revolution and the Industrial Revolution on one hand and the full emergence of the modern nation-state and mass society on the other. As was the case especially with the most idealistic and utopian of Europe's pre-1848 intellectuals, Dolci, too, believes that democracy and freedom need not be antithetical; that individualism and collectivism can be reconciled; that the people's material well-being and spiritual freedom do not form an insoluble conflict.

The thesis that Dolci is utopian can be supported on another plane of reflection. First, it can be argued that Dolci's thought is fundamentally ahistorical. That is, his social and political thought has not been developed in a truly critical dialogue with the past 200 years of Western historical experience. For instance, insofar as his thought is revealed by his writings, it is clear that he has not taken sufficient account of the reflections of that long, diverse, and distinguished list of liberals, socialists, radicals, anarchists, utopians, and union leaders, who in varying degrees also sought in thought and action, in solitude and community, to invent a new world. Nor, more generally, has Dolci amply tested his theories against the last two centuries of American and European experience which in themselves constitute a laboratory of unprecedented scale wherein people have experimented, violently and nonviolently, with finding solutions to such profound dilemmas as those which exist between individualism and collectivism, rich and poor, city and countryside, people and power. The ahistorical character of Dolci's thought is yet further testified to by the absence in his writings of any critical discussion of the meaning of revolution in the 20th century.

Instead of trying to deny the ahistorical character of Dolci's thought, by suggesting for example the "ultimate realism" of nonviolent practice or citing the concrete social analysis which underlay a portion of his work, it is more appropriate to affirm the proposition that, indeed, Dolci is a utopian. In truth, he is "a poetic modernizer." He belongs to that small group of persons—be they Christian or Marxist, liberal or conservative, socialist or democrat—who are driven by possibilities rather than compelled by necessities. In yet other words, Dolci takes his place with Gandhi, King, Chavez, and joins the ranks of those who believe that what is best in the human spirit should form what is most tangible in human existence. However Dolci is finally judged by his work and thought, he has given unique testimony to the belief that people can nonviolently reinvent themselves and their world.

Long Migrations and Less Than Gentle Conclusions

At the Palermo airport in 1974, at the end of my two week stay at the Center, I helped an old man board his sister on the plane. She looked terrible, and there was a good chance that she wouldn't survive the trip, he told me. It seemed that the stay in Sicily had seriously damaged her health. She went back, as many old Italian-Americans of the first generation do, like birds following the last light of their eyes: to see the place of their birth and childhood, to visit the graves of their parents, brothers and sisters, to be reunited in flesh to the family to which they are bound by blood but know only by letter. She had planned to stay several months, but her trip did not go well. Her gifts of fifteen and twenty dollars were mocked by her nieces and nephews who drove cars, and knew far more about the luxury of modernity than "this old peasant lady from America." She ran out of money, maybe even heart; her health failed, the relatives did not know what to do with her. Her brother had come to try to bring her home.

On the trip home, her deep and precarious breathing, sounding so much like my grandmother's during her death agony, constantly reminded me that there were two of us on this plane who had not found the Sicily we sought. There was so much that had disappointed me at the Centro. Dolci didn't want me to do a study of him and his work. He had so entangled himself in jargon-laden pedagogic theory of progressive education and the process of building a school (*un centro educativo!*, called "Myrtle") that the Center and Dolci were unquestionably detached in action and theory from the fundamental matter of the material transformation of Sicily. (The school, finally built after several years of delay caused by building strikes, absence of funds, and clear headed planning, was closed in 1976 because of teacher-administration quarrels, staffing problems, financial shortages, and a failure to secure adequate support for the state. It is presently scheduled to open in the fall of 1978.[37])

Particularly depressing to me, especially in light of intense involvement in the teacher union movement at home, was the discovery that Dolci had divorced himself altogether from the labor movement—and as far as I could discern, even from the co-op movement and the whole range of left wing politics associated with it. The Center was becoming a cultural center, focusing on the arts, with special attention given to the teaching of the recorder and recorder concerts by Dolci's talented son, Amico.[38] The recorder, *il flauto dolce*, seemed to rule all. Altogether unconvincing was Dolci's argument that as the people of Western Sicily once needed dams, they now needed culture.

It was particularly painful to discover that since my 1972 trip, certain older collaborators were gone. Franco, who so boldly pursued the Mafia was gone; so too was Orazio whose intimate work with the fishermen of Trappeto had so touched me. At the center now, there was no one either dedicated to and qualified for the study of Sicilian society. Aside from Dolci and his family, and a couple of long-time supporters, there was no one there who was committed to staying in Sicily and working for its social transformation. In residence there was, not to mention everyone, an American university couple who had donated a year to serve as the Center's hosts; one flute teacher from England and the English Friends who dedicated a part of every year for several years to teaching there; a retired and much esteemed Italo-American educator who sought to offer his help in the design of the school; a young Swiss engineer and his wife who were helping on a short-term basis with the building of the school; the head of American Friends who was at work on a money raising film; some Swedish students preparing to raise a substantial sum of money for Dolci; and individuals passing through for a day or two for a variety of purposes.

One person who has supported Dolci and worked with him a number of years says: "Dolci is lost in his own desires and dreams. He uses almost everybody and everything. Dolci, at best, is an egotist who luckily from time to time is in the service of the good. He may be too obsessed by himself to care about anything beyond himself."

Near the end of my notebook there are more comforting pages. Don't all strong individuals have their detractors? They become so much to so many, they must cause great dissatisfaction and disappointments, and therefore be subject to criticisms of all sorts. A fisherman tells how they still consider Dolci to be God's gift to them: He came, we didn't understand him, but he cared for us and helped us. Dolci has carried a heavy load, and maybe he has consciously chosen to draw a tighter circle, comfort himself in the arts and music he loves, nurture the youngest children in his family of ten. And just perhaps he should be measured far more by the ideals he evokes, than how well he meets their measure.

Notes

1. Joseph Amato, "Danilo Dolci, A Poetic Mordernizer," *World View*, December, 1973, pp. 28—34; "Danilo Dolci," *Street*, pp. 10—11, Summer/Fall, 1973, pp. 14—17, 42, reprinted in *The Minnesota Teacher*, Spring, 1974, pp. 7—11.

2. For a general introduction to Sicily, there are M. I. Finley and Mack Smith's three volume *History of Sicily*, New York, 1968; Renée Rochefort's excellent social geography *Le travail en Sicilie*, Paris, 1961; Charlotte Chapman's *Milocca: A Sicilian Village*, Cambridge, Mass., 1971; and S. Scrofani's *La questione agraria della Sicilia*, Caltanisetta, 1961; and Gavin Maxwell's *Ten Pains of Death*, London, 1959.

3. Aldo Capitini, *Danilo Dolci*, Manduria, 1958, p. 32.

4. Jerre Mangione, *A Passion For Sicilians. The World Around Danilo Dolci*, New York, 1968, (reprinted in 1972 with the title and subtitle reversed), p. 137.

5. Of general interest for Giuliano are E. Hobsbawn's *The Primitive Rebels. Studies in Archaic Forms of Social Movements in the 19th and 20th Centuries*, New York, 1965; and Gavin Maxwell's *Bandit*, New York, 1956.

6. For introduction to Mafia in Sicily, see Michele Pantaleone's *The Mafia and Politics*, London, 1966; and Anton Blok's *The Mafia of a Sicilian Village. A Study of Violent Peasant Entrepreneurs*, New York, 1974.

7. Mangione, op. cit., p. 6.

8. For descriptions of the strike see Danilo Dolci's *Outlaws of Partinico*, New York, 1961, pp. 215—296.

9. Mangione, op. cit., p. 144, and of special importance Aldo Capitini's *Rivoluzione aperta; che cosa ha fatto Danilo Dolci?*, Firenze, 1956. Of use also on Dolci's philosophy and its sources is Mario Delle Piane's "Aldo Capitini, Lettere per Nomadelfia," *Il Ponte*, XXIX, p. 9, Settembre, 1973, pp. 1228—1234.

10. The uniqueness of putting nonviolence in the service of the democratic modernization is established by measuring it against past

uses of nonviolent actions, as set forth in Gandhi's *Autobiography*, London, 1966; Bart de Ligt's *The Conquest of Violence*, London, 1937; Mulford Sibley's *The Quiet Battle*, Boston, 1963; Richard Gregg's *The Power of Nonviolence*, New York, 1959; H. Horsburgh's *Non-Violence and Aggression. A Study of Gandhi's Equivalent of War*, New York, 1968; and Gene Sharp's, *The Politics of Nonviolent Action*, Boston, 1973.

11. Danilo Dolci, *Banditi à Partinico*, Bari, 1955.

12. Danilo Dolci, *Inquiesta à Palermo*, Torino, 1956, available in English, *Report from Palermo*, New York, 1970.

13. Danilo Dolci, *Lo spreco*, Torino, 1960, available in English, *Waste: An Eye-Witness Report on Some Aspects of Waste in Western Sicily*, New York, 1964.

14. Danilo Dolci, *Chi gioca solo*, Torino, 1967, available in English, *The Man Who Plays Alone*, New York, 1970.

15. Danilo Dolci, *Verso un mondo nuovo*, Torino, 1964, available in English, *A New World in the Making*, New York, 1965.

16. The question of the Italian South has been a fundamental issue since the Risorgimento. It has elicited the attention of such masters of Italian thought as Salvamini, and Gramsci; been the subjects of such classic works as G. Fortunato's *Il Mezzogiorno*, 2 vols., Florence, new ed. 1926; L. Franchetti and S. Sonnino's *La Sicilia*, 2 vols., Firenze, 1877; and R. Romeo's *Risorgimento e capitalismo*, Bari, 1959. Useful starting for the study of the South are: Russell King's short guide, *The Questione Meridionale in Southern Italy*, Durham, 1971; Denis Mack Smith's *Italy*, rev. ed., Ann Arbor, 1969; Shepard Clough's *The Economic History of Italy*, New York, 1964; Vera Lutz's *Italy. A Study in Economic Development*, New York, 1962; and Gustav Schacter's *The Italian South: Economic Development in Mediterranean Europe*, New York, 1965; and Shepard Clough and Carlo Livi's "Economic Growth in Italy: An Analysis of the Uneven Economic Development of North and South," *Journal of Economic History* XVI, No. 3, September, 1956, pp. 334—349.

17. Criticisms of this sort surface in writing at several points in Mangione's work.

18. Criticisms of Dolci for his manipulation of opinions and impressions are written in Fernandez Dominque's, *The Mother Sea*, trans. Michael Callum, London 1967, pp. 171—173; Luigi Barzini's, *From Caesar to the Mafia. Sketches of Italian Life*, New York, 1971, pp. 78—80; and my review of his *Chissà se i pesci piangono? Minnesota Teacher*, Spring, 1975, pp. 11—13. What I found most disturbing about *Chissà: Documentazione di un esperienza educativa*, Toreno, 1973,

was that the dialogues between children and adults and children, which were Socratically to lay the theoretical basis for the *"Centro educativo,"* did not involve the poor children of the area but were restricted instead to Dolci's children, the children of other Center personnel and a doctor and dentist.

19. The grade school has been of engrossing importance to Dolci and the Center for the past five years. This *"Centro educativo"* is modeled upon "innovative" American and European pedagogy. Three of its essential features are: It gives primary attention to student experimentation and expression. It seeks full community involvement in the formation and direction of the *Centro*. And though it pursues the children's full personal and intellectual development, it is intentionally structured to the double end of making the children appreciatively aware of their Sicilian background, while preparing them realistically for the probability of their eventual migration from their native region.

20. Ironically, Dolci's heroic period was ending just as American supporters were, so to speak, starting to appreciate its beginnings. The further irony is: Dolci was entering the field of educational psychology, a field in which, for better or worse, Americans are pioneers and masters.

21. Dolci, *The Outlaws*, p. 251.

22. Hannah Arendt, *On Violence*, New York, 1970.

23. For short Thomistic definition of violence, see the subject "Violence," *New Catholic Encyclopedia* Vol. 14, New York, 1967, p. 690. For Mazzini's linking of man's historical realization of himself as a high ethical good and resistance to this progress as violence see his famous 1860 *Dei doveri dell' uomo* or his essay "From the Council of God," *The Duties of Man and Other Essays*, New York, 1966, esp. pp. 302—317.

24. Dolci, *A New World*, p. 7.

25. *Ibid.*, p. 30.

26. *Ibid.*, p. 65.

27. *Ibid.*, p. 303.

28. *Ibid.*, pp. 7, 12.

29. Dolci's close associate, sociologist Johan Galtung has written an article "Gandhi, Dolci e Nai, *Il Ponte*, XIII, No. 1, Febbraio, 1957, pp. 359—367.

30. Danilo Dolci, Speech in 1962 to the Anti-Nuclear Arms Convention in New Delhi, *"Instead of Violence*, Arthur and Lila Weinberg, (eds.), Boston, 1963, pp. 22—25.

31. Danilo Dolci, *"Per una rivoluzione nonviolenta,"* *Non sentite l'odore del fumo*, Bari, 1971, pp. 61—96.

32. *Ibid.*, pp. 61—63.

33. *Ibid.*

34. *Ibid.*, pp. 88—90.

35. *Ibid.*, p. 96.

36. *Ibid.*, p. 90.

37. This sad state of affairs is set forth from Dolci's point of view in not altogether satisfying terms in a fifteen page newsletter, "Appunti per gli amici," *Notiziaro del centro*, Aprile-Ottobre, 1977. An earlier statement was circulated in a four page mimeograph circular, dated Partinico, 24/6/'77.

38. For a work that offers an overview of Dolci's work and theory, based on the importance of a cultural revolution, see Giuseppei Casarrubea's *Una alternativa culturale dalla Sicilia Occidentale*, Trapani, 1974. There specific support is given to the proposition, "Nessuna rivoluzione e possibile nel Mezzogrorno e di consequenza in Italia, *senza una grande rivoluzione culturale*, pp. 11—66.

Chapter 9

Nonviolence in Africa*

Charles C. Walker

Traditions of nonviolent action, ancient and modern, are part of African history. They pre-date Africa's recent political awakening, and the story awaits the systematic chronicler and researcher. Accounts similar to the following could undoubtedly be found in many lands and cultures.

The Angoni tribe in Nyasaland, descendants of the Zulu conquerors, relied on an amalgam of ancient traditions and more recent Christian teaching in resisting Great Britain's imposition of the Central African Federation (circa 1952—53). At that time, Chief Phillip Gomani, along with 82 other chiefs, had organized a giant rally on the theme of nonviolent resistance. The authorities banned the rally and dispersed the crowd, later banishing Gomani and ordering him to leave his district within 24 hours.

People gathered from surrounding districts, at the chief's home, awaiting the police. Their tradition held that "their chief must at all costs not be taken captive; even if the people are killed, if the chief can be kept free, the tribe remains unconquered."[1] They had no warriors, and were urged to refrain from violence no matter how provocative the police became. It did not seem amiss that they sang an old Zulu warrior song "Inkosi Dinga Shawa" along with hymns and Bible readings from Isaiah.

When the police came, the crowd surged around to protect the

*The main text of this article was a preparatory paper for a workshop at the International Conference of Peace Researchers and Peace Activists, the Netherlands, July, 1975.

chief. When the police finally seized him, in the midst of a tear-gas attack (the people didn't know what it was, they thought it poison), the chief was suddenly and nonviolently "liberated" from the retreating police car. A group of youths physically stopped it, and spirited the chief away.

It was in South Africa, in the early years of this century, that Gandhi began his experiments with "satyagraha," a form of non-violent resistance. This experience was invoked in the 1952 Defiance Campaign and subsequent actions of that period. A more recent example was the enormously impressive and disciplined—and for a time effective—contract labor strike in Namibia (1971-72) involving 13,000 men directly, and many more indirectly.[2] This in turn influenced later strike action in the republic in 1973-74, refuting the prevailing view that such action was outdated and impotent.

Even in the midst of protracted armed struggles, there can be nonviolent phases and campaigns. In the Algerian uprising against the French, there was effectively disciplined nonviolent restraint in face of brutal provocation, by which the French were trying to incite violence "justifying" harsh crackdowns.[3] During the independence movement in Mozambique, farmers organized open boycotts for which they endured privations and reprisals.[4]

Transnational Actions

Two transnational actions, predominantly by Africans with non-African collaboration, had more than marginal effects. The first was the 1959 Sahara Project, a protest against French nuclear testing. The campaign, based in Accra, was supported by several countries in the area, and by nonviolent actionists in Europe and the United States. This effort, supported by rallies in other parts of Africa, was part of the developing international opposition to nuclear tests.[5]

The second was a broader coalition, based in Dar es Salaam, to support the movement for Zambian independence. It was composed of representatives and activists from political movements, governments and peoples organizations from Africa, to a limited degree elsewhere. It is this story that follows. It is recounted in such detail for these reasons: (1) the political implications of nonviolence are characteristically debated amid endless abstractions and imprecise images, but here the context is subject to examination; (2) the records of the World Peace Brigade (WPB) became available and stimulated the memories of participants[6]; and (3) so few political campaigns based on a strategic commitment to nonviolence have been published that more details rather than fewer promise to be useful to the inquirer.

As a result of these events, a beachhead for nonviolence was established in that region for a time. Without continuous initiatives and further political development, the conventional forces of politics gained ascendancy. At one point, Kenneth Kaunda and some World Peace Brigade leaders talked at length about the extent to which nonviolence could serve as an adequate and explicit basis for national policy. Despite his personal interest and background, Kaunda was not convinced.[7]

After independence, Kaunda asked the American Friends Service Committee (AFSC) to set up a national training center for nonviolence. The proposal envisaged work in border areas and tribal conflicts, with political activists, custodial personnel, educators and youth organizers. Initial steps to implement it were swamped in the sudden rush of events precipitated by Rhodesia's Unilateral Declaration of Independence.[8]

Bill Sutherland, the key WPB organizer, served for a time in the Tanzanian government. Since 1975 he has served as the AFSC's Representative in Southern Africa.

Attrition

National leaders such as Nyerere and Kaunda kept postponing hard decisions about the future of their military. (The parallel with Nehru in post-Gandhi India is compelling.) Each inherited a tiny military force, which they kept in the background as much as possible. In response, the Tanganyikan military rebelled. After some indecision, Nyerere announced he was upgrading the armed forces. Kaunda, apparently to forestall a similar problem in Zambia, followed suit. So a political watershed was crossed. The remorseless logic of military requirements could no longer be ignored or denied.

As the tempo of liberation struggles increased in southern Africa, concerted action by contiguous states created a new set of pressures. Several liberation movements formerly based in Dar es Salaam moved their offices to Lusaka after Zambian independence. Later the group called "frontline states" emerged: Tanzania, Zambia, Mozambique, Botswana and Angola. Botswana became a haven for exiles and refugees. It had no army at all but, like Zambia, its deeper involvement in guerrilla movements created pressure for a military establishment.

Primary attention could no longer be given to development projects and plans. The peremptory demands of onrushing events had to be met, for example, the crisis in Rhodesia (Zimbabwe). As one instance, an inordinate amount of time was spent trying to overcome the fragmentation of leadership, to cope with Ian Smith and his allies.[9]

By 1976 Kaunda, the most nearly a personal pacifist by inclination, abandoned his "moderate" role and became a vigorous advocate for arming the guerrilla movements.

Soweto

The rising in Soweto (a township adjoining Johannesburg) in 1976 may have marked another watershed. A new determination to act, come what may, became evident in particular among the black youth. In the first phase, violence was clearly improvised and peripheral. Stones hastily gathered were no match for guns and sophisticated equipment. Despite the African dead, (for months the only white person killed was a police officer in a motor accident during a disturbance), some of the signs carried by the protesters explicitly disavowed violence.

Leaders were picked off by the government as quickly as they appeared. The stage was thus set for clandestine forms of organizing. Books by Fanon were being circulated and read. Despite these currents of thought and action, and the meager results compared to so many sacrifices, restraint was a hallmark of Soweto rather than outbursts of frenzy or impotent rage.

Some universities are closed (as of this writing). Leaders such as Steve Biko still held open the possibility of militant action short of armed struggle. His death in custody is an ominous portent, but it remains to be seen how the Black Consciousness movement and other forces respond, after the initial outrage. A leading exile told me in mid-1977 that even now there is "scope" for nonviolent action, but where are the leaders?

A white South African minister, whose involvement dated back to the Defiance Campaign, put it succintly. He said the scattered forces of nonviolence have encountered enormous obstacles, some of their own making out of too little courage and imagination, most of them inherent in the situation itself. Campaigns had been sporadic; the famous Defiance Campaign lasted a little more than six months; organization posed massive problems, often became attempts to "build bricks without straw."[10] No one can gainsay nor should anyone minimize the costly efforts, the bravery and sacrifices and suffering. Nevertheless, he said, "we did not envisage a protracted struggle in the mode of Gandhi or even of conventional liberation movements; so today we and others must pay the price of our weakness, but nevertheless work in the hope that history will open another door."

Perhaps there is a counterpart of a traditional socialist issue: can there be nonviolence in one country for long? The key problems are multi-dimensional: personal, local, sectional, national, regional, transnational. The World Peace Brigade experiment revealed that truth again, and offered an intimation that militant nonviolent action, pursued assiduously and imaginately, can be a force for national liberation and reconstruction.

The World Peace Brigade in Eastern Africa

The World Peace Brigade was founded in Beirut, Lebanon, on the first of January, 1962, following an international conference called to prepare for its formation. The founding statement said that it intended to

> organize, train and keep available a Brigade for nonviolent action in situations of potential or actual conflict, internal and international . . . (and) against all war and preparations for war, and the continuing development of weapons of mass destruction . . .

> revolutionize the concept of revolution itself by infusing into the methods of resisting injustice the qualities which insure the preservation of human life and dignity . . .

> join with people in their nonviolent struggle for self-determination and social reconstruction . . .[11]

The organization was a natural outgrowth of internationalizing the forces of nonviolence. Multinational projects had been carried out, among them the Sahara Protest in 1959 against French nuclear tests in Africa, and the San Francisco-to-Moscow March beginning in 1960 opposing all nuclear testing. Gandhians in India were sometimes critical of Western movements for concentrating on resistance and protest, and for not developing a more comprehensive and integrated "constructive program."

The plan to form such an organization had been adopted at the triennial conference of the War Resisters International held in India in 1961. The four major components would be the Gandhian movement, segments of the peace movement particularly in Europe and USA, groups engaged in nonviolent struggles for social justice in local or regional campaigns, and movements for national independence and reconstruction.

Sponsors of the conference included notables from six continents, such as Martin Buber of Israel, Bertrand Russell of England, Martin Niemoller of West Germany, Leo Infeld of Poland, Vinoba Bhave of India, and Martin Luther King of the USA. Two were to become heads of state: Julius Nyerere, Prime Minister of Tanganyika and now President of Tanzania; and Kenneth Kaunda, leader of the United Independence Party of Northern Rhodesia (UNIP), and now president of Zambia.[12]

As early as 1906, Gandhi in South Africa had broached the idea of a "nonviolent army." In 1922 he first organized a corps of "volunteers for peace." He had invited some of his most trusted colleagues to a meeting to form a Shanti Sena (Peace Brigade) to deal with problems in an independent India. He was assassinated before it could be held. Vinoba Bhave revived the idea in 1957 in the context of the land-gift mission (Bhoodan).[13] The idea had been suggested elsewhere, for example by Maude Royden in the 1930s, but was never carried out successfully. More recently it was formally suggested to the United Nations, and followed up informally, so far to no avail.** Two themes characterized the intent of the organizers: (1) protest, resistance, nonviolent revo-

---

**Letter from the Shanti Sena to U Thant, 1971. Letter from the International Peace Academy to UN Missions, 1971. See *Nonviolence—International*, a documentation service edited by Charles C. Walker, No. 1, Haverford College, USA. Available from the Gandhi Institute, Box 92, Cheyney, PA 19319 USA. See also "A World Peace Guard," by Charles C. Walker, paper for the International Seminar on Training for Nonviolent Action, Mexico, 1977.

lution; and (2) a constructive program, the nonviolent transformation of society in the interests of freedom, justice and peace. At times the WPB might be partisan and join one side of a struggle, at other times it might serve as mediator or in some third-party capacity. What was needed, said Abbé Pierre of France, was not automatic partisans of governments or ideologies, but nonviolent defenders of the human race.

Elected co-chairmen were Michael Scott, A. J. Muste, and Jayaprakash Narayan. Scott is a legendary figure in Africa, known in particular for his dedicated work in the United Nations for African causes. Muste was a U.S. radical pacifist known internationally for his political and intellectual leadership in a variety of movements. Narayan is a Gandhian whose prestige among the Indian masses sometimes rivaled that of Nehru.[14]

One region where the WPB hoped to work was Africa south of the Sahara. Immediately after the conference, Siddharaj Dhadda, an Indian delegate and later secretary of the Asian Council, traveled in eastern Africa to describe the WPB and offer its services, perhaps to establish a training and action center in Dar es Salaam as a base for work in Africa.

Addis Ababa Meeting of Independence Groups

The organizational pace of WPB work in Africa might have been slower, involving numerous negotiations, but for a timely development. Meeting in Addis Ababa on February 2-10 were about 30 groups in the Pan-African Freedom Movements of East and Central Africa (PAFMECA, later Southern was added and the acronym became PAFMECSA). This was its fourth annual conference.

When Bill Sutherland arrived at that meeting, and Bayard Rustin a little later, they were greeted cordially by many who knew them from past associations and projects. Both had played major roles at the WPB conference. Sutherland had been secretary to the finance minister of Ghana when he served as government liaison to the Sahara Project. Rustin, a major U.S. civil rights leader, had also participated in that project, and had worked on several assignments in western Africa at the request of Nnamdi Azikewe, Prime Minister of Nigeria and the Cameroons, and Kwame Nkrumah, President of Ghana. Despite the suspicions of some, a WPB team of observers was agreed to: Sutherland, Rustin, Dhadda and Michael Scott.[14a]

The conferees at Addis Ababa were aroused by a formidable set of problems, among them postponement of independence, an increase in terrorism, and economic consolidation of European interests. Nonviolence was vigorously debated. Defeats and setbacks in South Africa were recounted, victories by violence described and promised. On the other hand, spokesmen such as Kenneth Kaunda presented a strong case for militant nonviolent action at that stage in political development and in the light of forces operating in the region. A resolution specifically commending nonviolence was narrowly defeated. Kenneth Kaunda was nevertheless elected chairman of PAFMECA, and support was pledged to his campaign for independence.

Crisis in Northern Rhodesia

Northern Rhodesia was one of three countries which the British had incorporated into the Central African Federation; the others were Southern Rhodesia and Nyasaland. UNIP had been agitating for independence with considerable effect, and Federation Prime Minister Sir Roy Welensky felt survival of this political unit was threatened. In 1961 the British Colonial Office had announced plans for a new constitution, one failing because of white opposition, the other because of bitter African resistance. Welensky said in February, 1962 that he was determined to maintain the status quo and implied he would do so by whatever means necessary.

The Federation appeared to many Africans as a way to slow down the coming of independence, and to maintain white settler control. Also at stake was the continued exploitation of the vast mineral wealth in areas stretching across the middle of the continent. Wielding major influence in the Federation were European and American interests which were part of the interlocking directorate of operating companies in the region.[15] Welensky had publicly supported the Katanga secession, and was friendly to the South African regime—a touchstone issue among independence groups.

Kaunda and UNIP proposed that if the Welensky forces remained adamant, and major disruptions appeared to block the scheduled election in Northern Rhodesia, then a general strike would be called. Coordinately, an international Freedom March would be mobilized, to cross from Tanganyika into Northern Rhodesia. Numbering in the thousands, it would be composed primarily of Africans but would be joined by supporters from many countries outside that continent. The March had been broached by WPB personnel, and the WPB was expected to organize the international contingent.[16]

Britain was feeling the pressure, and Colonial Secretary Reginald Maudling tried to find a formula. British officials reproved Nyerere for opposing the Federation, American officials warned Rustin about meddling as an outsider.

Welensky disdained the language of diplomacy and said, "The vicious influence of African nationalism has turned their bone marrow to jelly" and he declared flatly, "The Federation is mine" and that he would "go whole hog" implying armed force.[17]

Kaunda ordered food stocks prepared for the general strike. Beginning plans for the Freedom March were known to Federation authorities. Welensky stationed troops along the border between Northern Rhodesia and Tanganyika and numerous harassments were reported. (A few years later a former policeman in Northern Rhodesia who became a *Standard* reporter in Dar es Salaam told Bill Sutherland of the considerable preparations to deal with the marchers and the government's concern that the combination of the march and the general strike would be difficult to cope with. The plan: let the marchers cross the border into a desolate area and then seal them off.[18])

Some black African leaders echoed the speeches at Addis Ababa and pressed for violent solutions. Offers came to them for training in guerrilla tactics. On the other hand, if the independence struggle could succeed by nonviolent action, and establish a progressive society not based on racism, this could have a profound effect not only on other independence movements but on the whole of southern Africa.

Africa Freedom Action

To pursue nonviolent initiatives, and support the strike and march, a working committee was established called Africa Freedom Action. It was comprised of three representatives from each of four groups: UNIP, TANU (Tanganyika African National Union, leading party in that country), PAFMECA and the World Peace Brigade. It was pledged to nonviolent action and took action by consensus.

The rationale for the march was formulated in more precise terms:

1. It would be a significant act of international solidarity with those determined to achieve their independence

2. It might serve in some measure as a deterrent to the violence that was foreshadowed in incidents along the Northern Rhodesia-Tanganyika border, violence that might well intensify in face of thousands "invading" from the north

3. Marchers could help preserve a nonviolent discipline in Northern Rhodesian political rallies; not a few of these had ended up in violent incidents, and UNIP charged that provocateurs were responsible.

4. Marchers could help rebuild villages and areas destroyed in violent incidents.

Beyond this were other possibilities for action in the region, to be mentioned later in this report. One was a proposal by Michael Scott about Southwest Africa (Namibia).

Kaunda representing UNIP, and Rashid Kawawa, Vice-President of TANU after consulting with Nyerere, issued a statement which included the following:

> In the light of the grave struggle for freedom in Africa, we welcome and encourage the generous support offered by the World Peace Brigade in response to our appeal for cooperation from men of goodwill throughout the world.
>
> We are particularly heartened that a group whose members have engaged in positive action in so many countries should add their experience to our own long efforts to achieve freedom in Africa through nonviolent resistance and a direct economic struggle . . . In particular we are convinced that such action applied now in Northern Rhodesia may yet prove to be the key to the liberation of Central and Southern Africa.
>
> The active support and cooperation of freedom loving peoples everywhere is urgently needed if Africa is to move as quickly as she should toward true freedom; on the other hand, our

struggle for African freedom is not for Africa nor for ourselves alone. It is part of humanity's struggle for a just and peaceful world.[19]

WPB alliance with Africa Freedom Action was criticized from two sides. On the one hand, some militant Africans felt that an alliance with the WPB would impose restraints upon their freedom of action, and saw nonviolence only as a matter of immediate tactics. On the other hand, some pacifists criticized the coalition because they feared the fate of a nonviolent project was put into the hands of those whose commitment to nonviolence might weaken or change quickly.

The project moved ahead because of the following:

1. The Freedom March was a potent idea that required WPB help at the international level.

2. WPB leaders on the spot took the view that mass movements are working alliances of many forces.

3. It was clear that a nonviolent *strategy* would prevail for a time even as the crisis intensified.[20]

These judgments were quickly vindicated. Seldom in the life of Africa Freedom Action were the debates and discussions about nonviolence as the strategic option; rather they were about implementation, or on other questions of politics or organization.[21]

Brigade Mobilizes

WPB set as its initial goal getting teams of three people from ten countries each, to provide the core of the organizing effort. One of the three, it was hoped, would be a well-known personality. The AFA had urged this because the march was seen as a confrontation that guaranteed worldwide news coverage by the participation of an international contingent. Rustin drew up extensive and detailed plans for a dramatic event that could not be brushed aside by the press or the authorities.

A few volunteers were sent immediately, among them Quaker Philip Seed, a social worker and John Papworth, who had completed an extensive tour of Africa 18 months earlier—both were

from England. Another was Niels Mathiesen, WRI secretary in
Oslo for several years. Rustin, Scott and Sutherland pledged to
go. Jayaprakash Narayan and his wife Prabhavati would lead a
substantial Indian delegation. Responses also came from West
Germany, Italy, France, and Canada.

Bringing in these volunteers immediately was a way to show
seriousness about the action, generate intermediate publicity, and
to demonstrate the capacity of WPB to mobilize volunteers.

The march route was checked out, in Tanganyika by TANU
and in Northern Rhodesia by Anton (Ax) Nelson, who reported
that the 500-mile route was feasible despite the problems posed
by some desolate areas in the north.

In addition to the international aspect, the WPB was asked to
draw up plans for training "second echelon leaders" in the philosophy, strategy and tactics of nonviolent action. Such trained
cadres would be assigned a major role in the march, to cope with
the many problems that could arise in such a venture involving
many thousands from different countries, crossing a border without official permission.

The fast pace of these new developments posed a dilemma. It
put the WPB in business at once, in the midst of a struggle with
far-reaching implications. Serious theoretical questions about
power and nation-state politics had to be dealt with, organizational decisions made with little advance consultation at a time
when precedents were being set and morale tested. Improvisation
in the field is always necessary but groups differ on how much,
and tend to react strongly when they disapprove a decision. The
dilemma was posed: what was perceived as relevance vs. adequate
participation in decision-making at the start of the organization's
development. The peremptory needs of the Africa project also
gave impetus to organizing efforts in the other regions—Europe,
North America, Asia—despite the rumblings of disagreement on
politics, organization and to some extent philosophy. A difficult
problem to cope with was leadership style, which varies so much
between movements and cultures.[22]

PAFMECA Responds

While the WPB concentrated on non-African participation, Africa Freedom Action decided that the overwhelming majority of

marchers would be Africans, and most of these from the immediate region. (The WPB had adopted such a policy at its founding.)

To the constituent freedom groups in PAFMECA, from the Congo to Zanzibar, Secretary General Mbiyu Koinange sent a letter which included this remarkable statement:

> . . . Although this support from overseas is very encouraging, it is up to us, particularly those in PAFMECA, to be the first to respond to the call from our brothers in Zambia. We therefore call upon all our members to select three representatives, including one outstanding personality, to stand by ready for positive action which may involve civil disobedience such as crossing frontiers without official permission.
>
> Each representative must be so dedicated to the freedom and unity of Africa that he accepts without question the following risks: being shot at and wounded or killed, being beaten, being arrested, being brought to trial and imprisoned for a long time, or being held in jail for a long period without trial.

Thus the African militants in this organized expression of their work, far from diminishing the nonviolent character of the march, underlined it in unmistakable terms. The many thousands who attended rallies in Kenya and Tanganyika indicated the potential that could be mobilized.

The "Election"

The combination and accumulation of pressures made it apparent a new situation was in the making. Kaunda had testified before the UN Committee on Colonialism in New York. The various British proposals for a new constitution foundered. Publicity and knowledge of plans for the strike and march had some effect, according to reports reaching AFA from the region and elsewhere.

In a sudden move, Sir Roy Welensky handed in his resignation to the Governor-General on March 8. Under the British parliamentary system, this dissolved the Federal Assembly and set the stage for new elections on April 27. But it was to be held on the same old basis of discrimination against African voters. With a population of about 2.5 million Africans, Northern Rhodesia had about 5200 Africans on the Federal voters' roll. So complete was the election boycott urged by the African nationalists that fewer than 100 of the 5200 voted. Sir Edgar Whitehead, Prime Minister of Southern Rhodesia, said in a public speech the day before the election that it was "a bit of a farce" because the opposition refused to put up candidates. As expected, Welensky and the United Federal Party held 54 seats in the Federal Assembly of 59 members.

British authorities concluded that the situation could not be resolved in defiance of UNIP. New constitutional provisions were drawn up that "won the grudging participation of all political parties," as one observer put it.[23] UNIP was divided at first on whether to participate. This uncertainty had its immediate effect on plans for the march, and its planners were asked to await further developments.

A crisis faced WBP at this point. Mobilizing for such a venture, with the forces this released in various countries and in several organizations, was a formidable task. Expectations were raised, money collected, organizational staff adjusted to help out. Michael Scott wrote:

> We cannot switch peoples' enthusiasm and activities on and off. And to bring people from Europe and America on a venture that may cost them their liberty and perhaps their lives demands a lot of effort and organization at both ends, and the people who come may have to give up their jobs in some cases and make provision for their work and families, and have budgeted for a possible spell in jail or of being physically out of action . . . (all) for an as yet unspecified date.[24]

He suggested it might be necessary to arrange for supporting action after the strike has begun, or organize a symbolic action at the border and then call for volunteers if and when the strike began.

It would not have been surprising if some in UNIP regarded both the strike and march as threats, to be advertised or muted as the situation seemed to require. Kenneth Kaunda nevertheless wrote to Michael Scott:

> I must say at once that I admire your courage and determination to stand up to so many things. I do know that your waiting patiently for us to move in Northern Rhodesia takes a lot of courage and energy. I do hope, however, that you will not have

long to wait now before we decide one way or the other.[25]

The outcome of UNIP's decision would be a critical turning point
in the struggle, there were legitimate issues to debate, and dealing
with the British Colonial Office and the Federation was not a
simple matter.

On the other hand, WPB had no desire to impose its own organizational problems or needs on others. It was entirely in accord with the idea of self-determination, and had offered its
services to those with the prime stake in the outcome. An unin-
tended effect of forestalling the march was ironic: its possibility
had suddenly plunged the newly formed WPB into a significant
political struggle, and the postponement just as quickly put a dent
into its fortunes.

Kaunda repeatedly urged, even after deciding to cooperate in
the elections, that the march idea be held in readiness. Who knows,
he said, whether things will work out as promised? Will agent
provocateurs stir things up so badly that the election will be held
off? Will Welensky come up with some new gimmick? So the
march was neither cancelled nor called for; it was held in abeyance.

This seemed to vindicate the criticism of those who had warned
against putting the organization's fate in the hands of others.
Scarce funds had been expended on needless travel, as one example. Sutherland and others replied that it was precisely the
threat of mounting problems for the Federation and the British,
including the march, that had helped to produce the new situation, that the prospect of militant and dramatic action had enabled UNIP and its allies to keep initiative and move forward, that
it should be considered fortunate that suffering could be averted.[26]

Training Center

A training center, perhaps at Dar es Salaam, had been envisaged
as a base for organizing in eastern Africa. The experience of
organizing the Positive Action Center in Accra a few years earlier
was known to some of the principals. The training concepts that
prevailed at Beirut were not those that would envisage trying to
turn people into pacifists. Rather, training would be designed to
accord with the practical needs of the particular group or indi-

viduals who were involved. Action and training would reinforce each other, and hopefully be based in protracted campaigns or sustained efforts for development and social reconstruction.

The WPB set up a small center pending the availability of more funds and personnel. Its four main purposes were:

1. Explore the relevance of application of nonviolent action to issues at local, national and regional levels.

2. Serve as a forum for various socio-economic programs that would express African aspirations and meet needs of the people.

3. Help with immediate and intermediate action, provide some skill training, promote self-help projects.

4. Assist individuals and groups engaged in freedom struggles, in particular to develop international contacts.

A hostel was set up initially with four UNIP men, Sutherland and later Suresh Ram, who had been sent by the Asian Council as a full-time staff worker. Ram was a veteran Gandhian, arrested as a student during the "Quit India" campaign, active in the land-gift movement, sometimes a journalist and author of two books on Vinoba Bhave. (Prime Minister Nehru sat in on one of the meetings where it was decided to send Ram to the center.)

The work of the center was suspended for a time when WPB people became involved in daily meetings about the march and related matters. When the march was held in abeyance, the work began again. Time was taken up in finding a suitable location for an expanded center. In the meantime, discussions on independence issues were held, nonviolence examined in its African context, and current issues explored. Typing lessons were given to eight people each morning, self-help building projects undertaken nearby, speaking engagements carried out. Political refugees stayed there occasionally, some required emergency funds in straitened circumstances. It was called the Positive Action Center.

Africa Freedom Action was also considering action in other parts of Africa, notably Southwest Africa (Namibia). Refugees from that area who came to the center engaged in numerous discussions about action projects. PAFMECA included more than a dozen constituent groups, each with pressing problems. Work continued on aiding UNIP's election campaign, especially fundraising.

Rallies

Extensive meetings were held during May, 1962. PAFMECA planned a huge rally at the town of Mbeya, near the Tanganyika-Northern Rhodesia border. Planning for it provided the occasion for the three WPB co-chairmen to meet, the first time since Beirut, to re-evaluate the situation in consultation with African leaders.

A meeting of the Working Committee of AFA was held. Among those on hand were Nyerere, Kaunda, Kawawa (Tanganyikan Prime Minister), Munaka (his parliamentary secretary), Koinange (general secretary of PAFMECA), Makasa (UNIP representative), Scott, Rustin, Sutherland, Ram, Jayaprakash Narayan who had just come from India, and Muste from USA. Kaunda again emphasized the need to keep the march in the picture until the election demands were fully met, to raise money for the elections, to keep up the pressure through such occasions as the Mbeya rally, and to maintain morale and discipline among the people.[27]

A rally of more than 4000 people was held in Dar es Salaam on May 10, with Nyerere as chairman (an unusual size for a political rally in Dar, it was said).

A giant rally was held at Mbeya on the weekend of May 12-14. It was called the "PAFMECA Special Conference With Active Cooperation of UNIP and WPB." The crowd numbered perhaps 10,000 and included 140 Zambians who crossed the border for the meeting. They braved heavy downpours of rain to hear speakers from Kenya, Zanaibar, South Africa, Southern Rhodesia, Nyasaland, Ethiopia and Uganda (PAFMECA speakers). From the Peace Brigade were Narayan, Scott and Rustin. Nyerere, Kawawa and Kaunda also spoke. Not all spoke for nonviolence, of course; some held that if nonviolent means could not be mobilized or applied, then they would take other measures. Nevertheless, that such a gathering could be held in such numbers, and with endorsements of varying degrees in a nonviolent enterprise aimed at affecting the history of eastern Africa and neighboring regions—that was of no small significance. It was an enormous morale booster.

The WPB co-chairmen received the following letter from Mbiyu Koinange, secretary general of PAFMECA:

> The Co-ordinating Freedom Council sitting in special session at Mbeya, Tanganyika, on 14th May, 1962, asked me to convey to the World Peace Brigade through you its sincere appreciation for your wholehearted efforts in cooperating unselfishly with the United National Independence Party's struggle to free Zambia from imperialism, colonialism, neo-colonialism and European domination. The World Peace Brigade did a lot in initiating the Africa Freedom Action in Dar es Salaam and as one of its sponsoring organizations has helped in focusing world attention upon the cause of freedom in Central Africa . . .[28]

Later consultations indicated that further and more detailed plans for the center needed to be firmed up immediately, and then carried out effectively. Kaunda said he hoped the WPB could establish a powerful center in a free Zambia which would serve the whole southern region of Africa. When asked specifically if the nonviolence represented by the Brigade was a political embarrassment, he emphatically stated the opposite.

Nyerere urged the WPB to continue, and to lay before him specific plans for a new version of the center. He agreed that it should adhere firmly to nonviolence despite the problems that would inevitably arise. Others at various official levels endorsed these views.[29]

Educating, Organizing

J. P. Narayan and his wife Prabhavati spent five weeks in the area. A major part of the work was fund-raising, in particular among the Indian population. Funds were needed for the forthcoming election (he rather quickly raised 1000 pounds) and for WPB. In his talks Narayan emphasized the coordinate aspects of nonviolence: resistance to colonialism and suppression, as well as social reconstruction for a new society (the Gandhian term is *sarvodaya*, the welfare of all).

A side-effect of Narayan's efforts was that Asians in Tanganyika began to take an active role in TANU, whereas heretofore they had been criticized for not playing a more active part in political struggles. Good meetings were held in Kenya; Jomo Kenyatta acted as interpreter at a large mass meeting near Nairobi.

The feelings of many were expressed in this cable afterwards:

> We thank you for coming to our aid . . . stop . . . Your presence with the World Peace Brigade had had tremendous effects . . . stop . . . Your support draws our two countries closer . . . stop . . . The Peace March may still be necessary so Indian volunteers should be at the ready—KAUNDA.[30]

United Nations Testimony

The UN Special Committee on Colonialism met in Dar es Salaam on June 4 to accommodate petitioners who could not go to New York. On June 5 Michael Scott, Bill Sutherland, and Suresh Ram appeared as the first petitioners. Scott read a carefully drafted statement recounting the interlocking economic interests in the region, their political impact, and the need for drastic action to forestall violence and disorder in which the cause of freedom would be jeopardized further.[31]

That afternoon Narayan flew back from Nairobi to add impromptu testimony. He was questioned closely about the march and its possible consequences. (WPB learned the committee was pleased with the presentation.) For the next three days staff helped UNIP prepare documentation about harassment, even murders, of UNIP people. These documents were later used by Africa Freedom Action in educational work.

At this point, friendly critics said that the WPB had too uncritically enlisted on the side of UNIP, and ignored the violence and harassment of critics practiced on occasion by UNIP people. It appears in retrospect the charge may have had some merit. At the time of a public testimony may not have been the most appropriate occasion to ventilate such criticism. Kaunda was not averse to recognizing publicly the difficulty of restraining political workers even under harassment. Indeed, he said the presence of the march idea was a restraining force in face of such problems.

The New Center

Nyerere approved plans for an expanded center. A site was finally located near Kivukoni College. Freedom issues became the main focus of various kinds of work. Dar es Salaam was then the

major center in the southern part of the continent for political
refugees and their organizations. WPB staff was often in touch
with these groups, and contacts developed that could have been
significant for future work. John Papworth often used the center
for his organizing work for UNIP in the forthcoming election.

At the request of several groups, a seminar was organized by
WPB on the future of nonviolence and constructive development
in Africa.[32] Eduardo Mondlane, after several discussions with Bill
Sutherland, asked him to draft a program for nonviolent action
that could be used by FRELIMO, the leading resistance group in
Mozambique of which Mondlane was the acknowledged leader.
(It was from some of the Algerians that he had discovered the
role that nonviolent action sometimes played in that struggle.)
Sutherland and a colleague did draft a proposal but it was turned
down by the FRELIMO executive group.

Southwest Africa (Namibia) Project

From the outset of the Brigade's founding, Michael Scott, who
had worked arduously for Southwest Africa on several fronts,
envisaged some form of direct action project from outside, coordinated with internal action. In a political memorandum drafted
in January, 1962 (by Scott, Rustin and Michael Randle, the latter
the former director of the Accra Positive Action Center), the
march idea was first advanced on the basis of this perception:

> The fate of all these territories is bound up one with the other;
> a victory or defeat in one area has its repercussions in all the
> other areas. This is particularly true of South and Southwest
> Africa whose future may largely depend on whether Verwoerd
> and Welensky can succeed in establishing their stronghold or
> whether, on the other hand, the present Central African Fed-
> eration can be broken up and South Africa isolated. Northern
> Rhodesia is probably the key point as it is the most vulnerable
> area in the Verwoerd-Welensky axis.

After analyzing the futility of a military approach, they said:

> As the white extremists concentrate their economic and military
> forces, it is clear that to challenge them successfully positive
> action campaigns have to be developed with even greater effi-

ciency. Just as in violent campaigns strategy, tactics and discipline have to be worked out with care, leaders have to be trained and strategy studied, so in campaigns using nonviolent positive action there has to be intensive and special preparation and training.

They proposed Tanganyika as the site for a training and action center because "it is the nearest independent territory to the area concerned and adjoins Northern Rhodesia where the greatest chance of a breakthrough exists." The memorandum then suggested the coordinated plan for the march from Tanganyika into Northern Rhodesia, and then later a further march across the Caprivi Strip:

> ... into Southwest Africa demanding the return of the lands from which Africans have been forcibly evicted to their rightful owners and demanding that the territory be handed over to UN jurisdiction.[33]

At the London meeting of the International Council of WPB, a detailed proposal was drafted.[34] Coordinated with the march would be action by national groups in their own countries, deputations to governments and the UN, demonstrations at embassies and headquarters of mining companies or other commercial interests in London, Geneva, New York, and Brussels. At the initiative of some Germans in WPB, this idea emerged:

> Coinciding with the freedom march it is proposed that an internationally sponsored programme of land reclamation should take place in an adjoining African territory where the people and government are friendly towards the UN and the efforts of African states in experimenting in forms of cooperative agricultural enterprise. One object of this would be to provide land in at present unsettled or desert areas for settlement by African people who are denied land elsewhere and wish to experiment with new methods and forms of organization, and new agricultural techniques.

The proposal is presented in such detail here for three reasons: first, it was the focus of much discussion in AFA and the center; second, it illustrates well the twofold emphasis of WPB, on both resistance and social organization interacting; and third, it is a valuable scenario illustrating the possible application of a nonviolent political strategy—with further implications apparent—in a politically sensitive and pivotal area on the world scene.

At the request of SWA leaders, on occasion the North American Council organized demonstrations in New York, at embassies and elsewhere, on behalf of issues that needed more visibility and international support. Michael Scott and A. J. Muste met with U Thant at the United Nations about ways the WPB could be useful to the UN in the areas of its work in Africa. The SWA proposal remained only that, for lack of agreement among African groups, even if it could be staged from an independent Zambia.[35]

UNIP Wins Election

In the October election UNIP emerged as the clearly dominant party, which ended the march idea. Inasmuch as the Southwest Africa project didn't prosper, no direct action program appeared relevant. So the work of the WPB, the center in particular, took on a more conventional character. Statements by African leaders and organizations were solicited for the 1963 March on Washington, and against the Vietnam War. Educational work continued, but without a dramatic project at hand money was hard to come by. Appeals from Sutherland and Ram for help yielded limited results. The WPB mounted another major project in Asia: the Delhi-Peking March in the wake of the Sino-India border clash in 1963. This absorbed the energies, funds and work time of many in the North American Council which had the major responsibility for aiding the Africa project.

As part of a re-assessment, a WPB delegation which included Bayard Rustin and Bill Sutherland had a long interview with Julius Nyerere. He paid tribute to WPB work, wished it could be of larger scope and impact, and in an unusual comment, expressed appreciation that some WPB people had several times expressed serious concern about dilemmas he would face if he moved in a more authoritarian direction.[36] Sutherland was asked to take a government post in Tanganyika.

Fade-Out

The WPB as an international organization began to lose momentum in 1964. The voyage it sponsored from London to Leningrad to protest Soviet nuclear testing (late 1962) had some effect but did not put the European groups into business as happened in Africa. In the U.S. the civil rights movement was burgeoning and absorbing the energies of nearly all the WPB people there, some of whom were key fundraisers for WPB too: Muste, Rustin, Robert Gilmore of New York Friends Group. Michael Scott did not find it possible to use the Dar center as an African base of operations for a time. Requests from Dar for staff additions and replacements could not be met.

The base of the WPB did not expand significantly. It was maintained largely by radical pacifists in the U.S., the Shanti Sena in India, and by European groups, English in particular. As the civil rights movement turned U.S. leaders inward to an increasing degree, the Indians were caught up in problems arising from the Sino-Indian conflict, and the WPB march there. The competition for funds was also intense.

Some of its proposals erred because they tried to transpose to the international scene action methods more appropriate to a national setting. The WPB was unable to commit key people to assignments at critical times. Perhaps the main reason for the demise was simply the fact that no action program finally emerged. Narayan believes that, in addition to these reasons, the two main reasons for WPB's problems and inability to become a viable organization were lack of funds—it underestimated the cost of international organization—and the lack of mechanisms to consult enough at the international level.[37]

The WPB was never formally laid down. It fell into disuse, leaving an ambiguous legacy of what Theodore Olson called "vision and failure," but perhaps invaluable experience on which to build at a more propitious time.[38]

In recognition of what the WPB contributed to the struggle for independence of Zambia, Michael Scott and Bill Sutherland were invited at the 1964 independence ceremonies.

What Was Gained?

What follows is a personal evaluation. It is based on participation in the founding conference as one of its training specialists, membership in the North American Council, and participation in the Delhi-Peking March. I have interviewed most of the principals in later years. Jayaprakash Narayan in 1971 and Sutherland and

Scott more recently. I have examined the extensive files of the
Africa project recently obtained by the Swarthmore College Peace
Collection, made available by Bill Sutherland.

1. The WPB helped, if modestly, in the unfolding events leading
   to Zambian independence.

2. The march idea was an antidote to the frustration and bitter-
   ness that were affecting groups in PAFMECA, as evidenced at
   Addis Ababa. The idea was new enough and sufficiently dramatic that it added a new dimension to some of the political
   dialog.

3. By Kaunda's testimony, the march idea provided help in maintaining morale and positive movement at a critical time in Zambia.

4. By Nyerere's testimony, and from what Michael Scott learned
   later in London, the march combined with the threatened general strike was a factor in the British revised attitude toward
   the viability of the Federation, if Welensky persisted in the old
   ways.

5. The idea of militant nonviolence was projected in a particular
   context so that its potential could be better understood by
   thousands of Africans.

6. Jayaprakash Narayan's travels, speeches and fundraising activities produced positive effects, direct and indirect, among
   groups and political leaders in the region. They also led to
   more Asian participation in TANU. (Narayan, Sutherland and
   Ram raised about 5000 pounds for UNIP.)

7. In later years, Kenneth Kaunda carried further his hope for
   a training center in a free Zambia. He asked the American
   Friends Service Committee to establish a center in Lusaka to
   give specific form and direction to the general ideas of nonviolence associated with the Kaunda regime and the independence movement. Implementation was interrupted by UDI:
   Unilateral Declaration of Independence by Southern Rhodesia.

The fact that nonviolent actionists could work out practical
strategies regarding resistance to colonialism, develop tactics ap-

plicable on a mass scale, and establish a cordial working relationship with a variety of independence groups is perhaps some indication of the potential of nonviolence, if it is more assiduously pursued in its organizational and political aspects.

Notes*

1. Michael Scott, "African Episode," reprinted in 1976 by the Gandhi Institute, Cheyney, PA.

2. Peter Jones, "Nonviolent Aspects of the Liberation Struggle in Namibia." A background report written for the Gandhi Institute, July, 1975.

3. Reported to the author by Bill Sutherland, from his conversations with Algerian leaders, early 1960s.

4. Recounted by Janet Mondlane, of Frelimo; Driebergen Conference, The Netherlands, 1972.

5. April Carter, "Sahara Project." A chapter in *Liberation Without Violence*, A. Paul Hare and Herbert Blumberg, (eds.), London, Rex Collings, 1977.

6. World Peace Brigade Papers. Peace Collection at Swarthmore College, Swarthmore, PA.

7. Among those on hand were A. J. Muste, Bayard Rustin and Bill Sutherland.

8. The proposal was negotiated by Lyle Tatum in Lusaka, formulated by the AFSC Program on Nonviolence in which the author participated, started by AFSC staff member James Bristol—until UDI.

9. The author was in Dar es Salaam immediately after a 1976 conference of frontline leaders, and learned that about a half hour was spent considering the proposals of U.S. Secretary of State Henry Kissinger, the rest on trying to develop a common political front.

10. Organizational tribulations, and the scope of the task, are described in a book by Albert Lithuli, Let My People Go, New York: McGraw-Hill, 1962.

11. "Statement of Principles and Aims," by the World Peace Brigade For Nonviolent Action. 1 January 62, Beirut, Lebanon. For ref-

*Unless otherwise stated, all references can be found in the World Peace Brigade Papers at the Swarthmore College Peace Collection, Swarthmore, PA.

erences to documents, see World Peace Brigade Papers, at the Swarthmore College Peace Collection, Swarthmore, PA.

12. Some other sponsors: Prof. Iwao Ayusawa of Japan, Bernhardt Jensen of Denmark, G. Nadjakov of Bulgaria, Alan Paton of South Africa, Tibor Sekelj of Yugoslavia. Few of the sponsors could attend but it is difficult to imagine that the outcome of the conference would have been substantially different.

13. Narayan Desai, *Towards a Nonviolent Revolution*, Sarva Seva Sangh Prakashan, India, 1972, Chapter XIV.

14. For an account of the conference, see Barbara Deming, "International Peace Brigade" in *The Nation*, 7 April 62. The official founding meeting was held in Beirut on January 1. The preparatory conference was held at Brummana, a suburb, December 28—31, 1961. The founding parley is usually referred to as the Brummana Conference.

14a. Some of the same people in the WPB had been involved in the Sahara Protest in 1959—Scott, Sutherland, Muste, Rustin, Randle. See "Sahara Action" by April Carter. Nonviolent Action Research Project, Haverford College. To appear in Liberation Without Violence, A. Paul Hare — Herbert Blumberg, (eds.), Collings, London.

15. Documentation by Alvin W. Wolfe, "The Economics of the Jungle," Liberation Magazine, January, 1962.

16. "Memo on Project in Africa from Policy Group D," proceedings at the Brummana Conference. "Memorandum on Positive Action In Southern Africa" by Michael Scott, Michael Randle and Bayard Rustin, January 1962. Also "World Peace Brigade—Africa Freedom Action Project," a reflective memorandum by Bill Sutherland, 8 January 63.

17. TIME, 9 March 62, pp. 35—36.

18. Tape recording No. 1, Beverly Sterner interviewing Bill Sutherland in Dar es Salaam, 1975.

19. Quoted in "World Peace Brigade Submission To UN Committee On Colonialism," page 1. Dar es Salaam, 5 June 62.

20. Interview with Bill Sutherland by the author, at Wayne, PA., 19 December 74.

21. Tape Recording No. 2, Charles Walker interviewing Bill Sutherland, Philadelphia, PA, 19 December 74.

22. Reflected, for example, in Minutes of Meeting No. 7 and Meeting No. 9 of the London Working Committee of WPB.

23. Lyle Tatum, American Friends Service Committee representative stationed in Salisbury. May, 1962 report.

24. To Bayard Rustin, 8 April 62.

25. From Lusaka, 2 May 62.

26. Interview with Bill Sutherland by the author, 19 December 74, Wayne, PA.

27. "Report of the Chairmen," WPB, 23 May 62. Dar es Salaam. Prepared after several meetings and interviews with African leaders.

28. On PAFMECA stationery, 19 July 62.

29. "Report of the Chairmen," WPB, 23 May 62. Dar es Salaam.

30. "Newsletter," Positive Action Center, 30 June 62.

31. "World Peace Brigade Submission To UN Committee on Colonialism," 8 pages. Dar es Salaam, 5 June 62.

32. "Proposed Seminar On Basic Problems of New African Societies," by Bill Sutherland, attached to letter to Kenneth Kaunda, 31 January 63. Expanded in another undated memorandum.

33. Michael Scott, Michael Randle and Bayard Rustin, "Memorandum on Positive Action in Southern Africa," January, 1962.

34. "Africa Freedom Ride," a confidential memorandum. Perhaps during WPB Council meetings in London, 30 July to 2 August 1962.

35. Discussions with Southwest Africa people and others in PAFMECA reported in Newsletter No. 2, Africa Freedom Action Project, 1 September 62.

36. For example, letter from Bill Sutherland to Julius Nyerere, 17 January 63.

37. Interview with Jayaprakash Narayan by Charles Walker, New Delhi, Summer 1971.

38. See the chapter called "Vision and Failure," by Theodore Olson, in *Our Generation Against Nuclear War*, Montreal, June 1964.

Chapter 10

Nonviolent Resistance to Occupation: Norway and Czechoslovakia*

Paul Wehr

In the past decade, nonviolent national defense has become the object of serious analysis for a growing number of social researchers. A dual-image scenario of the future guides the research. One image has weapons systems of major military powers becoming so formidable and limited in applicability that governments seek alternative means of national defense. This "transarmament" process relies heavily on civilian, nonviolent national defense.

The second image has the major powers increasing their military, technological and economic control over lesser states to such a degree that violent rebellion or national defense becomes unfeasible and new forms of nonmilitary struggle develop of necessity. Under such conditions, nonviolent civilian resistance is that weapon which denies control of a state's social, political, and economic institutions to an oppressor.

Research on civilian defense is not idle speculation for at least two governments, Denmark and Sweden, have commissioned feasibility studies of it.[1] While no nation has yet developed a policy of civilian defense—which implies preparation and training as does any defense policy—there are historical cases of nonviolent civilian resistance to foreign occupation which suggest the major dynamics, potential, and limitations of such resistance. This paper

*This research was made possible by a grant from the National Endowment for the Humanities.

examines two of the more interesting examples—the Norwegian resistance to German occupation in World War II and the Czechoslovak resistance to Soviet intervention in 1968. In both cases, a highly literate population with strong democratic traditions was invaded and occupied by masses of foreign troops. In Norway the resistance movement was slow in building but was sustained throughout the five year occupation. In Czechoslovakia, the initial resistance was immediate and widespread but diminished and disappeared within a year. Through a comparative analysis of the two cases, it is possible to identify certain essential components of successful nonviolent resistance.

Polarization

Resistance of a population to occupation rests, of course, on its perception of the invaders as the enemy—the out-group. There must develop a dichotomous image in the public mind of "them" and "us"—with the latter encompassing not only the nationals of the occupied state but the complex of social, political and economic institutions and values which defines the nation. In short, there must be a clear conception both of what they are to defend and how they will defend it.

In the case of Czechoslovakia, polarization occurred easily. The liberalization period (1967—68) had already reinforced Czechoslovak nationalism and renewed basic democratic and socialist values. The enemy was any nation that threatened those values and the freedom to exercise them. Still, the establishment of a collaborationist regime could have created ambiguity by placing the legitimacy of the Dubcek government in doubt. The refusal of telecommunications leaders, early in the day of invasion, to broadcast the "Appeal to Citizens" calling for support of a collaborationist regime was essential in polarizing the situation.[2] There was little confusion about the identity of friend and enemy.

In Norway, polarization was more difficult to bring about. The nation's governmental leaders had withdrawn to England with their king. The Allied cause seemed certain to fail. Public morale was extremely low. While the Norwegian Nazi party, the Nasjonal Samling (NS), was despised by the majority of Norwegians, it was an indigenous group and cleverly emphasized those aspects of Norwegian culture, such as Nordic mythology, which were at least not inimical to Nazi ideology. Unlike the Czech situation, Norwegian national values and beliefs were not explicit and pronounced at the time of invasion, and the people came dangerously close to acquiescing to the nazification of Norwegian society during the first year of occupation.

By early 1941, however, the dynamics of polarization had begun to operate, largely because of the Nazis' heavy-handed attempts to transform Norway into a corporate state. The vehicle for transformation was to be the private and quasi-official voluntary associations—a foundation block of Norwegian society. Initial targets were organizations that were thought to be more politically conservative or tractable—the health professions, civil servants, agricultural and sports unions.

As the Nazis pushed, leaders resisted, often mobilizing their constituencies to protest specific government policies which controverted national values and political norms. The letter-writing campaign of communal administrators, in January, 1941, was a response to the Interior Minister's demand that all civil servants swear loyalty to the Nazi state. Most people—up to 98 percent in certain communes—sent letters of protest and refusal.[3] The creation, in February, 1941, of an NS office with the authority to appoint all public officials at any level threatened and activated the values of appointment by merit and through local autonomy.

Ultimately the resistance became open and public as national representatives of 43 professional organizations sent an open letter protesting nazification to the German Reichskommissar. Consequentially, some of the signatories were arrested and all of the organizations were placed under NS tutelage. In early September of that year, a period of martial law, arrests, and executions, underscored both the growing threat to the Norwegian way of life and the risks of participating in resistance activity. The battle lines were now clearly drawn for clandestine leaders. Their task was to draw the lines as clearly for the larger population.

Leadership

The existence of on-site clearly identifiable and popular leadership is a second requisite for nonviolent resistance. For the Czechoslovak movement this was not an initial problem. The Prague Spring had produced a set of contemporary national heroes whose very names—such as Dubcek (Little Oak, in Slovak) and Svoboda (Freedom, in Czech)—encouraged resistance. Czech leadership was highly visible and, through speeches and other communication forms in the mass media, provided both motivation and direction for the resistance. The identification with and confidence in their new and popular leadership which most Czechs and Slovaks felt, were major determinants of the immediate, spirited and nonviolent resistance that developed. The leaders became the symbols of resistance—models to emulate.

In Norway, resistance leadership had quite different origins. The government in exile could provide only nominal leadership. Most of the established leaders of political parties, business and other professional groupings were too old, too involved with the Nazi war effort, or too unwilling to expose themselves to risk to shape the resistance. This task fell to the younger, second-level officials in the secretariats of the many professionally-oriented voluntary associations. These persons cemented contacts with reliable people at all levels in their organizations and built webs of relationships linking these contacts across organizational lines. These "faceless" leaders were already key people in their organizations by virtue of middle-level positions which gave them greater access to communication and control. The central communication function of the strategic middle-level personnel in organizations, as indicated by Karl Deutsch is underscored by the activator role of these second-level officials.[4] Because of former intermediary positions in their associations, where they were crucial both vertically—linking top level and rank-and-file membership, and horizontally—permitting sufficient contact with large numbers of members to permit them to organize effectively—they were able to perform the same function for the resistance movement within their organizations—sometimes clandestinely.

These middle-level people initiated resistance by forming "action committees" within their respective organizations which ". . . sounded out opinion among the membership, gave directives to members, led cooperative action among the extreme factions, and kept in contact with each other . . . and to continue contact [with members] down the line, each built its own communications apparatus.[5] By the end of 1941, these new leaders began to integrate their various webs and networks to exercise activation and control.

Middle-level leaders were vital for the Czechoslovak movement as well—some of them as occupants of positions in governmental structures, and others in improvised roles created by the resistance itself. The first group included broadcasting and press editors and journalists, military officers below the general staff level, local and regional labor leaders, heads of student organizations, and regional party and administrative functionaries. In the second group, resistance roles developed around individuals likely to have sustained authority contact with a sizable number of people. Many leaders developed spontaneously in response to a crisis, had no formal positions, but nevertheless acted as information disseminators and resistance activators.

Persons in both of these leadership categories monitored information and opinion passing between system levels—a predominantly downward movement at first but with increasing amounts of feedback from below as resistance grew. They relayed public opinion upward, leadership decisions and statements downward, and translated the latter into specific and imaginative instructions for resistance. When there was inadequate direction from above—as when national leaders were absent from the country—intermediate-level leaders took the initiative in leading the resistance.

Communication

An interesting characteristic of both the Czech and Norwegian movements was the authority of anonymous or little-known leaders whose power was insured through a unique legitimization process. This authority rested largely on a leader's access to an effective communication system. Communication is, of course, of central importance for any social movement. One can view the movement as a developmental process by which communications networks are modified and built—to mobilize and sustain popular resistance.

These two resistance communication systems used both conventional and innovative techniques of transmitting information. Where established media remained beyond the occupier's control, they were an essential tool for organizing resistance. Mass media communication, for example, was the prime activator of Czech resistance. Shortly after the initial border crossings by Warsaw

Pact armies, Czech broadcasting had begun a continuing account of the invasion, analyzing important political events, such as the refusal of national leaders to collaborate or resign, and monitoring and reporting international reaction to the invasion. Knowledge of the government's anti-invasion posture, and the decisions to resist issuing from the emergency session of the Fourteenth Party Congress, strengthened the popular will to resist. Since that will presupposed an informed population, the mass media information-gathering and -transmitting functions were vital. Uncertainty and confusion rapidly demoralize and paralyze a society and rumor and distortion of news are forms of social transmission that weaken a political system. The invasion could have presented the population with a totally chaotic and ambiguous situation. It did not.

Information about the maintenance of rail transportation and urban tram service, and provision of food, fuel and medical supplies during the first days of occupation, contributed substantially to calm and determination among the population.

The mass media, and particularly radio broadcasting, were also instrumental in instructing in resistance techniques—encouraging widespread use of such tactics as obscuring street signs and building numbers, painting wall-slogans, staging symbolic demonstrations, and giving occupiers the "cold shoulder." Warnings to those sought by the KGB, radio frequencies the invaders were using, messages to pharmacists, food suppliers, "ham" operators, blood donors, medical personnel—and other emergency information was transmitted by radio.[6] Perhaps most striking, was broadcasting's relative spontaneity and its technical mobility. Through a combination of broadcaster ability to capitalize on the ignorance of the invading troops, the existence of small mobile transmitters, and the extensive public use of transistor receivers, broadcasting continued for several days after the whole of Czechoslovakia had been occupied.

The press, too, played its role. At the height of the resistance, an estimated 400,000 newspaper copies were circulating daily in Prague.[7] In a highly literate society it was natural that in crisis the press would meet needs that telecommunication could not. Through satire, reprints of leaders' statements and speeches, and unequivocal editorial policies, the press helped shape a unified public viewpoint. Distribution was imaginative. When occupiers made on-the-street peddling and open delivery to central locations impossible, foot-peddlers distributed papers in trams and shops and central deliveries were made in ambulances and police cars. The press also mass-produced the leaflets, wall-newspapers, petitions and other duplicated material which fed the resistance.

In Norway, the mass media played a less spectacular but nevertheless important role in the resistance movement. The B.B.C. Norwegian section, with its programs of news, propaganda, and speeches of Norwegian leaders in exile served to moderate the sense of isolation and despair which made resistance difficult. The anticipation of ultimate liberation was kept alive. In addition, the B.B.C. was essential for the success of specific resistance actions as will be shown later.

With the legitimate press in Norway tightly controlled, the underground press played a most important resistance role. The most influential paper was *Bulletinen* which first appeared in mid-November, 1940. By late 1941 it had wide distribution in cities throughout Norway. The most authoritative papers came out of Oslo and Bergen and had nationwide distribution systems later incorporated into the resistance communication network.

Interpersonal Communication

While the influence of the mass media in the resistance is more visible and more easily documented in retrospect, interpersonal communication was very important in both the Norwegian and Czech movements. Such channels not only transmit information quickly, if not always accurately, but function to integrate a population as well. In Czechoslovakia such communication came easily, where during the months of liberalization preceding the invasion, the people had once again learned to trust and talk among themselves.[8] In the face of invasion, this interaction became interdependence which both lent itself to and depended on word-of-mouth communication. Coleman observes that in time of social crisis or controversy ". . . the formal media of communication. . . . are simply not flexible enough to fill the insatiable need for news which develops as people become more and more involved. . . . Word-of-mouth communication gradually fills the gap, both in volume and in content. . . ."[9]

This observation holds more for the Norwegian situation, where severe constraints inhibited mass media communication, than in Czechoslovakia, where the media demonstrated extreme flexibility and an ability to expand coverage with the developing crisis. Even there, personal communication refined and discussed the views and transformed attitudes into action.

In the Czech case, other factors facilitated personal communication. Intergenerational and inter-class contact is great in Czechoslovakia, where class distinctions are muted, literacy universal and wealth more equitably distributed than in most countries.[10] The absence of such interaction and egalitarianism was a major reason for the rapid collapse of World War II resistance in France, according to Ophuls' documentary film, "The Sorrow and the Pity."

In Norwegian society there was likewise a strong tradition of democracy and classlessness. At that time, Norway was still largely a rural society with many *gemeinschaft*-like personal networks. With the tight control prolonged occupation placed on communication of all sorts, the least controllable was this interpersonal exchange. In the Norwegian movement, personal contact and communication determined both who would lead and who could stimulate and control resistance. In analyzing political movements, as Deutsch points out, we may err

> . . . in overestimating the importance of impersonal media of communication, such as radio broadcasts and newspapers, and underestimating the incomparably greater significance of face-to-face contacts. The essence of the political party, or of an underground organization, consists in its functioning as a network of such face-to-face contacts. [They] determine to a large degree what in fact will be transmitted most effectively and who will be the "insiders" in the organization, that is, those persons who receive information and attention on highly preferred terms.[11]

The mainspring of Norwegian resistance was the Coordination Committee (KK) comprising representatives of various professional/occupational associations in Norway. At its initial meeting were present an engineer, the chief of communal administrators, a lawyer, a pastor, a school principal, a university lecturer, and a teacher—each of them an important man in his field.[12] It seems, however, that personal acquaintanceship among these men was as influential in their selection as were considerations of strategic representation.

The group decided that a nationwide network of reliable contacts was needed to receive directives and organize local resistance to nazification. For two months a young physician travelled about Norway doing "research" for a nonexistent thesis on bone diseases, setting up 21 "contact points," each of which brought a particular region into the national network. By early 1942 the net was operative. It was a multiplex information-gathering and -diffusing system which depended, strangely enough, on a mix of personal and anonymous communication. At the center of the net—the KK Operating Group—and at its periphery—the villages and valleys—communication travelled through stable personal relationships. The intervening channels operated through anonymity—no one knew anyone else. This unusual mix worked well, for the network was never broken.

It was used primarily to disseminate the *paroles*—directives to resist particular actions of the Nazi government. A *parole's* effectiveness was measured by the extent of its coverage—how many people were reached and how rapidly—and the authority and authenticity accorded it by receivers. To insure proper transmission and to foil Nazi counter-*paroles*, directives were sent to the contact points via four routes—personal courier, the underground press, a coded B.B.C. broadcast and personal letters with messages written in invisible ink from KK Central to contact points. The authenticity of a *parole* was established by (1) its arrival through all four channels, and (2) by the distinctive handwriting of a KK secretary who wrote every message and provided continuity as successive coordinators were forced into exile.

> Neither her conduct nor her manner suggested that she had the remotest connection with illegal activity. Ostensibly she was a secretary in a doctor's office on Storting Street in Oslo. The other floors (in the building) had been expropriated for Hird (Nazi SA) offices. Who would suspect that the medicine bottles contained chemicals for clandestine writing and "prescriptions" were resistance directives.[13]

There was a unique reciprocal relationship of leadership to communication in the Norwegian case. *Paroles* would be followed only if the public sensed legitimate authority behind them—yet this authority for a group of anonymous men in Oslo depended on the directives being obeyed. What occurred was a delicate spiralling process of authority and leadership-building in which the KK carefully conceived and phrased the *paroles* to maximize their chance of being followed. Each successful *parole* enhanced the authority of the leaders which in turn increased the success probability of subsequent directives. But at any point, through overconfidence, or misreading of public attitudes, the spiral could be reversed downward. The system then presupposed (1) obtaining precise information about government plans with sufficient leadtime to move a directive through the network, and (2) formulating the *parole* so that it would be followed.

The teachers strike illustrates the process. On February 4, 1942, the Ministry of Religion and Educational Affairs required teachers to join the national teachers union. Membership implied willingness to teach Nazi ideology. In the first major test of its system, the KK dispatched a *parole* to the 14,000 teachers urging them to send a standard letter of protest on a certain day. As in all *paroles*, the emphasis was on threatened national values, moral responsibility and group solidarity. Twelve thousand letters reached the ministry, most of them on the same day and all resisters were threatened with dismissal. Despite the subsequent internment and abuse of 1,100 teachers, the protest continued for weeks and the government backed away. From early 1942 one could plot a credibility curve for *paroles* with initially 70—80 percent of the target group responding and the curve moving upward toward stability at around 90 percent or better thereafter.

Social Defense of Institutions

The basic objective of nonviolent national defense, once national territory has been occupied by an alien force, is to protect social and political institutions through (1) denying their use to the invader, and (2) reinforcing them to persist in modified ways during the occupation. Denial and reinforcement can be achieved through the same process, as both the Czech and Norwegian cases illustrate.

During Dubcek's liberalization period, the political and social institutions of Czechoslovakia had been reborn in a socialist humanism resting on restored free speech, anti-bureaucratism, and grass-roots participation in decision-making. Each of these revitalized institutions (e.g., the press and broadcasting, labor organizations, the Communist Party, the arts and literature, and the universities) now had energetic and popular leadership which made the resistance possible and strengthened their own organizations in the process.

This duality of function—denial and self-renewal—which prominent institutionalized segments of society assumed, was even more pronounced in the Norwegian case where nongovernmental organizations were the core of resistance. Norwegian society is one of voluntary professional associations—very similar in this respect to American society. The most important of these represented occupational groupings, while others were centered around avocational activities such as sports and the arts. In addition to professional communication and training functions, these organizations had political functions as well

> . . . through the activities of the pressure groups at different State levels, through contacts with the parties, as administrative bodies working for the State, as sources of recruitment to public bodies, as groups supplying experts, and as elements in the general political context. In conjunction with the organs of the State and the political parties, the organizations had come to play so important a part in the underpinning of the democratic structure of the State, that one can without exaggeration describe the Norwegian system of government as an "organization-democracy."[14]

The transformation of these organizations into resistance networks permitted the denial of the use of such institutions as the schools, churches and the arts to further an alien ideology, and the simultaneous protection and reinforcement of the traditional values those institutions made explicit. The strategic significance of the initial nationwide protests by the clergy and the teachers is obvious. Those two professions were the caretakers of the national normative order, so to speak, and their early organized resistance had an activating effect on the resistance of other groups to the corporate Nazi state.

Through the integration of these various networks in the KK, the *holdningskamp* or "battle of the wills" as it was called, had by late 1942 blocked incorporation and other nazification objectives. It was, by and large, the modification of extant social organization to protect and renew itself that won the *holdningskamp*.

I have earlier referred to similarities in the Norwegian and

Czechoslovak social and political institutions and values, such as a strong democratic tradition that regards violence as a negative value, and to the great popular support of both socio-political systems.[15] While these similarities help to explain the many common characteristics of the two movements, there were widely disparate international and geographical contexts in the two cases which determined that one would survive and the other crumble. The Norwegian movement had support from the Allies, the promise of eventual liberation, links by sea with friendly nations, and a long common border with Sweden which provided comfortable exile. Czechoslovakia, by contrast, could expect nothing but moral support, and its geographical position, surrounded as it was on all sides by hostile governments save one, was hopeless. Dubcek and Svoboda, realizing the futility and risk of prolonged resistance agreed, under duress, to call for an end to resistance, and it died down rapidly. In Norway, resistance leadership gradually shaped the popular will to resist and the movement's momentum increased steadily until liberation.

Strategy and Tactics

Objectives of the resistance—corresponding in the two movements—were to isolate the invaders socially, and to deny them the profitable use of national resources—personnel, technology, and goods. Consequently, certain common tactics developed in both countries. The "cold shoulder," or social quarantine, was one—a technique having serious effects on occupier morale. Warsaw Pact troops were rotated out of Czechoslovakia regularly, primarily for this reason. Czechs went so far as to turn their heads away as occupation vehicles passed by. Norwegians carefully maintained both physical and social distance from Nazis and occupation soldiers. Official signs posted in Oslo trams which read, "Warning: Anyone leaving his seat next to an NS party member will be put off at the next stop!" suggest how effective this social boycott was. Nor was the quarantine a purely public exercise. A special service was organized for the care of hundreds of Norwegian unwed mothers whose fraternization with German soldiers led their families and friends to reject them.

Schweikism[16], or the ostensibly unwitting frustration of enemy objectives, was a popular tactic in the Czechoslovak resistance.

One illustrative instance involved a trainload of jamming equipment sent from the Soviet Union to block resistance broadcasting. The equipment took several days to travel 200 miles and then had to be airlifted by helicopter when it ended far from its intended destination. In Norway too, work slowdowns, unexplained delays in German shipments, and other obstructionist tactics, grew increasingly common as the occupation progressed.

Schweikism is difficult to detect and punish, particularly when it is done in good humor. The Czech case is particularly illustrative of the potential of spontaneous public mischief and its value in frustrating invaders. An invading force which does not know its way around a society can be literally at the latter's mercy. The catalogue of tactics developed by Czechoslovaks to frustrate, outwit, mislead, and ridicule their occupiers is a study in itself.

Finally, open refusal to render services or goods to the occupiers was widespread. This was more than the organized resistance of professionals cited earlier. It was an individualized withdrawal of cooperation with the occupation and its agents. Czechoslovak farmers refused food, drink and information to troops. Norwegian engineers refused German tunnel construction contracts and laborers rejected military construction jobs. Artists declined to perform for Nazi audiences. One of the most revealing sets of documents for this research was an exchange of letters between the Nazi communications minister and the manager of a cinema in southern Norway over the latter's refusal to admit censors, show propaganda films, send in requested information and the like. The dynamics of patient and persistent noncooperation is documented therein. By no means did a majority of Norwegians resist in this manner initially, but exemplary individual acts of noncooperation had a cumulative effect and set a normative tone that ultimately swayed the population to public and private resistance.

Symbols

Something should be said here about the role of symbols in nonviolent resistance—the symbolic act, the heroic figure representing certain national values, the commonplace object which suddenly takes on a new significance for national identity. So in the Czech resistance did Jan Hus (symbolizing national resistance and self-sacrifice), King Wenceslas (known for his courage and anti-war sentiments), and Franz Kafka (satirist of unproductive and dehumanizing bureaucratism) become symbols with great affective power. In Norway, a paper clip worn on the lapel meant, "Norwegians must keep together against the enemy," and the traditional long winter stocking cap and the royal insignia were powerful unifying symbols.

It seems that such symbolism is particularly important for unarmed resistance, which is largely value-centered with implicit national values and norms being both the defended and the means of defense. Such struggle needs constant referent points—visible reminders of what is being defended and why. Hugh D. Duncan sees a society existing around the communication of "significant symbols." To define and preserve it, some sort of dramatic model of that society built around those symbols is necessary. A community, in his view, needs to "dramatize itself before its people" from time to time.[17] The Czechoslovak and Norwegian societies both dramatized and protected themselves through resistance, and symbols were essential to this dramatization.

Conclusions

Admittedly a two-case study provides insufficient data from which to generalize but I would like to summarize by stating propositionally certain observations about nonviolent resistance.

1. *Nonviolent resistance movements are first of all communications systems.* The ease, accuracy and security of the flow of resistance information are primary determinants of its success or failure—determining even the structure and effectiveness of movement leadership. In both cases presented above, existing communications networks were modified for resistance purposes.

2. *Psychological polarization is essential for resistance development.* In both cases—immediately with Czechoslovakia and gradually in Norway—as the threat to national integrity, values and institutions became clear, the in-group/out-group dichotomy grew to isolate occupiers and collaborators. As Coser[18] points out, however, this attack/solidarity dynamic operates only under certain conditions—where the basic social structure is stable and central values are not questioned—conditions which obtained in both set-

tings. Even where such conditions do exist, polarization may not necessarily occur and requires a movement to bring about a confrontation of in-group/out-group values.

3. *The clarification and reinforcement of indigenous values and norms is essential to nonviolent resistance.* Military occupation generally creates a temporary anomie in which societal values must be redefined and reactivated, and norms of acceptable behavior under new and stressful conditions clarified. In the Czech case, the preceding liberalization period had made very explicit the basic values, thereby providing an operating guide to resistance behavior. In Norway, the *paroles* clarified the values and set the normative tone.

4. *The establishment of leadership legitimacy is a prerequisite for large scale resistance.* To whom people should give the right to lead, under a suspension of normal political life, is a difficult problem. In our two cases, legitimacy was ultimately accorded those who controlled the face-to-face and mass media communication channels, but whose directives and leadership drew unequivocally on legitimate values. As Deutsch observes, it is in the *"coincidence between legitimacy beliefs and social communication channels that political power can be found."*[19]

5. *The role of the sub-national organization is vital for resistance mobilization.* Voluntary and professional associations, and professional groupings within administrative structures seem especially important in that they merge sub-group and national identities and loyalties and activate them on behalf of resistance. They also lend decisional and communication structures to the resistance.

6. *The emergence of nonviolent, civilian resistance depends partly on the existence of a propitious combination of geographical, political and socio-cultural factors in the victimized nation.* In both cases in point, a literate population, a relatively restrained occupying force, an egalitarian social structure, a cultural past which discouraged violent response, peculiar geographical and topographical characteristics, and the futility of armed resistance were all important in determining the nonviolent character of the resistance.

7. *The intensity and duration of nonviolent resistance depends in large measure on the links the communications system has with external systems and the possibility for ultimate liberation.* In the Czechoslovak case, resistance was intense initially, with excellent communication with friendly political systems—but lasted only a week as the futility of further resistance without assistance from outside was acknowledged.

8. *The influence of incidental and situational factors in nonviolent resistance is assumed.* A personalization of resistance makes the movement much less vulnerable to counter-strategy, and strategies of nonviolent national defense will have to anticipate and exploit such factors.

The Future of Nonviolent National Defense

It is perhaps premature to suggest a future for nonviolent resistance as a respectable component of a nation's defense policy. In an age of "thinking the unthinkable," however, it seems to me we need to exploit the imagination in conceiving alternative defense strategies supplementary to traditional and increasingly ineffective ones. The skeptics' query—but could nonviolent defense really defend?—is a hard-headed one and the response depends on how one defines effectiveness. In the short-range, the Czechoslovak resistance was effective and in the long-range the Norwegians were successful, given goals they set for their movement. Success indicators are not limited to ejecting or deterring the invaders but will include such things as better bargaining positions gained for indigenous leaders, the survival of national values, and the defeat of occupier values within the occupied system.

We have no historical validation of the deterrence capability of nonviolent national defense because deterrence is only credible if a nation has trained its people and created strategies and tactics before the fact. Our two cases are not, strictly speaking, civilian defense, which like any good defense policy is anticipatory and most successful if it deters attack.

It is possible that nations will develop nonviolent resistance within a mixed defense strategy, with the former becoming more dominant as new developments in weapons technology make armed defense less secure, less effective and more costly. It will be, as it always has been, a strategy of last resort. The initial adoption will be by smaller nations whose armed defense capabilities are already negligible and for whom the risks of transarming are minimal. Yet even first-level powers such as Japan might conceivably consider civilian defense as a realistic policy. Planning now for future defense, Japan is caught between its growing stature as an economic and political force in Asia and the world, and its adherence to a minimum armed defense policy.

What is needed is more and better research on the form, dynamics, strategy and tactics of civilian defense. This will be part of a more general body of research on both defensive and offensive forms of nonviolent struggle.

Notes

1. A. Boserup and A. Mack, *War Without Weapons: Nonviolence in National Defense*, New York: Schocken, 1975; A. Roberts, *Total Defense and Civil Resistance: Problems of Sweden's Security Policy*, Mimeo, Stockholm: Research Institute of Swedish National Defense.

2. R. Littell, *The Czech Black Book*, New York: Avon, 1969, p. 89.

3. O. J. Malm, "Orientering pa Landsmotet for aden Sivile Hjemmeledelses Kontaktpunkter." Report made June 8, 1945 to Norwegian national investigative commission on the resistance and occupation, Norwegian National Archives, p. 4.

4. K. Deutsch, *The Nerves of Government*, New York: Free Press, 1966, p. 154.

5. T. C. Wyller, *Nyordning og Motstand*, Oslo: Universitets Forlaget, 1958, p. 277. Here, as elsewhere in the paper, translations from the Norwegian are mine.

6. R. Hutchinson, Czechoslovakia, 1968: The Radio and the Resistance, Monograph. Copenhagen: Institute for Peace and Conflict Research, 1969.

7. C. Menges, Prague Resistance, 1968: The Ingenuity of Conviction. Santa Monica, CA.: RAND Corporation, 1968, p. 7.

8. M. Mayer, The Art of the Impossible. Santa Barbara, CA.: Center for the Study of Democratic Institutions, 1969, p. 16.

9. J. Coleman, The dynamics of community controversy. In R. Warren, (ed.), *Perspectives in American Community*, Chicago: Rand-McNally, 1966, p. 553.

10. P. Machonin, et. al., "Vertical social differentiation and mobility of

the Czechoslovak population," *Co-Existence*, 1968, pp. 5, 7—16.

11. Deutsch, op. cit., p. 152.

12. Malm, op. cit., p. 7.

13. S. Steen, (ed.), *Norges Krig*, III. Oslo: Gyldendal, 1959, p. 299.

14. Wyller, T. C., op. cit., pp. 315—316.

15. Theodor Ebert concludes that civilian defense is a natural strategy for socialist states where, according to this view, the sense of participation in and ownership of national institutions is great. T. Ebert, Conjectures about the dialectical process to civilian defense. Paper presented to the Conference on Nonviolent Struggle, Uppsala, Sweden, August, 1972.

16. The term originates with the Czech folk anti-hero Josef Schweik, who survived through the cultivation of the art of dim-witted obstructionism Jaroslav Hasek, *The Good Soldier Schweik*, Harmondsworth, England; Penguin, 1951.

17. H.D. Duncan, *Symbols in Society*, New York: Oxford University Press, 1968, p.94.

18. L. Coser, *Functions of Social Conflict*, New York: Free Press, 1956.

19. Deutsch, op. cit., p. 153.

Part IV.

The Future of Nonviolent Action

On the basis of nonviolent actions in this century, we can see how the nation of the future may employ defense against invaders without military arms, how a whole new meaning to personhood may become introduced through the culture of new nonviolent action movements, and, finally, how the seeds of a new "nonviolent revolution" are being sown in this century. These are perspectives generated by people who are active in the social change movements today.

Gene Sharp shows us the political significance of creative resistance against invasion and international aggressions. He points toward the development of a whole new collective tactic for nonviolent defense at the level of the nation. Like the concept of a democratic state in the 18th century, the concept of nonviolent national defense is only beginning to be seen for its power as an idea whose time has come.

Mary Roodkovsky describes how the feminist movement now joins with movements for nonviolent action to introduce new integral values into human interaction. We have known since the protean writings of George Herbert Mead that the human self, the person, is symbolically defined in culture. Now we see how the culturally defined male powers of aggression and the culturally defined female powers of human sensitivity for life and tenderness are both requirements for participation in radical movements for nonviolent action. The feminist movement for liberation links with nonviolent movements to show the "self" in a new creation. We are neither male nor female in our essence but a whole person beyond the social roles that people are taught in modern society. This fact, Mary suggests, has yet to be realized in the changing institutions and structures of the post-modern society.

Louise Bruyn describes how theater is relevant to the new revolution in the making. That revolution is based on the principles of nonviolence. She describes the many ways that theater can be consciously used to further that revolution—to raise consciousness to mobilize energy and to create a vision of the future. The arts and theater gain a new place in society helping to transform the lives of people toward a new age.

Chapter 11

The Significance of Domestic Nonviolent Action As a Substitute for International War[1]*

Gene Sharp

A re-examination of the problem of war and the possible means for its solution needs to begin with the recognition of the failure of past movements and proposals for the abolition of war, despite the widespread understood destructiveness of modern war. Few people believe that we are on the way to end war. Military technology is at its highest stage of development in history. During this decade and the previous one, military institutions in many countries have been the most powerful and productive in comparison to the civilian branches of government and to the rest of society. Except for world wars, a higher proportion of resources has been devoted in the period to military purposes than ever before. More lives can now be threatened and destroyed faster than it has ever been imagined.

Defenders of the status quo are not the only practitioners and supporters of war and other political violence. Political movements and governments which espouse change, as in Viet Nam, are often equally committed to military means. Nor are we on the verge of a popular rebellion against war as such. The time when the general public might have been capable of feeling significant shock and revulsion at the nature of modern weaponry to rebel against it—as in its early atomic and thermonuclear forms in the late 1940s and the 1950s—has gone.

True, there are anti-war groups. For example, there are objectors to all war, perhaps even more than there used to be: the perpetually small minority which opposes all war by a refusal to participate in it. Also, many other people oppose a particular war, as in Viet Nam, which is perceived as especially unjust or inhuman (although some of these are silent about, or support, the war effort of the other side). Still others, including governments, seek to limit the development, manufacture, spread and use of certain military weapons while accepting that serious disarmament is outside the realm of reality.

But, with very, very few exceptions, the dream that many people only a few decades ago firmly believed, that war, along with certain other objectionable aspects of society, could and would be abolished, is no longer even dreamed. If it is still being dreamed and voiced by a few, those persons are perceived as out of touch with political reality. Yet, if there ever was a time in world history for a proper awareness of the destructiveness and brutality of war, and when one might have expected an increase in the efforts to abolish the military system and to increase the prospects for doing so, it should have been by now! Instead, we have witnessed the demise of even major efforts to end war.

Reexamining The Problem

It is possible that one or several of the previously proposed solutions to the problem of war may have been partially or largely valid. Those more orthodox approaches will continue to receive attention, as they generally should. However, our further examination of the problem should not be limited to those past approaches. It is not reasonable to presume that the answer must lie in a proposal, or course, or system, which has not yet moved us perceptibly closer to the resolution of the problem. A careful and critical re-examination of those earlier proposals for peace and to abolish war is impossible here, although it is important that it be done. Since the past proposals have not yet worked, we shall instead concentrate on developing a different analysis of the nature of the problem of war, which will point the direction toward a possible alternative policy. We are unlikely to find a solution to the problem of war if we do not understand adequately the nature of that problem. We need to examine once again whether war might be abolished for particular societies, groups of societies, or generally—and, if so, how.

Distasteful "Givens"

A new effort to abolish war will require a prior rejection of any romantic illusions that we may have and a willingness to recognize certain premises which are often distasteful to exponents of peace. The following is assumed here:

1. There will always be intra-societal and inter-societal conflict.

2. In any such conflict, some type of power will always be present and needed, on both sides.

3. That what is crudely called "human nature" need not, and most likely will not, be changed.

4. That people and governments will not, and should not be asked to, sacrifice either freedom or justice for the sake of peace.

5. Peace is not identical with maintenance of the status quo, or with revolution.

6. Individual conversions to pacifism are not going to happen by the hundreds of millions, and world peace will have to come in a different way.

7. There is no break in the spiral of military technology within the context of military technology and military assumptions.

8. There have been and are ghastly dictatorships and oppressive systems in the world, which may continue and recur, use new forms of control, and may expand against other countries in various ways.

9. The abolition of capitalism does not produce the abolition of war (the military system is more powerful now in noncapitalist states than before the change, and military action is even threatened and used by noncapitalist states against each other).

10. Negotiations are no substitute for the capacity to wage con-

flict (a capacity which itself is a crucial factor in negotiations).

11. "Disarmament" (understood as the major reduction or abandonment of defense capacity) on a unilateral basis is not possible (for reasons which will be discussed).

12. Major multilateral disarmament is nearly as unlikely because
of the fear of every country to be at a relative disadvantage,
and also because of the constantly changing nature of the
international situation.

13. National independence is not the origin of war, but instead
reliance on military means as the ultimate sanction of the
independent nation.

14. Peace through world government is either a dangerous illusion because it is unrealizable, or, if achievable, a severe danger to world peace (likely to produce a world civil war), to
freedom (if capable of preventing war it would be capable of
tyranny), and to justice (who would control, to what ends,
and how could shifts of control and ends be prevented?).

There are other such factors that need to be recognized. Our
search for an understanding of the problem of war, and for a
solution to it, must not rest on utopian illusions. Neither must
our search be naive concerning the political intentions of protagonists to international conflicts.

Nor should the role of the basic nature of certain social and
political systems be neglected. This does not require agreement
that any particular system be identified as "evil." Critical analyses
of any and all such systems are desirable; it is unnecessary to gloss
over their unsatisfactory characteristics in order to contribute to
peace. However, this should not lead us to neglect the military
system itself. Without elimination of reliance on military means,
structural or systemic change is unlikely to be very complete, and
the new system is likely to find itself distorted or controlled by
the military system it accepted.

Functional Alternatives

One approach which has rarely been applied to the military
system is to analyse its function of providing defense and to ex-

plore if defense could be provided in some other way. Functional analysis is sometimes dismissed as a status quo approach, but it is utilized here as a tool precisely because it may provide insights making possible fundamental change which may otherwise not be possible. Here the sociological terminology of "function" and "structure" will be used, which might instead be called "need" or "task" and "instrument" or "institution" for the particular purposes of this discussion.

A. R. Radcliffe-Brown defined function as the part something "plays in the social life as a whole, and therefore the contribution it makes to the maintenance of the structural continuity. Bennett and Tumin wrote that to ask the function of something is to ask "What does it 'do for' people and groups." Recognition that human institutions have functions and do certain jobs for society in no way blocks the way to change, even fundamental change. Instead, examination of the existence and possibilities of "functional alternatives" opens the way for basic change. Functional substitutes have been referred to by various analysts and theorists, including Theodore Newcomb, Talcott Parsons, Parsons and Edward A. Shils, Lewis Coser, and especially Robert K. Merton.

Merton pointed out over 20 years ago that the existing social structures—that is, patterns of action, institutions, instruments, or "means" to a social goal—are not the only possible ones. There also exist other ways of fulfilling the function served by the present structure. The specific existing social structures, he insisted, are not functionally indispensable. Merton offered "as a major theorem of analysis": *the same function may be diversely fulfilled by alternative items*. Functional needs are here taken to be permissive, rather than determinant, of specific social structures." In fact, alternative social structures have served the functions necessary for groups to continue to exist. This, he wrote, "unfreezes the identity of the existent and the inevitable." Since there may be a range of ways in which particular functional needs may be fulfilled, we should look for functional alternatives. Merton insisted that this was relevant to conscious efforts to produce social change, and offered also as "a basic theorem":

> any attempt to eliminate an existing social structure without providing adequate alternative structures for fulfilling the functions previously fulfilled by the abolished organization is doomed to failure.

Parsons similarly wrote: "There must be a development of 'functional alternatives' to the structures which have been eliminated. Coser also argued:

> In realistic conflict, there exist functional alternatives as to means. . . . there are always possibilities of choice between various forms of contention, such choice depending . . . on an assessment of their instrumental adequacy.

Functions of War

War is such a prominent institution of modern society that if these theoretical views are valid they must apply to the military system. Let us therefore explore such an application.

Such a complex and diverse structure as the military system has served many purposes. A careful analysis of all of them is needed (a task which is not attempted here), including examinations of alternative ways of fulfilling those functions which seem lasting, and explorations of whether some of the functions of the military—especially those deemed undesirable—may be required only under specific conditions and not universally, and may hence be removed, reduced or dealt with in some other way.

We shall here identify four functions of a military capacity which are primarily political and are associated with national policy of governments:

1. *To attack.* Especially international aggression, motivated or justified variously, as for: economic benefit; power expansion; egocentric aggrandizement of rules; "liberation"; extending "civilization"; seizure of territory; extermination of "inferiors"; and the like. Sometimes the attack is internal on the governmental system of that very country, or on another part of the society, as in a *coup d'etat* or civil war.

2. *To dominate.* The home population, or foreign populations and countries, or both, also with diverse motivations remarkably similar to those just listed.

3. *To deter.* That is, to prevent attack by possession of sufficient capacity to cause the potential attacker to anticipate greater losses than gains, and hence to decide against the venture.

4. *To defend.* That is, to "defend" in the literal sense of the term, as to ward off, to protect, to resist against attack, to deny the objective of the attacker, to uphold or maintain against the attacker. This includes both defense against genuine attack and preparations to defend in case of attack. Also at times the excuse of "defense" is used to assist in internal domination or is used to disguise for the home population what is in fact an attack on another country. (This last point is very important, and the following analysis is by implication relevant to it, although that specific kind of situation requires separate full analysis.)

The relative importance of each of the several functions of war may vary from case to case, culture to culture, and time to time, although certain ones may be both far more persistent and perceived as more generally justifiable than others. Let us now look at these four functions more closely, in two groups.

Functions of Attack and Domination

It appears that the functions of attack and domination may be dealt with in other ways than by providing substitute nonmilitary means of attacking and dominating, functions which are in any case undesirable. These functions might be removed, or attempts to carry them out might be frustrated, and thus the functions in practice finally drastically reduced in two ways:

1. Changes may be carried out in the society which is, or potentially is, the origin of an attack, to reduce or eliminate both motives and ability to attack, by changes in its social institutions, distribution of power, economic system, beliefs and attitudes as to legitimacy, acceptable policies, and the like. Those social changes require separate attention which unfortunately is not possible here.[2] If attacks can be reduced or eliminated by social changes which remove the "need," functional alternatives are not needed here.

2. The capacity of the attacked society to defend itself by some means might be increased, so as effectively to deter attacks, to defeat attacks if they occur, or to liberate itself from the oppression caused by past attacks. Successful and repeated defense (and liberation) to such internal or external attacks, denying the objectives to the attackers is likely to reduce the frequency with which military systems are used to attack, provided that the defense is by means which do not confirm the attacker's belief in the omnipotence of the military system to gain ends. In other words, in the case of this function, it may not be a functional substitute means of attack which may be needed, but a functional substitute means of defeating the attack. There are very important reasons (which cannot be developed here) why such deterrence and struggle against internal or external attacks may be more advantageously and effectively achieved by means other than the military forms of conflict.

Functions of Deterrence and Defense

Military systems also are widely used to deter and to defend. The reasons offered by most ordinary people, policy makers, and government spokesmen for keeping and relying upon the military system are that a strong military capacity can, better than anything else, deter and defend against the attack. In the face of these perceived functions of military systems, pleas to abandon military capacity on moral, religious, humanitarian or political grounds have historically been accepted by only a small minority, which the general population has overwhelmingly, with few exceptions, rejected the anti-military pleadings. War may be brutal, immoral, and even suicidal, but people have seen that it provided an ultimate sanction and means of struggle for which they have perceived no alternative. Even where deterrence or defense are not the real motives for military systems, popular support for those systems and war efforts will be forthcoming even if they are for aggressive purposes as long as people believe they have no alternative means of defense.

Whether to be held in reserve to back up one's position in international negotiations, to deter attack by adequate preparations, or to defend in case of attack, military systems have been believed necessary since no other way to fulfill those functions of deterrence and defense has been seen to exist. It has been com-

monly believed that the alternative to war is impotence, cowardice
and passive submission, and that the perception of ordinary people has been shared by statesmen, policy makers, intellectuals and
academics. Even nuclear weapons have not changed this, for people believe that, though they normally ought not to be launched,
their existence will prevent attack, and thus provide safety and
avoid helplessness.

All this is fully compatible with the application of Merton's
"basic theorem" to the problem of war. For Merton postulated
that efforts to remove a basic structure without providing an alternative structure for fulfilling its function would be doomed to
failure. The need for defense of a society, its populace, its institutions, way of life and the like, is such a basic societal need that
in conditions of perceived and actual threats of attack, the military
system will not be abandoned when it is perceived that this will
leave the society helpless and defenseless in meeting real or imagined dangers. Yet this is what proposals for abandonment of war
and the military system have almost always meant or been perceived to mean.

Separating Structure and Function

Peace movements and most peace proposals have, in their assumptions and analyses, often confused structure and function,
or, putting it in other ways, confused institution and job, or instrument and task. Exponents of peace have largely accepted the
identity of the structure (the military system and war) with its
perceived most justified functions (deterrence and defense), just
as have the exponents and practitioners of the war system itself.
It has been assumed that effective defense and strong military
capacity were synonymous. Whether judged by Merton's theorem, by statements of political officials, or by the views of ordinary
people, it was predictable and inevitable that past efforts to abolish war would fail, and this explains why present and future efforts which are primarily anti-military and anti-war cannot succeed
either.

The simple distinction between structure and function, or instrument and task, applied to war and defense may free us from
the axiomatic presumption of the identity of defense with the
military system, and enable us to ask whether there can be alter-

native means of defense which are not military, a question which to most people has been inconceivable.

This ought not to be as ludicrous a question as it might appear to others, since, even with present policies, defense and military capacity are not identical. First of all, the growth and development of military technology means that in its extreme forms the actual use of military means can in some cases provide only vast destruction and death, not actual defense. Second, in some cases, the advance perception of such possible destruction, or of overwhelming military capacity by the attacker, may lead to a realization that military resistance for defense is futile and hence to a decision not to attempt it. Third, and most important, is the existence already in some international conflicts of the improvised use for national defense purposes of nonmilitary means of resistance, and a much larger, though also still crude and underdeveloped use of such nonviolent means of struggle in domestic conflicts.

The analysis in this section of the paper has pointed in this direction:

The path to the abolition of war may lie through the substitution of nonmilitary means of defense, if these exist, can be created or refined, and if they are, or can be made to be, at least as instrumentally effective as military means of defense have been and now are.

Nonviolent Struggle

The world, much less politics, is not divided neatly into violence and nonviolence. There are many intermediary phenomena, and many which are neither violent nor nonviolent. But in terms of ultimate sanctions and means of struggle, which are used when milder means are judged inadequate or have failed, there do appear to be two broad techniques: one is violent action, which includes several types of violent conflict, among them conventional and nuclear war; the other, nonviolent action, which is also a broad and diverse technique. It is to the nature and potential of this nonviolent technique of struggle that our attention now turns.

Our awareness and understanding of the nonviolent counterpart of violent struggle is generally sharply limited and filled with many serious distortions and errors of fact. An initial effort is therefore usually required to free our minds from inaccurate perceptions of this type of struggle which we have accumulated from a culture in which belief in violence as the ultimate form of power and as the most significant single fact in history (both of which are now challenged) are fundamental axioms. This belief in the omnipotence of violence, and ignorance of the power of popular nonviolent struggle, may have also been compatible with the interests of past dominating elites who did not want people to realize their power potential.

Unfortunately, it may be necessary to indicate some of the things that nonviolent action is not. This technique is the opposite of passivity, submissiveness and cowardice. Nonviolent action uses social, economic, psychological and political power in the matching of forces in conflict, and is not to be equated with verbal or purely psychological persuasion. This means of struggle does not assume that man is inherently "good." This is not "pacifism"; in fact, this technique has been used predominantly by "ordinary" people who never became pacifists and some pacifists find it offensive. Nonviolent conflict may operate even in cases of extreme social distance between contending groups. This technique is probably more "Western" than "Eastern." It is designed to combat a violent opponent, and does not presume a nonviolent response to the nonviolent challenge. This technique may be used for both "good" and "bad" causes, though the social consequences of its use for "bad" causes differs sharply from that of violence. While violence is believed to work fast, and nonviolent action slowly, often violence takes a long time and nonviolent struggle may operate extremely quickly. Finally, and most importantly for this paper, nonviolent action is not limited to domestic conflicts within a democratic system; it has been used widely against dictatorial regimes, foreign occupations, and even totalitarian systems, and it has already been used without advance preparations internationally even in improvised national defense struggles.

Our recent studies of this technique have revealed it to be infinitely richer, more variable and powerful than hitherto dreamed. It has been widely thought that, for the most part, politically significant nonviolent struggle began with Gandhi. We now know that it has a rich and vast history. We are only beginning to piece together, how it goes back at least to several centuries B.C., and ranges over many cultures, continents, countries, historical periods, issues, and types of groups and opponents. Instead of the list of specific methods, or forms, of action included within this technique being relatively few, a dozen or so as was once thought, we now know that even with a partial listing the number is at least 198, arranged in three main classes of nonviolent protest and persuasion (the milder forms), noncooperation (including boycotts of social relations, economic boycotts, strikes and political noncooperation), and nonviolent intervention.

It was thought by some that conversion of the opponent by the sufferings of the nonviolent actionists was the only, or at least the best, way in which nonviolent action produced change. We now know that this is not true, and that nonviolent struggle can also be coercive, possible even more so than violence against an obstinate opponent. This is because nonviolent struggle is capable of severing the various sources of the opponent's power—by massive civil disobedience of the population as a whole paralyzing the political system, strikes by workers and noncooperation by management paralyzing the economic system, noncooperation by civil servants paralyzing the governmental structure, mutiny by soldiers destroying the repressive capacity, and in many other equally important but more subtle ways.

Comparisons with Violent Struggle

A survey of the knowledge that we now have of the history of nonviolent action would facilitate our consideration of this largely neglected socio-political technique, but that is not possible within the scope of this paper. Suffice it to say that it is a remarkable history which when more fully revealed will require and produce major re-examinations of not only social but political history, and fundamental reinterpretations of very significant historical cases where violence is widely presumed to have been the only form of struggle, or the only possible successful one. In this, the American Revolution, the Russian Revolution, and struggles against Nazism are only three of the more dramatic such cases.

This new understanding and information about the nature, history, dynamics and existing capacities of nonviolent struggle is of a magnitude as to require major reevaluation of the judgments which have been made or assumed as to its effectiveness and potential in comparison with violence. However, that is but the beginning.

Nonviolent action has almost always been improvised without significant awareness of the past history of this type of struggle. It has usually been waged without qualified leadership, or without compensating wide popular understanding of the technique, without thorough comprehension of its requirements for effectiveness, without preparations and training, without analyses of past conflicts, without studies of strategy and tactics, without conscious development of its "weaponry," and often without a consciousness among the actionists that they were waging a special type of struggle. In short, the most unfavorable circumstances possible have accompanied the use of this technique. It is amazing that the significant number of victories for nonviolent struggle exist at all, for these conditions of the lack of knowledge, skill and preparations have been to the highest degree unfavorable.

In contrast, for many centuries military struggle has benefited from conscious efforts to improve its effectiveness in all the ways in which nonviolent action has lacked.

International Relevance

Some people assume that the nonviolent means of conflict used predominantly in domestic conflicts are intrinsically limited to that range of conflict situations, while military struggle is the means obviously appropriate to the international level. On closer reflection it becomes obvious that this distinction is by no means so clear-cut as is often assumed. Violent action, of course, is also widely used internally in repression, resistance, *coups d'etat*, revolution, guerrilla war, and civil war. Also, certain forms of nonviolent action are used internationally far more frequently than usually recognized such as embargoes, freezing the assets of another country, economic boycotts, cancellation of planned conferences and diplomatic visits, and refusal of diplomatic recognition. Other forms, that are far more relevant to our analysis, are the cases of widespread civilian resistance against invasion forces and occupation regimes.

The reality may be that whether a given technique is applicable to domestic or international conflicts is not determined by whether it does or does not use physical violence but by whether people have tried to adapt it as effectively as possible to that type of conflict situation. The presumption that nonviolent struggle is only appropriate to domestic conflicts is not valid.

Nonviolent struggle has already been applied in international
politics without planning or preparations or at times even advance
decision (all of which are regarded as essential for maximum effectiveness). These international struggles do not refer to international economic boycotts and embargoes. Those, although
important, are (contrary to Thomas Jefferson) probably not
models, or even primitive prototypes, upon which to build a nonviolent, functional substitute for war. There have been other cases
which, although not models, might be early prototypes upon which
to build more successful prepared and trained nonviolent defense
capacities.

The case of Czechoslovakia in 1968—69 is the closest to what
is envisaged—a nonviolent war of resistance which in the end
seems to have been lost. But we learn from lost military wars and
we can learn from lost nonviolent wars. According to some reports, the Russians anticipated military resistance from the able
Czechoslovak army, and expected they could overcome it and
install a puppet government within four days. Despite very considerable Czechoslovak military capacity based on years of preparations and training, the obvious futility of military resistance in
face of five invading armies including that of the Soviet Union
produced a decision not to resist with military force.

Instead, an unprepared, improvised nonviolent resistance occurred which despite serious problems, and apparent major strategic errors, and sometimes without adequate assistance from the
official leadership, managed initially to frustrate completely the
Russian efforts to install a puppet government in spite of the
distribution of troops throughout the country. It forced negotiations with leaders (some, as Dubcek, already arrested and kid-
napped) whose country was already totally occupied and whose
army had never entered the field—conditions under which negotiations should not have been required or expected.

Even after those negotiations, such resistance in less dramatic
forms maintained the Dubcek regime, so hated by the Russians,
in power (after their release from arrest and imprisonment) until
April of 1969—eight months! Even then, it can be argued, the
demise resulted more from the collapse of resistance by the government and Party at a time of anti-Russian riots (a break in the
nonviolent discipline, possibly caused by agents provocateurs) than
it did from any intrinsic weakness in the means of resistance.

That initial week of unified nonviolent resistance and complete denial of political victory to the Russians, and the eight-month life of the very regime which was the motivation for the Russian invasion, are achievements of immense proportions. This is especially so considering that this nonviolent, civilian, resistance capacity was unprepared, and hence probably less effectual and certainly less reliable than if it had been adequately prepared. Had unprepared military struggle against such odds held off the Russians for eight months it would have been hailed as victory even in defeat, with courage and historical significance comparable to Thermopylae.

There have been other cases, such as the struggle in the Ruhr against the French and Belgian occupation in 1923 in which nonviolent resistance was launched as official German government policy. (The situation became mixed with sabotage later with detrimental effects on the German cause.) This case is widely regarded as a complete German defeat. Nevertheless, it led to an end of the occupation, and disastrous economic consequences for France (as well as Germany), and French revulsion against French repression policies toward their former enemies, which is said to have contributed to the unexpected electoral defeat of Poincaré's government in the next election—achievements which Germany was militarily unable even to attempt at the time.

Significant other cases of nonviolent resistance can be classed as nonviolent struggle for national defense. These include the Hungarian struggle against Austria for home rule from 1850 to 1867, and Finland's struggles against Russification, especially 1898-1905. Even the Gandhian struggles in India against British rule are those of an occupied country seeking restoration of independence—surely an international conflict. (Gandhi was far from the first Indian nationalist to advocate or organize nonviolent struggle for independence.) During World War II, Norwegian, Danish, and Dutch resistance against the Nazi occupations and certain other anti-Nazi struggles, including limited efforts to save Jews, produced some modest but significant victories. Some of these actions had the support of, or were even initiated by, governments-in-exile.

A Basis for a Substitute for War?

Generally, nonviolent action and its use for national defense purposes have never even received systematic efforts to develop its capacity, to increase its effectiveness, and to expand the areas of its utility. The nonviolent technique is thus an underdeveloped political technique, probably at the stage comparable to violent group conflict several thousand years ago, hence, nonviolent struggle to date may only have revealed a small fraction of its potential fighting power and effectiveness.

The challenge now is to bring to nonviolent struggle research, analysis, experimentation, planning, preparations and training. This will provide greater knowledge and understanding, facilitate our ability to evaluate it fairly, increase the effectiveness of this technique, and, finally, explore its progressive extension to serious conflict situations where most people have presumed that only military, or other violent, conflict was adequate.

Specifically, the question posed is whether a national defense policy for both small and large countries can be created by the capacity of the civilian population, trained, prepared, knowledgeable, in the wielding of nonviolent struggle, to make impossible the consolidation and maintenance of control by an invading force of a *coup d'etat*. Even cursory examination of strategies for civilian defense lies outside this paper. We note only that they are diverse, and flexible, and always need to be related to the specific situation, and the objectives of the attacker, so as to defeat his specific aims as effectively and efficiently as possible.

The question arises whether such preparations can be perceived as sufficiently effective in order to deter invasions and coups. For the present nuclear powers, an important question is whether a country that has gradually built up its capacity to wage civilian defense by nonviolent struggle, and hence has gradually phased down and dispensed with its military weaponry as unneeded, including its nuclear capacity (the latter either by unilateral action or negotiations), would be likely to be subjected to nuclear threat or attack. (This needs careful attention even though today it is generally the nuclear powers that fear attack, and the non-nuclear powers generally do not expect it.)

In comparing nonviolent struggle with military struggle for defense capacity, the same criteria must be used in evaluating both, in terms of the degree of risk, what is risked, the costs if it comes to an open clash, the nature of failure and success in such a clash, and the possible gains in case of success.

Is it Possible?

This type of policy is called *civilian defense*. It is a direct defense of the society, its principles, people, way of life, chosen institutions, right to maintain or change itself, by action of the civilian population as a whole, and their institutions, using civilian (non-military, nonviolent) means of struggle. It should go without saying that this is not a panacea and diverse other programs are needed to help meet many other needs.

Remarkably, this approach—on a serious level of policy presentation—is only about 15 years old. It has thus far received the most serious attention from people regarded as hard-headed realists, strategists, defense analysts, planners, and military officers, and least serious attention from people who have thought themselves peace minded, liberal, radical and humanitarian. The response is as yet small, but it includes the official research interest and efforts of one nation's Defense Department—Sweden. In that country it has also become a major topic of public discussion. In various countries there are now books and other publications on the subject in several European languages and Japanese. Thus within 15 years, this idea has been transformed from the realm of a "crackpot" notion to a strategic proposal receiving serious thought from most unlikely people.

There are some people who still see this as a romantic conception unassociated with the real and the possible. Yet, there is profound truth contained in what Kenneth Boulding calls "Boulding's First Law"; "That which is, is possible." Nonviolent action exists. It has occurred in human history on a scale, seriousness, and with a degree of success (nothing is ever always successful) which has hitherto been unrealized (despite the noted lack of understanding), even against ruthless tyrants, and (as we observed) has already been used for national defense. Social science research also exists and can be applied to this phenomenon. There is more evidence today that a civilian defense policy is not only possible but if adequately prepared could work more effectively than military means for real defense at this stage of history, than there was in August 1939 (when Dr. Einstein wrote the famous letter to President Roosevelt) that atomic energy could be made into atomic weaponry.

It is popular today to pronounce that war is inevitable because of man's aggressive nature, and hence some conclude that this nonviolent thing is all nonsense. That is not the view of significant writers on aggression. Konrad Lorenz has insisted: "modern war has become an institution and . . . being an institution war can be abolished." Robert Ardrey, no less, has asserted: "We must be nonviolent. Yes, we can do it—but we are going to have to work at it."

Civilian defense is set forth for study and research as a possible functional substitute for war, as a means of abolishing war while providing real defense by nonviolent means against tyrants and aggressors. If it could be made to work at least as well as military means, it would be possible for individual countries, alone or in groups, without waiting on others, to *transarm*—that is, to change over to this defense system. This would be possible (in contrast to disarmament) because if it works civilian defense will maintain or increase defense capacity while making possible abandonment of military means. It would thus by-pass the most serious blockage to disarmament proposals, fear of reduced fighting capacity or an unfavorable relative fighting capacity.

Four Tasks

A vast amount of research, analysis, and problem-oriented investigations is required to examine whether this approach to provide a functional substitute for the military system is indeed a fruitful one, and whether, and if so how, the multitude of difficult problems associated with it can be solved. These problems include such questions as the means of training and preparation, how to handle the transarmament period, ways to meet the particular defense needs of particular countries, and the potential of this policy (compared with violence) in confronting successfully the most extreme and ruthless regimes.

Four tasks now urgently need to be tackled simultaneously to determine whether the approach to the problem of war presented in this paper contains the basis for its solution:

1. A major program of research, analysis, and problem-oriented investigation, involving thousands of scholars of many disciplines, analysts and other specialists. Outlines of some general

research areas which might be tackled have been already proposed, and others are needed. Dozens of research centers and programs will be needed. The equivalent of one percent of the military budget can be used effectively, and this should be a short-term objective in all countries.

2. Public and private discussion and evaluation of this substitute-for-war-policy, the problems it attempts to deal with, existing knowledge relevant to whether it could work, and the difficulties which must be overcome if the policy is to be viable, and its potentialities and possible consequences.

3. Serious investigation and evaluation of this policy by civilian governmental bodies, defense departments, private institutions and groups, organizations, institutions, and individuals.

4. High school, college, university, and general public education courses on the nature of nonviolent action, its potential as an alternative to domestic violence, and on the potential and problems of civilian defense as a substitute for war.

Each of these four tasks will require major financial resources that may sound rather large, but considering the seriousness of our problems, this is a very modest proposal. If the research should reveal this to be a false hope, it would be worth the money and effort to know. But, after all, what if we could develop an effective substitute for war?

Notes

1. This article was originally a paper presented at the meetings of the American Association for the Advancement of Science, Section on Social and Economic Sciences, Dec. 28—29, 1972, "The Future of Collective Violence: Societal and International Perspectives," organized by Joseph D. Ben-Dak, an official session of the American Orthopsychiatric Association, cosponsored by the American Sociological Association and the American Psychological Association. This article is being published as a chapter in Joseph D. Ben-Dak, (Ed.), *The Future of Collective Violence: Societal and International Perspectives*. Lund, Sweden: Studentlitteratur, 1973. The article appears here with kind permission of Joseph Ben-Dak and Studentlitteratur, Magistratsvagen 10, Lund 1, Sweden.

2. However, the view that institutional or systemic changes (with or without accompanying attitude changes) will lead to the abandonment of the military system without specific attention to that task is rejected here. In fact, social changes and social revolution may increase the military system, and popular support for it, because of perceived greater need to defend the changes against counter-revolutionary threats (domestic or foreign), because the society is perceived as more worthy of defense, etc. If violent struggle has produced the social revolution, the relative role of the military system in comparison to civil branches of the government and other institutions is likely to increase. If the struggle was largely nonviolent but with confidence remaining with military means for defense, an increase in the military system is also likely, only to a lesser degree. Almost without exception, those countries that have undergone avowed social revolutions possess stronger military systems than they did under the old order. Therefore, further attention should be given to other means of abolishing war.

This chapter was originally published under the title, "An Examination of the Significance of Domestic Nonviolent Action for Development of a Substitute for International War," in Joseph D. Ben-Dak (Ed.) *The Future of Collective Violence, Societal and International Perspectives,* Lund, Sweden, Studentlitteratur, 1974; and also appears in Gene Sharp, *Social Power and Political Freedom,* Porter Sargent Publishers, Inc., 11 Beacon Street, Boston, Ma. 02108, 1979.

References

Bennet, J. and Tumin, M., *Social Life: Structure and Function*, New York: Knopf, 1948.

Coser, L., *The Functions of Social Conflict*, New York: Free Press, 1956.

Frank, J., "Breaking the Thought Barrier: Psychological Challenges of the Nuclear Age." In Thomas Merton (ed.) *Breakthrough to Peace: Twelve Views on the Threat of Thermonuclear Extermination*, Norfolk, Conn. and New York: New Directions, 1962.

Frank, J. *Sanity and Survival: Psychological Aspects of War and Peace*, New York: Random House, 1968.

Leakey, L. S. B. and Ardrey, R., "Man the Killer" (a dialogue). In *Psychology Today*, 1972, 6, no. 4 (September).

Lorenz, K., *On Aggression*, New York: Harcourt, Brace and Jovanovich, Inc., 1963.

Merton, R. K., *Social Theory and Social Structure*, Glencoe, Ill.: Free Press.

Newcomb, T., *Social Psychology*, New York: Dryden Press, 1950.

Parsons, T., *Essays in Sociological Theory, Pure and Applied*, Glencoe, Ill.: Free Press, 1949.

Parsons, T., *The Social System*, Glencoe, Ill.: Free Press, 1951.

Parsons, T. and Shils, E. A., *Toward a General Theory of Action*, Cambridge, Mass.: Harvard University Press, 1951.

Radcliffe-Brown, A. R., *Structure and Function in Primitive Society*, Glencoe, Ill.: Free Press, 1952.

Roberts, A. (ed.), *Civilian Resistance as a National Defense: Nonviolent Action Against Aggression*, Harrisburg, Pa.: Stackpole Books, 1968.

Sharp, G., *Explaining Nonviolent Alternatives*, Boston: Porter Sargent Publisher, Inc., 1970.

Sharp, G., "The Need of a Functional Substitute for War." In International Relations, London, 1967, *3*, pp. 187—207. Reprint series of the Center for International Affairs, Harvard University.

Sharp, G., "The Political Equivalent of War—Civilian Defense." In *International Conciliation*, 1965, no. 555. New York: Carnegie Endowment for International Peace (Whole number).

Sharp, G., *The Politics of Nonviolent Action*, Boston: Porter Sargent Publisher, Inc., 1973. Prepared under the auspices of the Center for International Affairs, Harvard University.

Chapter 12

Feminism, Peace, and Power

Mary Roodkowsky

> *"Who then will do it? The men are all fighting, and some women, too."*

——Betty Williams,
Nobel Peace laureate,
when asked why women
created the People's Peace
Movement in Ireland.

Fighting, vanquishing, attacking and counterattacking are so-called masculine skills shed of the metaphors of business, sports, and social competition which usually clothe them. War creates heroes, supermen, known by their performance: true men, on whose chest medals and stripes glitter and ribbons flap. Strong men, whose very survival proves brains and brawn. Men-in-charge of their own lives, and with the power and authority to direct and mold the lives of others.

Victory in war derives from comparative advantage—no stronger or wiser for the battle, perhaps poorer than before—the conqueror is defined by his superior position, his lower losses. The loot consists mainly of positional goods, those which can be held only at the expense of others. Use and control over the opponent's natural resources and social status—the ability to determine if and how others will share in those resources.

Because it seems that conflict's only rationale is acquisition of goods or power from another, only those who are enfranchised, or who might hope to be, need involve themselves. No wonder, then, that women neither profit from nor join in wars. The round tables where strategic decisions are made never include women—in fact, women rarely approach them save with memos or coffee for the real decision makers.

While men wage war, women keep house and also the economy. Their perpetual care of the hearth and of the children maintains a social structure and ensures a home where soldiers may return. Women labor in factories and offices, in seats left vacant by men called to the front.

Women also take on new burdens in wartime. They sacrifice butter to churn out guns in factories, they expand their roles as society's washers, nurses, and caretakers, to include the extra destruction created by war. Women make and roll bandages, and then use them to bind wounds they never inflicted. At the war's close they comfort combat tattered psyches, of both sides. Their wartime jobs—and the newly acquired earning power it brought—are preempted by those to whom they really belong, the boys back from the front.

Thus, wars that are fought for goods and position benefit women little. In fact, rather than acquiring goods or position in war, women often *are* the goods, the spoils, acquired by war. Rape has been standard operating procedure during armed conflict, from the Trojan War to the Viet Nam War.[1] In her book *Against Our Will*, Susan Brownmiller suggests that soldiers' abuse of women ranks along with looting, burning and bombing as a means of subduing the enemy. Later, the women become part of the victor's booty:

> The body of a raped woman becomes a ceremonial battlefield, a parade ground for the victor's trooping of the colors. The act that is played out upon her is a message passed between men—vivid proof of victory for one and loss and defeat for the other.[2]

Some of glory's light does shine on women, but indirectly and through their relationships to men, as in so many other areas of life. Army nurses who have bravely cared for wounded men may receive medals, and exceptional female military personnel may also be rewarded for their contributions. But that "glory" comes mostly through their men—the fathers, husbands, sons—"given" to the effort. All women in wartime must sacrifice those men's presence, as well as their contributions to home and family. Later, the ultimate honor consists in welcoming back the womb's fruit like the Spartan woman who will only greet her son with his shield, victorious, or on it, dead. Today's reward consists of a body in a bag, and a yearly appearance in the Memorial Day parade. While triumphant men split the spoils and bask in power, women replace their life's love and the result of their caring work with a Gold Star banner fluttering in the wind. Only one-half of the men in a battle can win, one side must lose; however, no woman, on either side of the battle line, can ever claim victory or its prerogatives.

Women Propose Peace

Given their suffering—in themselves, in the destruction of what is most important to them, in the violation of their bodies—and given that women receive little compensation for what they give, it is not surprising that many peace movements and movements for nonviolent change throughout history have been led by women. A history of such involvement might include the imagery of Euripides' *Lysistrata*, or the way that Pilate's unnamed wife tried to save Christ; it could also tell of Angelina Grimke's impassioned pleas that women work for an end to slavery, without bloodshed; it might discuss Mrs. Rosa Parks' refusal to move to the rear of a bus in Montgomery, Alabama, sparking the civil rights movement; it might document the women's strike for peace during the Viet Nam War years, and describe Betty Williams and Mairead Corrigan and the other women in the Irish People's Peace Movement. It might discuss how the woman's suffrage movement of the 19th and 20th centuries in America deligently overturned law and social order, without violence. Given the deep state of powerlessness of most women and the extra effort it takes for women to work in the organized realms of government, law, and broad scale organization, this record is even more remarkable.

Such facts do not declare that an absolute majority of women openly oppose militarism—although they suggest that implicitly, women do despise it. Virtually all who discuss women's roles, from Mary Daly and Adrienne Rich to Phyllis Schlafly and other ERA opponents, agree that war is men's work. Anti-feminist reactionaries cannot imagine an end to war, and so argue against an Equal Rights Amendment that would require women to take arms. Progressive women work to stop violence, either as reformers who call for women in power structures where their perspective as women will help to prevent wars, or as radicals, like Daly and Rich, who call for new social structures whose repertoire need not include such destruction. The grass-roots of the women's movement took pains to discuss peace and disarmament during the November, 1977 National Women's Convention in Houston. The conference rejected arguments that that plank did not deal with women's issues, which should therefore not concern the gathering, in favor of a feminism whose broad social critique necessarily includes the topic of war.

Winning Over Others

Nonviolence not only opposes war; it also upholds a way of living where conflict creates rather than destroys. Feminism, too, goes beyond its rejection of arms and battle, to suggest and to practice nondestructive patterns of conflict resolution. It is perhaps rooted in women's socialization, or perhaps due to women's economic and political powerlessness, or perhaps because of the common female roles. But whatever its source, feminist understandings of conflict can help to clarify and expand nonviolent theory.

One major aspect of Gandhi's nonviolence embodied a stance of non-injury, or *ahimsa*, to the enemy. Destruction of the opponent merely perpetuates the injustice one tries to overcome. Instead, the goal is to win the opponent over to one's own side. Gandhi wrote:

> We must try patiently to convert our opponents. If we wish to evolve the spirit of democracy out of slavery, we must be scrupulously exact in our dealings with opponents . . . We must concede to our opponents the freedom we claim for ourselves and for which we are fighting.[3]

Ahimsa has been very much a part of women's attitudes, even with respect to the most emotional, basic issues of feminism. For instance, at the national convention sponsored by the State Department, the most volatile issues included abortion rights, the Equal Rights Amendment, and freedom for sexual preference (lesbian rights). All three passed, but not without debate, debate which adhered in various ways to nonviolent principles, of respect for the opponent, and of winning over those with whom one disagrees.

The chairperson of the convention, former congresswoman Bella Abzug, outspoken proponent of abortion rights, gave equal floor time to the opposition, who in turn used that time well and with minimal disruption. And although a counter-conference, insisting that women's place is in the home, was held across town, overt disruption between the two did not occur. Perhaps the atmosphere surrounding the third of the resolutions mentioned above best depicts the spirit of the convention. Lesbian rights are a potentially explosive issue, not in the least because the popular press and anti-feminists delight in characterizing all "women's libbers" as man-hating and gay. Despite such sentiment, the largely heterosexual convention refused to buy into either stereotype, and the lesbian minority, which had refrained from disruption, broke into a song as that resolution passed. Women—both heterosexual and homosexual—were refusing to oppose each other; they knew the credibility of one group need not be bought at the other's expense. Betty Friedan, founder and former president of the National Organization for Women, said that she had learned a new side of sisterhood—that it would have been "immoral, wrong, to sacrifice the civil rights of lesbians to appease the right wing."[4]

Women's response to tough issues at the Houston convention grew from women's roles in the world. Because of socialization from girlhood on, reinforced by the expectations of womanhood, a woman perceives her fate as intimately tied to that of others in a variety of ways—her choices are not always hers alone. A woman has far less decision-making power in the social structures that govern her, whether she lives in the United States, Ireland, Egypt, or India. Likewise, on an individual level, her husband, children, and other family steer her life's course. What happens to these people and to the dominant social structures, affect her with a more conclusive impact than they do a man with more autonomy. Economically, for example, when a woman depends on a man for her sustenance, the political or social factors which increase or decrease his status will likely do the same for her—either directly, when he gets a raise, or indirectly, when a slow economy pushes the "least important" elements out of the work force, as after a war or when labor is costly. He may have alternative choices in his job, and hers depend upon his. Women's relationship to men, for better and usually for worse, is a derivative one. For women as a group this has led to a greater cognizance of the interrelatedness of all humans, with each other and with the earth. Women's relationships to other women likewise recognize such interrelatedness, but on a far more egalitarian basis. Contrary to stereotypes of calculating, competitive women, documentation of women in developing nations and histories of women in Western Civilization demonstrates norms of cooperation, caring and nurture among women.*

For example, female midwives through the Middle Ages often expertly delivered children at minimal cost. When two male doctors introduced the forceps, many midwives scorned them—for their expense, and for the fact that they foresaw an era when less compassionate, more technological childbirth would become the norm. Women in many developing nations sustain informal exchanges of goods and services among themselves, swapping household foods and childcare on a cooperative, nonprofit basis. In contemporary society, wherever neighborhoods still exist and women's communities live despite pressures of urbanization, such bartering still occurs, despite the counter pressures of consumerism.

An adherent of nonviolence cannot injure another, because their fates intertwine. How, then, can women make a policy of winning their needs and more by destroying or subjugating the adversary, when so much of their own well being so clearly depends on the welfare of the adversary.

Not only are women's fates combined with those of their community, but women's roles in society are constructed with a notion

---

*Women do sometimes act aggressively, or destructively against each other. In many cases, as in Chinese mothers binding their daughters' feet, such behavior against self interest can only be explained in the larger context of the standards of male-dominated society.

of responsibility to others and to the physical world—such accountability intrinsically leads to nonviolence.

Women bear the brunt of their own actions more directly than do men. Men's work is supported by others—by those lower on the social ladder, by secretaries and subordinates in the workplace, by women at home. A woman's work, however, receives no such subsidy. She takes final responsibility for the children's and the men's lifestyles and daily physical and material needs, as well as for her own, since there is no one further down the ladder to whom she can shunt the blame or the chores. Cooking dinner, washing laundry, feeding the baby, are all tasks created by the needs of many but only met by the work of one woman. Such "women's work" is not the whole of the females' responsibilities. The world over, women perform not only such womanly chores, but other "male" work as well. In Africa, 80 percent of the farmers are women[5]; in the United States, 48 percent of women work or need work outside the home.[6] Dual workloads complicate women's accountability and burden. A woman doctor in a remote Himalayan mountain area comments that women in her district "work three times as hard as men," for they must do all the things men do, and then care for the family.[7]

Without someone down the line to blame, the unpleasant, ugly fallout of violent action might deter more women from participating in it. The desecration of the earth in strip mining, for example, is encouraged and financed by those not displaced or living near the site, but by corporations in cities. Nuclear power, irresponsibly manufactures energy, allowing others—future generations?—to grapple with the radioactive waste it creates. No one thoroughly socialized in female responsibilities could ever dream such a system.

Feminism, Advocacy, and Nonviolence

Nonviolent action asserts the value and necessity of acting in support of the truth (the *Satyagraha* of Gandhi), that doing for self means also doing for others. The U.S. peace group, Mobilization for Survival, made four demands in 1977, the first three were all injunctions against violence: zero nuclear weapons, ban nuclear power, and stop the arms race; the fourth demand was the advocacy for the justice central to nonviolent action: fund human needs.

The psychology of women supports this policy of non-injury. A woman judges her own worth, and others judge her in terms of how well she serves others. Rather than basing her worth on the domination of others or on comparative strength, the normative criteria have been sacrifice and service.

Such advocacy is in many ways the raison d'être of the traditional female role. Psychoanalyst Jean Baker Miller states:

> In our culture 'serving others' is for losers, it is low-level stuff. Yet serving others is a basic principle around which women's lives are organized; it is far from such for men. In fact, there are psychoanalytic data to suggest that men's lives are psychologically organized *against* such a principle, that there is a potent dynamic at work forcing men *away* from such a goal.[8]

When conflict produces an either/or, have/have-not situation, a woman is apt to opt for the subordinate role. The ideal of service is so firmly inplanted in the consciousness, in letting the other win—tennis, an argument, or a job—that *not* to do so is unfeminine, and therefore attacks the core of the woman's worth. Women's spirituality is beautifully described by the French mystic, Simone Wiel, who states that love is merely attention to the other's needs.

However, in doing such service, we can make another kind of connection between feminism on the one hand, and nonviolence on the other. This ideal of living-for-others not only has avoided overt violence aimed at others by women, its reverse side is the exploitation of that service by men, to hurt women, and women's extreme internalization of that ideal and the negation of their own needs.

Because nonviolence *promotes* action for justice, nothing can be less passive than its "truth-force." For their own sake women need to emphasize this active side far more than the avoidance of violence to others. Many ethics, nonviolent codes included, speak largely to the male psyche: to its aggressive, competitive, against-others nature. Applying ethical principles of self-denial and service to the already self-sacrificing woman can sometimes overwhelm her into increased living-for-others to the point where any living-for-self seems invalid. Jean Baker Miller writes that the unilateral assignation of women to a service role is the source of overwhelming problems for men and women alike, denying to the former (men), their justly due community responsibility, to the latter (women), a necessary and realistic understanding of self-worth.

Gandhi sometimes glorified suffering for the cause of truth. But he, and other nonviolent activists, also stressed the need for non-cooperation with the forces of evil. Angelina Grimke urged her Christian sisters to throw away their submissive behavior in order to work to end slavery. Peace activist, Dorothy Day, illegally asserted herself against nuclear armaments, and for the United Farm Workers' union struggle. Women can apply this principle of non-cooperation to their oppression, and to those who hurt them. Nonviolence never assents to the demands of the oppressors, even though it may cause anger or resentment. It strips the oppressors of authority to which they are not entitled, at the same time ascertaining that all enjoy what they rightfully own.

Feminist and nonviolent activist, Barbara Deming, connects feminism with nonviolent cooperation in application of *ahimsa* to both the other and the self:

> We act out respect for ourselves by refusing to cooperate with those who oppress or exploit us. And as their power never resides in their single selves, always depends upon the cooperation of others—by refusing that cooperation . . . refusing our labor, our wits, our money, our blood upon their battlefields, our deference, we take their power away from them.[9]

Our actions bear upon ourselves as well as on others. Injuring others means injuring ourselves—our capacity to love, to care, to create and learn. And this dynamic works in reverse: to respect ourselves will mean to respect others, to *expect* them to respect, learn, and create in return. Feminism has set in motion a process by which women—in caring, nonviolent ways—are learning to respect themselves, value their own work, and to evoke, expect, and demand that respect from others. In this way, another dichotomy—that between oppressor and oppressed, powerful and powerless—dissolves.

For women, such non-cooperation with the degradation of sexism and the self-hatred it brings is nonviolent to others and to self. Doubtless, non-cooperation with sexist structures—refusal to make coffee; criticism of policies made by men with high-ego involvement in their work; insisting on equal wages; or going to school—will be threatening to men, who will then accuse women of being angry and even violent. Affirmative action in the U.S.A., for example, is really such non-cooperation with the male WASP workworld. Yet, if women are not to continue to judge themselves with violence, non-cooperation is essential.

Using Power Creatively

At their cores, both feminism and nonviolence perceive power differently from male-centered ideology and are alien to the reality principle that directs our world and which encourages violent struggles for position.

Power, as the dominant ideology understands it, cannot co-exist with love or caring—it is an imposition over others, rather than a force to help us compose, or create, together.

Those who know that only one side can be victorious in war can well understand the corollary of this truism: that any concept of a loving or interdependent ethic must mean a relinquishing of social and positional goods and therefore, powerlessness. Power so conceptualized cannot be used for the general good of the society—only for the aggrandizement of an individual or state—hence, a state of war. Feminist philosopher, Mary Daly, suggests that this split degrades humanity: "Power split off from love makes an obscenity out of what we call love, forcing us unwillingly to destroy ourselves and each other."[10]

Feminists and advocates of nonviolence live by the contrary force, the power of love, which compels us to *ahimsa*. Learning to use our human energies as a loving force is the process of *empowerment*—a process which enables us to act critically and creatively to end injustice, not accept it. Empowerment comes both from the community—in the consciousness-raising group or the affinity group—and in the individual's new reconceptualizing of his/her own loving capabilities.

For poet and feminist, Adrienne Rich, motherhood dissolves many dichotomies between power and powerlessness. While a mother has ultimate power over responsibility for and control over her baby, since the baby depends on the mother for all sustenance and warmth, the baby also controls the mother—her psyche and her body, as in the flow of milk from her breasts. Rich writes of the sense of confused power and powerlessness, of being taken over in the one hand and of touching new physical and psychic potentialities in the other, a heightened sensibility which can be exhilerating, bewildering, and exhausting. For Rich, motherhood dramatizes the interactions of "exclusive" opposites, impresses upon us, for example, that "love and anger can exist concurrently."[11]

The women's health care movement generally, and feminist attitudes toward both specifically, understand the concurrence of power and powerlessness and use it as a principle in developing nonviolent attitudes toward the body. The women's health care movement seeks to change the physical alienation affecting women, replacing a variety of attitudes that deny the body's goodness and fear of its functions. Rather than labelling menstruation "the curse," women are learning to accept and celebrate their cyclical rhythms. Instead of birth control pills which, although "sure," chemically dominate and sometimes injure the body, women are turning to methods that are perhaps more limited but far safer.

The movement toward home births, and toward "childbirth without violence" integrates many principles of nonviolence in the relationships involved in childbirth. Modern technological obstetrics sterilizes, shaves, and generally obfuscates the nature of childbirth, dehumanizing the most profound of human experiences. Mothers become passive observers, while their bodies become objects. Babies likewise are objectified, not considered to be people affected by their environment. The goal of such obstetrics is, of course, total control through the domination of the doctor. The entire birth experience is subject to manipulation—its labor and its pain, but also its passion, creativity and satisfaction. Home births have developed an alternative to this, where midwife, mother, child, father, and others all participate and cooperate with natural forces. The benefits of such non-injury to mother and child alike include physically healthy birth without drugs, less birth trauma for the baby, early development of emotional ties between mother, father, and baby. Beyond these, new attitudes toward birth signify the development of supportive and less destructive attitudes toward our bodies, and to the natural environment generally.

Feminism and Nonviolence as Creativity

New thinking by women shedding old oppressive roles, yet retaining the real joys of womanness, can become one of the most creative political forces society has ever known. Women, like all oppressed groups, have had to know well, and bargain with, the structures which hurt them. Feminism has helped to evoke new social understandings based on women's experience and sisterhood. Many of these are implicitly grounded in nonviolence. Sisterhood implies democracy, for the needs and points of view are all-important in community. Women's responsibility provides a rationale for self-reliance and an end to exploitation.

Perhaps, as men take on new roles which encourage human values, nonviolence will seem more realistic to them too. Those who care for children and who understand their value as derived from caring, will be less willing to kill. Environmental accountability will be encouraged when men take more responsibility for their day-to-day actions, and deal more closely with the consequences. Competition may lose some of its importance to those with other priorities.

Life is not a zero-sum game, where some *must* win at the others' expense. Violence and sexism in their many forms destroy our bonds with each other and our standing on the earth. They are ideologies which deny the ways in which we need each other and our natural order, and attempt to do what cannot be done: discard human needs and emotions and the natural workings of the earth. Theologian, Rosemary Ruether, knows that a new social, non-hierarchical order is the only way to survival:

> Such solidarity is not utopian, but eminently practical, pointing to our actual solidarity with all others and with our mother, the earth, which is the actual ground of our being.[12]

Many parallels exist between nonviolence and feminism. Each hopes and struggles to encourage cooperation and discourage competition; to create community and sisterhood and discard isolation; to make crippling social structures obsolete and reconstruct them in a non-hierarchical way. Together, the two can appreciate each other's value and strengthen each other's strategies, for a new world order needs them both in order to bring peace to all people.

Notes

1. Conversation with author, Boston, Mass., May 18, 1977.
2. Susan Brownmiller, *Against Our Will*, Simon & Schuster, New York, 1976, p. 31.
3. M. K. Gandhi, *Non-Violent Resistance*, Schocken, New York, 1962, p. 142.
4. Betty Friedan, "The Women at Houston," *The New Republic*, Dec. 10, 1977, p. 18.
5. Ester Boserup, *Woman's Role in Economic Development*, St. Martins Press, New York, 1970, p. 22.
6. New York Times, September 12, 1976.
7. Conversation with Doctor Dolma Tsering, Srinagar, Kashmir, India, August 2, 1977. Dr. Tsering believes that one solution to area's development problems is that the men must help the women in their chores.
8. Jean Baker Miller, *Toward a New Psychology of Women*, Beacon, Boston, 1976, p. 60.
9. Barbara Deming, *We Cannot Live Without Our Lives*, Grassman Pub., New York, 1974, p. 9.
10. Mary Daly, *Beyond God the Father*, Beacon, Boston, 1973, p. 127.
11. Adrienne Rich, *Of Woman Born*, New York, Norton, 1976, p. 52.
12. Rosemary Reuther, *New Woman, New Earth*, Seabury, New York, 1975, p. 211.

Chapter 13

Theater for the Living Revolution

Louise Bruyn

Introduction

For some years now I have been interested in the connection between theater and social change. I used to see theater as an egocentric art—it was the star system, the promise of riches if one "made it," the "big time," personal success or personal failure, "Broadway." Theater meant lights and makeup, "getting a part," and hearing applause. It meant being someone in a special way. Gradually I began to see the deeper meanings of theater, the way it is a channel of communication, a method of transmitting meaning, the way it is itself symbolic of life and death through the raising and lowering of the curtain.

I have been intrigued by the two meanings of the verb "to act." Why is the same word used to refer to both that which is symbolic and that which is real? Webster defines one meaning "to perform on the stage; as, to act in a play; hence, to behave as if acting a part." And in the second meaning he defines "to act": "to exert one's powers in a way to bring about an effect." Perhaps at the core the first meaning includes the second. "To exert one's powers to bring about an effect." How basic this definition is to social change. For change cannot come about without people exerting their powers. It is not enough to think about how change should come or whether change should come. It is necessary "to act" in order to have an effect.

By acting symbolically, one can encourage action in reality. The theater is not just a mirror of the world—it has a holy obligation, and in those moments after the ritual curtain has lifted there is a special time of communion between the actor and the audience. It is a time to pass on hope, possibilities, truths, energy. It is a time of renewing, intensifying, clarifying life, relationships, responsibilities, and community.

But if we take on these weighty tasks, it is important to know our direction. Which way do we want to move? If we talk about social change, what kind of change do we want? What process might we follow? How does theater relate to these goals and processes?

In this paper I want to say something about the role of theater in the nonviolent revolution. I believe that theater and the arts will be taking an increasingly important role in helping to bring about social change in the decades ahead.

The Goals and Concepts of Nonviolence

I believe that a fundamental goal of nonviolent action is liberation of all people, liberation from all that oppresses them. John Swomley puts these goals succinctly:

> Liberation . . . implies a quality of life that asserts the importance and worth of persons in such a way that they are free from poverty, from control by more powerful interests, from superstition, fear, hostility, or from anything that enslaves them.[1]

But liberation cannot exist without order. In the arts, freedom is achieved when one learns the discipline of the medium. The artist must control the brush, the musician the instrument, and the dancer the body. Not until then can the artist be liberated to express the nuance, the tone, the line. In a social order, freedom is achieved when one learns the discipline of living in a caring relationship with others. The discipline involves being as concerned for the welfare of others as one is concerned for the welfare of oneself.

Liberation as a quality of life is different than liberation as an act that happens once and then is accomplished. It resembles more the idea of the "continuing revolution." Liberation is both a goal and a process. It should be consistent in its means and ends.

Utpal Dutt, director of political theater in Calcutta, India, has argued for a revolutionary theater which "preaches violent methods of overthrowing the present setup."[2] His hope is to achieve a people's democratic revolution by "violent smashing of the state machine."[3] He admits that is considered "left wing adventurism" but he claims that this is the kind of heroism that India needs today.[4]

The problem is that Dutt is equating nonviolence and passivity. If passivity were the only alternative to violence, then perhaps we could agree with him on the necessity for bearing arms. Gandhi himself agreed that it is better to fight than to be a coward. He said once to Richard Gregg, "If you have a sword in your bosom, take it out and use it like a man."* Gregg elaborates on this theme by writing the following:

> Courageous violence, to try to prevent or stop a wrong, is better than cowardly acquiescence. Cowardice is more harmful morally than violence. The inner attitude is more important than the outer act, though it is vitally important always to be true to oneself, to make one's outer conduct a true reflection and expression of one's inner state. Fear develops out of an assumption of relative weakness. Since all men have the innate possibility of moral strength, to be afraid is really a denial of one's moral potential powers and is therefore very harmful. Violence and anger at least show faith in one's own moral powers and thus provide at least a basis for further growth. He who refrains from fighting because he is afraid, really hates his opponent in his heart and wishes that circumstances would change so that he could hurt or destroy his opponent. The energy of his hate is present but suppressed. If one lacks the discipline or conviction to resist wrong or violence without counter-violence, then I agree with Gandhi that it is better to be violent than to be cowardly.[5]

If we accept liberation of all people as a goal of social change we must become aware of the many levels of enslavement or oppression of people. People can be enslaved by their feelings, by habits, by systems such as war and racism, and by the economy.

---

*Editor's note: The language imagery used by nonviolent activists and leaders unfortunately has not always been sensitive to the oppression of sexism.

The range of oppression extends from their private, personal lives to their public, corporate lives.

Swomley adds another element to his definition of liberation which I think is essential:

> Yet liberation is an impossible goal so long as men (people) seek freedom for their own group at the expense of others. The truth evident in the fact of thermonuclear weapons and in the growing worldwide air, land, and water pollution is that we are all under the ax. All of us are likely to be doomed or saved together.[6]

This means that in the process of defining a strategy, we must look for methods that emphasize our commonality. We must not see people as our enemies, but see that the enemy is composed of systems, of which war is one, racism another, capitalism another. Formulating a strategy to combat or transform these systems means dealing with specific situations. To say one wants to bring about the liberation of people by nonviolence is as meaningless as it would be to say one wants to bring about liberation by violence. It does not tell us what to *do*. We need a strategy that suggests specific actions.

Since systems can enslave people, it is necessary to turn one's attention to changing those systems rather than placing "good men and women" in positions of power in the existing systems. Lately, we have heard much of the violence of systems, as well as individual violence. How do we deal with that violence? Do we ask ourselves to overthrow our oppressor through the use of violence? Do we turn the tables, putting the one on top who had been on the bottom? What kind of discipline must we expect of ourselves in order for us to achieve and maintain our liberation?

The answers to the following questions will tell us the extent to which nonviolent action is achieving its goals:

1. Does it lead to shared power?
2. Does it lead to sharing resources and opportunities?
3. Does it lead to simplicity?

The desegregation of public schools by busing is an example of an issue which has aroused the threat of civil disobedience by those who feel aggrieved. Civil disobedience is considered a non-violent action. One then must ask the question, "Does the action (Civil disobedience) lead to shared power? Does it lead to shared resources and opportunities?" Disobedience of the busing order does not lead to sharing of resources or opportunity. Busing is aimed at sharing those elements. Yet part of the strong reaction of the parents is due to a sense of powerlessness. The decision which affects their lives is handed down from a higher authority, power is taken away from the local neighborhood. However, this is done in order for power to be shared among a larger group, a group that includes blacks. Based on this view, it is in the interests of everyone that interracial busing be promoted.

Another criterion involves simplicity. Schumacher speaks of the relationship between simplicity and nonviolence.

> Simplicity and non-violence are obviously closely related. The optimal pattern of consumption, producing a high degree of human satisfaction by means of a relatively low rate of consumption, allows people to live without great pressure and strain and to fulfill the primary injunction of Buddhist teaching: "Cease to do evil; try to do good." As physical resources are everywhere limited, people satisfying their needs by means of a modest use of resources are obviously less likely to be at each other's throats than people depending upon a high rate of use. Equally, people who live in highly self-sufficient local communities are less likely to get involved in large-scale violence than people whose existence depends on world-wide systems of trade.[7]

His concept of simplicity involves self-sufficiency and modest use of resources. Busing does not lead to that; it makes life more complex. Motor vehicles must be used to take children to school instead of their walking. It would be simpler to attend neighborhood schools, and in terms of immediate simplicity, busing is not an ideal solution. But when looked at in the larger picture, busing is simpler in achieving racial integration than is moving families into integrated neighborhoods. The larger injustice is the de facto segregation which perpetuates the racial fear and the bigotry patterns. Busing is an attempt to break through that. It is a creative solution; no other method to break down segregation has been found that will do the job. Therefore, opposing the busing order does not lead toward liberation through nonviolence.

Jonathan Kozol has this to say about the possible use of civil disobedience by Boston parents against busing:

> We're seeing today not civil disobedience in its classic sense—moral action taken by choice, driven by love, devoid of fear—but mob terror and decades of miseducation, stirred by demagogues, preplanned by those who feed on hate . . .[8]

Howard Zinn states, "If racial segregation is wrong, then disobedience in support of racial segregation is wrong."[9] George Wald, noted Nobel Peace Prize recipient, has affirmed that defiance of the law is only justified when the cause is just.

In terms of types of protest, civil disobedience that has an absence of overt violence is far preferable to violent rioting or murder. One may not agree with the goals, but one can certainly accept the methods.

Nonviolent action has been viewed from different perspectives. It can be simply a technique without any reference to principles or ethics; it can be viewed as a method based on principles; and it can be conceived as a complete life style. A person might *live* "nonviolence." The latter perspective is the closest to Gandhi's. If one is living "nonviolence" then one is concerned with all personal relations, all use of resources, all involvement in institutions in whatever society a person lives. Each action, including diet, is scrutinized by the "satyagrahi" so that it conforms to basic beliefs about truth and love and respect for life. It is this form which is so deeply spiritual and enriching. The spirit of a person embarked on this path cannot help but grow. Perhaps because this form seems too distant from our western, materialist life, people react with a sense of defeatism if they think of themselves needing to be so totally devoted. If people think that this total approach is necessary in order to use nonviolent protest, noncooperation, or intervention, they could never bring themselves to engage in it. For this reason Gene Sharp's arguments that nonviolent action can take place without reference to moral or ethical principles has merit. One does not have to live the life of a satyagrahi in order to take nonviolent action,[10] but it helps.

It is a long way from the pragmatism of nonviolent action to the living of satyagraha of Gandhi. The former calculates the risks, measures the successes, estimates the cost-benefit so to speak. The latter accepts suffering as part of the search for Truth and lives in a spirit of love. However both ways, and all the gradations in between, are on the same side of the chasm that divides the nonviolent method from the method of retaliationg against injustice through further violence.

With these basic concepts in mind, let us now look at the strategies outlined by George Lakey that he sees as necessary stages in the nonviolent revolution and see where theater fits into those categories.

Future Strategies for the Nonviolent Revolution: Theater in Action

George Lakey, in his book, *Strategy for a Living Revolution*, outlines five stages necessary for the nonviolent revolution. They are (1) Cultural Preparation, (2) Organization, (3) Propaganda of the Deed (or symbolic, dramatic action), (4) Political and Economic Noncooperation, and finally, (5) Parallel Institutions.

Stage 1: Cultural Preparation

The first stage involves "raising consciousness," or education. People must become aware of themselves as being oppressed and aware of those people and powers most responsible for the oppression. It is necessary for people to regard themselves as having worth in order to engage in struggle, whether violent or nonviolent. This first stage is the development of self-respect, and at the same time, a feeling of oneness with all people, with all nature.

This is the level at which so much has been done in theater. Black theater, Chicano theater, Woman's theater, Gay theater—each area of oppression has been illuminated by those against whom the repression is perpetrated. Through the medium of theater, feelings once thought to be private come to the surface and people say, "Aha, others have had this experience, it is not just my individual problem." They become aware of the social framework that surrounds those feelings. Through theater, alternatives can be suggested, analyses can be offered.

To the extent that theater explores cultural roots it adds to Cultural Preparation. Awareness of one's cultural heritage adds to one's sense of dignity and therefore to an unwillingness to endure degradation. Singing songs, performing dances, reviving myths all add to the sense of solidarity among people and give them the strength to continue the battle for rights, perhaps just the battle for life itself. Maxine Klein writes of Indian theater in Guatemala:

> The Indian theatre—the fountainhead of all Guatemalan the-atre—lives in its place of birth, in the streets and on the church steps of villages scattered throughout the highlands. This still primitive theatre is a theatre of dance, of mask, of ritual, and of magic. . . . This indigenous theatre, moreover, is a theatre of direct social involvement—an involvement rendered possible by the fact that it exists not for profit or even for art's sake, but for people's sake. For in a country which denies the Indians pride, theatre is their pride. In a country which starves them to death in a bloodless genocide, theatre is their recognition of individual and collective worth. In a country which works them to an early death, theatre is extra life.[11]

Maxine Klein suggests that the Indians in Guatemala may not have long to enjoy their theater, that the pressure put upon the Indians to abandon their old ways and join the move toward industrialization, or to extermination by the ruling class, does not leave them much time. It is not the same as revolutionary theater but it is close—it maintains their identity as a people and therefore makes it more difficult for other groups to oppress them.

Carol Benglesdorf traveled in Cuba as part of a theater group. The Escambray Theatre Group, as they called themselves, trav-eled into little villages of 20-40 families and would remain in each village for about 15 days. They would establish certain links be-tween the population and themselves. Upon arrival the group went to the village school where they would make contact with the children, teaching them skills concerning puppet plays; sub-sequently, they were often invited into the homes of the children. When they were not involved in the production of plays they worked in the fields or in the dairies, alongside the villagers, in an effort to understand the villagers better. The Group then in-vited them to attend their performances.

One of the techniques they used in presenting a play was leav-ing the ending open; the play was stopped before the conclusion and the people would discuss what endings might be appropriate. In the process, the villagers learned more about their own atti-tudes. The following is an example:

The play shows the problem of individual responsibility in the
person of a young soldier who has to make the choice of whether
to be in the group that executes the bandits. The first part of
the play depicts the hunting of the bandits, which is easy for the
young soldier. But in the second part of the play, he can't make
up his mind to shoot the bandit in cold blood. Then the two
bandits fight among themselves and the young soldier listens to
them discuss all that they have done against the Revolution.
Then the play ends. Then there is a discussion and the audience
is asked, What would you do? Could you make the decision to
execute, as is required in a revolutionary situation? How they
react depends on their own conscience, but the dilemma of the
young soldier occurs for those who don't hate the enemy
enough.[12]

By presenting the dilemma in this way, alternatives were open
for dealing with the problem. However, it would seem from this
example that the actors felt that hating the enemy was a good
thing. The Revolution "requires" it. I believe this is a fallacy in
the violent revolution. But whether one believes one should hate
the enemy or transform the enemy, this method of presenting
the dilemma in play form is excellent. It allows people to explore
the attitudes they have concerning human life and, in this example, the process of the Revolution.

Theater can be used consciously to educate people to care for
their needs. Barney Simon experimented in South Africa with
the creation of a show based on health information. The troupe
traveled to many outlying districts in Zululand. Their songs and
dances imparted simple rules for good health and child care, and
because the people knew the forms of the songs, they were able
to quickly learn the chants and songs which required that they
repeat information given by the leader. The performers varied
the program with skits and dances. The traveling show was both
popular and educational.

The performers were not actors as such but were nurses and
health care people; their own knowledge of dance and song was
called upon. Besides benefitting the communities, there was a
benefit to the performers. These nurses felt a value placed on
them through helping to formulate the show which they had not
felt before in their work with white doctors in the mission hospital. By bringing them into the creation of the theater piece, the
communities benefitted in better health information arising out

of the nurses' special knowledge of community needs, and the nurses benefitted in self-confidence by being given the responsibility for this project.

Stage 2: Organization

Lakey's second stage, Organization, is one in which people realize that they are not alone in the condition of oppression and therefore, make alliances with others. They are now aware of themselves as part of a group. The group may be based on race, sex, class, belief, or status. Whatever the category, the members of the group desire equality with other groups; they give up the individual route to honor and dignity in favor of group mobilization.

There are several ways of looking at organizing for the "revolution." One is to see how theater can be used to organize communities so that people can better articulate their own problems; another is to see how theater itself can be organized to gain greater strength for the task at hand.

Using Theater to Organize Communities. A group that has tried to pay attention to the "tactical and strategic considerations in using theater as a tool for community building and organizing" is the Quaker Project on Community Conflict in New York City. They have devised a training program to "use street theatre and puppet shows as tools to enable aggrieved groups to dramatize their grievances and help to bring about needed changes nonviolently." They cite four goals of this program:

1. To place in the hands of aggrieved groups the powerful tool of the dramatic art as a means for the nonviolent education of authorities and the general public on the sufferings and needs of the aggrieved groups.

2. To establish a model for training members of such groups to present in public places short dramatic skits which will have a persuasive impact on viewers and to follow these up with discussions and leaflets designed to further persuade viewers and to encourage them to organize and take other action to get grievances redressed.

3. To spread this model of training and organizing both region-
ally and nationally by training groups in different places to
perform this type of theatre and to train others to do so.
Printed manuals and instructive videotapes will also be distributed to interested groups.

4. To interest people concerned with conventional theatre to become involved in this type of street theatre and to contribute
their talents and know-how to its improvement.[13]

They recognize the way in which theater can "strike home on
a very deep conscious and subconscious level with messages which
can alter people's images of values, traditions, institutions and
norms."

The Quaker Project states ten areas that require transformation:

1. Personal relations.

2. Group activities.

3. Economic institutions, including production, distribution,
housing, labor/management relations, financing and the profit
motive.

4. Political institutions, including the executive, legislative and
judicial branches of government and taxation. This also includes changes in the law, penal system and police.

5. International institutions, including the abolition of war.

6. Educational institutions.

7. Health care institutions.

8. Transportation and communications institutions.

9. Science and technology.

10. Ecology.[14]

A way of integrating theater into the fabric of an organization
has been practiced by the Mobilization for Survival since its in-
ception. The Mobilization for Survival is a coalition of groups and
individuals, formed in 1977, to work toward four goals stated as

follows: Zero Nuclear Weapons, Ban Nuclear Power, Stop the Arms Race, and Meet Human Needs. From the very beginning, organizers within the coalition have been conscious of the special role theater and the arts would play in the achievement of those goals. In the Boston area, the Arts Committee has met regularly to both reach out to artists with informational materials as well as to try to make it more possible for artists to use their talents to further the four goals. The meetings have drawn poets, dancers, actors, musicians, sculptors and graphic artists into active participation. The participation has varied from the creation of a short theater-music piece performed at a teach-in/community forum to a "die-in" on the sidewalks of Boston—a protest against the neutron bomb. The committee has helped locate artists who would perform at community meetings. Artists have designed posters and flyers and created masks for processions. In conjunction with the Fundraising Committee, the Arts Committee considers part of its function to be arranging for benefit performances by performing artists and theater groups. Similar committees exist in other areas where the Mobilization has been organizing.

Organizing Theater Transnationally and Nationally.   Lakey talks of transnational organizing that is already going on among scientists, artists and writers, religious workers, and students. This organizing is also going on among theater people.

The Second Third World Theatre Conference held in Shiraz, Iran, in 1973 testifies to the importance attributed to theater in developing the awareness of a group and also of developing a sense of dignity. The main topic of the conference was "Third World theatre as a creative force for education and social development." It was attended by delegates and observers from thirty participating countries.

The First Third World Conference, held in Manila in 1971, adopted the following resolution:

> In order to fulfill its essential function in the cultural life of society, theatre must aim at becoming an instrument of social change and progress. Thus, it should develop ways and means to bring its performances to popular audiences in both urban and rural communities and should endeavor to give expression in its artistic work to the needs and aspirations of these popular audiences.[15]

The pieces performed at the conference were totally traditional in character. This is in line with the previously expressed idea that in order to throw off the oppressive rule of another people, the aggrieved group must have a sense of its own worth in terms of its own culture.

In terms of organizing related to the Third World Conference, it was agreed that the next step would be the organizing of workshops in the different participating countries. They would be focussed on the concrete tasks of training teachers in theatre and on the preservation of cultural traditions. Following that step would come multinational workshops and the crossfertilization of experience.

An example of organizing at the national level is the Chicano Theater Festival in San Jose, in 1973. Twenty five separate groups participated. Most of the *teatros* were from California but Chicago, Colorado Springs, and Ann Arbor were also represented. Some of the troupes ordinarily play to urban audiences, some to suburban, some to college students and some to fieldworkers.

An important aspect of the festival was the kind of self-criticism that participants engaged in. Performances were given at night. Critiques of those performances written by other groups were submitted the following day and discussed. Those groups were then criticized by others after their performances. It would seem that it would be extremely important to organize theater in such a way that everybody learns the most possible from the experience. In order to learn one must be open to criticism and yet be able to make critical judgments of one's own, as well as others' work. This theme comes through in this short statement that preceded one of the plays that was given:

> This play deals with us, and with the many times we criticize other people and organizations, but fail individually to look at ourselves so that we may see if we are coming from the best direction we are able. In other words, are we just as wrong, through our ignorance, as the people we criticize. We must all remember that before social change is a possibility, individuals must be transformed and this necessitates a personal change.[16]

The purpose of organizing theater would be to learn better from one another. If all can hold to a common purpose, much can be gained from helping one another examine our works in relation to this purpose in order to see if we are, in fact, moving toward that goal. The following criticism of a play called *Moloch*, performed at the Chicano Theater Festival, is an example of holding productions up to a measure.

> Since the performers were university students, it was reasonable to expect some sophisticated analysis from them even if they had no theatre experience. What are they creating for? "Art for art's sake" is useless. You are workers of the culture, not priests. The workings of society are no mystery. The class struggle can be dramatized in many different ways, but it must not be obscured. Which class are you dealing with? Are you supporters of the productive class or the oppressors? From whose point of view do you perform? If the audience does not understand your work, forget it. It is the people that you are doing theatre for. There was no special impulse visible in this play; you were trying to be 'above' politics. Now there's nothing wrong with using abstract figures, but their actions must be made concrete. But where is the oppression? Who is the oppressor? Who is the victim? All this is not clear in *Moloch*.[17]

If our measures of a nonviolent and liberated society are based on truth, simplicity, sharing of resources, opportunity and power, then theater pieces could be held up to that measure to see if they reflected these basic tenets. Bringing together theater groups that were trying to affect social change in these directions would inspire them to greater performance and clarity. This would be a way in which organizing within the theater community could further the nonviolent revolution.

Stage 3: Propaganda of the Deed

Lakey's third stage is what he calls the Propaganda of the Deed. This is the stage where symbolic action is taken. It is not enough to talk about ideas or alternatives, they must at some point become acted upon. "In the drama of action and counter-action the people can see more clearly the brutality of the old order and the virility of the new."[18]

At this level, the deeds themselves become drama. There is an element of theater in them. They become events which are watched by others, either by people who are directly at the scene of action or by those who are informed about them through the media. The action involves a challenge to the status quo—a conflict is set up between the demands of the oppressed or aggrieved and the laws of those in power.

Such a case was the sailing of the Phoenix in 1967. It carried medical supplies to Haiphong for the Democratic Republic of Viet Nam in violation of the United States "trading with the enemy" law. The venture sparked the imagination of thousands as a direct way to confront the United States government over a war which few wanted. The United States government and the South Vietnamese government were put in a position of refusing medical supplies to a people, a negative position to be in, or else of allowing the boat to get through and provide help to the North Vietnamese.

Another example was the attempt to draw attention to chemical warfare. The campaigners tried to plant a pine tree, "a symbol of the American colonial struggle as well as life and ecological sanity,"[19] at Edgewood Arsenal, a chemical weapons factory in Maryland. The commandant refused permission to plant the tree on the arsenal grounds. "In the course of the confrontations twenty-nine demonstrators and several pine trees were arrested."[20] Finally, after a week of embarrassing media coverage, the commander of the Arsenal told the press, "We'll accept the tree as a tree." Here the action was staged not just because the demonstrators wanted to plant a tree on the Arsenal grounds, but because they wanted an audience, the public, to be aware of the existence of chemical warfare. By comparing it with the life symbolized in the tree, a dramatic point was scored. It was a dilemma situation in which, either way the officials acted, the point would be made.

In speaking of actions that present a dilemma situation, Lakey says

> Since the heart of the dynamic is in the contrast, it makes sense to increase that contrast by initiating the encounter with nonviolent action. Nonviolent struggle is so clearly consistent with the goals of the revolution that the movement using them is likely to achieve not only most of the support which the guerrillas gain but also the support of elements which remain uncommitted in a violent struggle.[21]

During the summer of 1974 a number of people from all over

the Eastern seaboard took part in a vigil and fast on the steps of Congress to draw attention to the civilian detainees in South Viet Nam and the continuing war in Viet Nam and Cambodia. A simulation of a "tiger cage" (a cement cell used on Con Son Island) was erected daily at the top of the stairs, and demonstrators took turns sitting in it, shackled to an iron bar, while other passed out leaflets or lobbied. The fact that people were sitting in the cage brought the demonstration to the level of theater. Onlookers' reactions ran the gamut of feeling, from deep concern for the prisoners to disdain at the method used to publicize the problem. Some were angered to think that people were "acting as if" they were prisoners. Yet those people in the cages were specifically trying to use the time only to identify with the condition of the prisoners, not to "act as if" they were the prisoners—a fine distinction, but one necessary in order to maintain integrity. Children were the first to ask, "Are those people *really* prisoners?" It was explained to all that the action was symbolic. The presence of the tiger cage created a forum in which the problem of United States aid to Indochina could be discussed.

Lakey's examples go beyond those actions seemingly staged for their propaganda value, to those in which direct confrontation takes place in order to change a law or injustice. He mentions the case of Amritsar in India, in 1919, when a crowd of 20,000 had gathered to protest Gandhi's arrest. The British military officer, with fifty troops, machinegunned the crowd and left 1200 dead and 3600 wounded. Though the results of that demonstration had not been planned, the violence that was unleashed became a factor in triggering a nationwide campaign of noncooperation against the British government. The dilemma created by the demonstration can cause the authorities to reveal their most brutal side, and thereby give strength to the movement.

While this action was dramatic, I cannot consider it an example of theater. The concept of theater suggests a willful staging of an event and a sense of responsibility for the outcome of the "script." It would have been a most callous manipulation of the participants if the organizers of the demonstration had known that officers would shoot into the crowd and had not so informed the demonstrators. To inform people that violence or arrest is expected is essential in organizing. It is then the responsibility of the demonstrators to judge for themselves whether they want to join the action.

The organizers, to the extent that they are able, and to the extent that they believe in nonviolence, must help prepare those who will join the action to use nonviolent methods of dealing with the expected violence. This leads us to another way in which theater relates to the Propaganda of the Deed. It can be used to role play in preparation for an action. If nonviolence is to be adhered to as a principle, people need to practice nonviolent responses, since many of our responses are conditioned by our "John Wayne culture"—the smart retort, the recourse to physical attack.

During the Montgomery, Alabama, bus boycott, role playing was a device that was used to help train people for the battle to come.

> Dr. King and the other leaders explained the philosophy and methods of the movement night after night. It was a combination of Jesus' ethic of love and Gandhi's nonviolent resistance. Dr. King explained in great detail its effectiveness and applications, emphasizing the essential importance of love and nonviolence, no matter under what provocation. To make the method more vivid, they acted out possible situations where violence might be used against them, and how to behave under such circumstances.[22]

The testing of responses can be a very important part of the effectiveness of an action. Training sessions can submit a person to the indignities of name-calling, of verbal threats, of physical threat by a person or group such as hecklers, extremists or police. A person can try out new responses through acting them out in a group. Because of this prior training, those demonstrating for equal rights in the South were able to withstand cigarette burns, hosing, and beatings without giving in to their violent responses. Theater, then, can act as a trial run before action is initiated in order to explore emotional and physical possibilities.

There is still another way in which theater can be effective during the Propaganda of the Deed stage. It can lift the spirits of those who are engaged in an action, and keep their morale high to encourage a successful conclusion of the action. During a sit-in at the Federal Building in Boston, a theater group performed their skits for those who were blocking the entrance. It had the effect of "entertaining the troops," a device commonly used by the military. In California, Luis Valdez first organized El

Teatro Campesino in 1965 to play in the fields for the *huelgistas* (strikers) of the United Farm Workers in support of the strikes and boycotts against table grapes and lettuce. At a demonstration, a theater group can also help interpret the action to onlookers.

The Propaganda of the Deed stage exposes the violence of the system. It becomes clear that all is not well when blacks are hosed down, when Indians are massacred, when innocent college students are shot. A mass base has then been prepared for the fourth stage of nonviolent revolution which is that of Political and Economic Noncooperation.

Stage 4: Political and Economic Noncooperation

Lakey states that the purpose of this stage in the nonviolent revolution is to resist the system which has become oppressive. Resistance can be effected through tax refusal, segments of civil servants going on strike, draft resistance, refusal to vote. Lawmakers might resign from governing bodies in protest or boycott sessions. "Where the government found compliance it now finds defiance."[23]

This type of activity depends on unity for its success. It seems that theater can be of the most benefit during this stage by building unity behind the movement. It can offer interpretation of the action to the people who are not sympathetic. It can build the morale of those who are sympathetic and involved.

At this stage, theater itself can feel the effects of repression. It will be directed at the actors if they become effective in maintaining the spirit of the resisters. This has been the case of performers in coffee houses which encouraged defections or at the least, independent thinking, from members of the armed forces. Many coffee houses were raided or harassed by authorities because they were places where theater could affect the thinking of the soldier. The Jane Fonda-Donald Sutherland show, FTA, was restricted from performing on certain bases because it fostered resistance.

There is a close tie between noncooperation and the next stage which Lakey describes as intervention and parallel institutions. Because of this close tie, I would like to discuss the way in which theater can be useful to both these stages within the framework of the next section.

Stage 5: Intervention and Parallel Institutions

This final stage of the nonviolent revolution is the most important and the most difficult. This is the stage in which it is not enough to say "no" to something. One must have an idea of what one is saying "yes" to.

> Our struggle cannot end with mass noncooperation; we need a revolution. The warfare states which hold small nations down and prepare ecological disaster must be radically changed, not only shaken up.[24]

Judith Malina, of the Living Theatre, deeply committed to liberation and the nonviolent revolution says

> We have to build another reality. And I'm not talking about Utopias, about the creation of paradisical ideas, because then we're attacked for that. But if we have an agreed-upon goal, then we can begin to build agreed-upon steps. Otherwise all we can do is fritter away the frenzy in specific protests.[25]

Lakey suggests that part of the process is that the counter-institutions which had been set up during the organization stages would begin to take over the functions of the prevailing institutions. Radical caucuses will have grown in strength and numbers. They can, in the fifth stage, intervene in the old order so as to disrupt it.

> Radical political scientists can occupy and begin to dismantle the State Department; radical workers can occupy factories and set up workers' councils to reorganize and operate them; social workers can occupy the cathedral, the free press can occupy the capitalist press . . . and inter-tribal revolutionary league of native Americans would probably want to dissolve the U.S. Bureau of Indian Affairs.[26]

These transfers of power will be legitimate if people accept them as such. Neither the caucuses nor the counter-institutions would have used violence to coerce the people.

Imagining the many ways that the social order can be changed—projecting different possibilities—is a mind-stretching process. Here is again where theater can fill a need. Theater can act as a spur to the imagination and it can act as a means of documentation. Revolutionary theater is intent upon dramatizing those episodes in which people have taken up arms in pursuit of revolutionary goals. However, we have seen relatively little theater dealing with methods of nonviolent intervention and possibilities of parallel or alternate institutions. Theater provides an excellent tool by which to "expand the mind" because it deals in symbols that are nonverbal. Through theater, we can experiment with new ideas, new feelings. We can develop new models for society. We envision a society in which there is liberation for everyone, in which power is shared, resources are shared, in which change happens nonviolently. We want theater to help our society move toward these goals. In order to do that, theater must somehow reflect that which is desired. It can do that partly through subject matter and partly through methods.

Paul Goodman discusses methods of using film to educate for nonviolent change. He rejects the use of violence on film to show how bad war is, because of its tendency to appeal to the "pornographic" emotions—sentimentality, pity, guilt. He comes to the following conclusions:

What, then, are the available resources of pacifist persuasion that can be used for the pacifist film? They can be roughly classified as:

1. Factual education.

2. Analyses of character-neurotic and social-neurotic war ideology, and the withdrawal of energy from the causes of the war spirit.

3. Opportunities for positive action, and pacifist history and exemplars.[27]

Under point (1) he suggests that "It is best if the facts, of the senselessness of it, (war) are allowed to speak for themselves, without admixture of moral or emotional appeal or any grandiose references to saving the human species." Rely on "logic, statistics, and history." "The framework must be an irrefragable and unmistakable structure of verbal propositions, even printed subtitles, however 'uncinematic': for we are dealing with a deeply neurotic and even schizophrenic phenomenon, and the *reality of ordinary reasoning, and ordinary dismissal of stupidity,* must be strongly affirmed." At the same time, the dangers of the pacifist position must not be minimized. ". . . the risks involved in unilateral disarmament should also be dispassionately and *fully* presented . . . *It is not necessary to have an answer for every argument.*" He feels that the facts about war policy, war makers, and war economy ought to be exposed "with unsparing honesty and detail, at the risk of inevitable censorship. . . . The immense network of the power structure must be made clear and diagrammed, so that a person comes to realize how nearly every job, profession, and status is directly involved in making war.[28]

Concerning conclusion (2), he talks of the importance of analysing the types who live in the "war spirit," the Marine, and the underprivileged gang "tough." One must analyse their backgrounds, their families, the relationship of the Organization Man with the military, the notion of the Enemy as a scapegoat, but most important, analyse "the paralysis with which the vast majority of people of all countries accept the war that they oppose both by conviction and feeling." Here, Goodman makes a strongly stressed point:

> Social and psychological subject matter of this type is sufficiently interesting in itself and is only confused by attempts at drama or case history; a straight classroom approach, the illustrated lecture, is most quietly effective.[29]

Goodman feels that factual education and analysis of the war ideology will release energy that has been bound up in the traditional way of doing things. There must be an outlet for this energy. He says that "pacifists do well to invent and support programs for the use of our wealth and energy freed from the expense, fear, and senselessness of war." He suggests the availability of nonviolent direct action to exert social force.

Goodman's analysis can be carried beyond his focus on war. Hunger, poverty, police repression, bigotry, sexual harassment—are all areas in which social action needs to be taken. War is not the only violence.

I have quoted a great deal of Paul Goodman's work because I think it is so insightful. It speaks not only to what our concern is about creating works that move people to solve problems nonviolently, but it also speaks to the constant barrage of violent television shows.

Defenders of television violence say that it helps people live out violent feelings, so that they won't need to express them in real life. Even Artaud, who writes with such inspiration concerning the power of the theater, describes his theater as the Theatre of Cruelty. He hopes that by exposing the audience to the cruelest part of humankind, the audience will never want to participate in violence again. My sense is that wallowing in the cruelty of which people are capable brutalizes the audience and kills hope. Without hope we cannot act. It is essential to realize that cruelty exists, and that the possibility for it exists in us, but we must know the alternatives, and we must act on the alternatives. That is why nonviolent theater must present constructive models.

It is an interesting point of Goodman's that social and psychological subject matter is confused by attempts at drama or case history. "Straight classroom approach, the illustrated lecture, is most quietly effective." This is Brechtian to the extreme. The result of his "illustrated lecture" would be that people would not identify with the victims. They would certainly remain rational, but do we still have theater?

Connections can be made between his requirements for nonviolent film and similar techniques used in theatre. The factual element he mentioned is present in "The Trial of the Catonsville Nine." The lines spoken had really been those of the defendants, given as testimony during the trial. Daniel Berrigan writes of his process:

> In composing this book, I have worked directly with the data of the trial record, somewhat in the manner of the new "factual theater." As I understand it, that form requires essential adherence to the letter of a text (in this case, some twelve hundred pages, supplied to us by the court stenographer). I have been as faithful as possible to the original words, spoken in the heat or long haul of the trial, making only those minute changes required for clarity or good sense.
> In condensing such a mass of material, it was predictable that a qualitative change would occur, almost by the law of nature, as the form emerged. And this of course was my hope: to induce out of the density of matter an art form worthy of the passionate acts and words of the Nine, acts and words which were the substance of the court record.[30]

Documentary film has been combined with theatre and with fictional film to achieve the effects of which Goodman writes. In one production of "The Trial of the Catonsville Nine," a film clip was shown at the end of the play of the nine actually burning the draft files with napalm. That final touch brought the audience back to the awareness that the act was specific at a time and place. They could deal with it more rationally. That production was responsible for at least one person deciding she must be more political in her theater work. It was a turning point for her.

The film "Z" used a similar ending. The reality of the oppression in Greece was brought out at the end of the film by having photographs of the real people, who had met violent death by "accident," flashed on the screen along with the printed details of their demise. Through this device, one could bridge the gap from the fantasy world in which the movie seemed to be, to the real world. The same thing followed "Executive Order," a film about the possible way in which President Kennedy had been assassinated.

An interesting reversal of this method was used by the "Spring Revels," an annual celebration of the return of Spring by Boston area performers. Traditionally, the program has consisted of singing, dancing, the playing of music on medieval instruments, and the dramatizing of old tales. Near the end of one program, a film was shown on the back wall of the stage. It was of an actual festival in England, the Padstow Hobby Horse ritual. The audience was taken out of the immediate "revelry" into a rational awareness of something that had happened in the past. Suddenly, through doors at the back of the stage on which the film had been shown, burst a real-life Hobby Horse with real people dancing. The effect was electric. Now it was a ceremony in which the audience could really take part. It was happening "now." The dancing continued through the aisles and out into the lobby and finally onto the green in front of the theater.

This last example illustrates the power of the "nowness" of theater as distinct from film. Action on film must necessarily have happened in the past, but theater takes place in the present. Because of that, the audience can be moved to participate in action, allowing for their free will. The action must be present and ready for them. In the case of the "Revels," it was dancing and celebrating life. In the case of protest plays, it might be signing petitions, donating money, or going as a group to participate in a demonstration or civil disobedience action.

A different method was used by the Living Theatre Collective in their play, "Seven Meditations on Political Sado-Masochism," which they performed in Boston in March, 1974. The physical imagery was symbolic. The actors used ritual movements or slow-motion realistic movements. During the movements, readings were presented based on factual material that the Collective had gathered, which pertained to that phase of slavery under consideration. At the same time as one received kinesthetic and emotional messages, one heard factual texts being read. The physical images were much stronger than the auditory images, but the auditory images filled them with more meaning. The conclusion of the play brought the actors directly into the audience for a "rap" session with members of the audience on the problem of what people can do to change our conditioning to hierarchical and sado-masochistic forms of organization.

Another production of the Living Theatre Collective is "The Money Tower." The set is a 35-foot high tower that has five levels. On the ground level are 10 actors who represent the "Lumpen-proletariat," the poor, and the unemployed. On the next level are 8 performers who represent the working class. The third level is for the middle class or management class (6 actors), the fourth level has 4 actors representing the police and the military, and at the top are two performers, representing the ruling class elite. Using this basic structure, the Living Theatre demonstrates how ore extracted from the earth becomes money, how the elite accumulates most of the money, and by wanting to make more and more profit, how a depression is caused. What is ordinarily a very abstract problem becomes concretized in this form of theater. At the end of the play the actors briefly examine the possibilities of doing without money, in a completely anarchic way.

Focusing more specifically on models, there are two ways of presenting them. One is by describing something that has happened in the past, and the other is by describing what might happen in the future. The model of the past would have really happened. Therefore, it is believable. That of the future can be imaginative, can deal with what might be if one followed a certain path.

Paul Goodman writes of the importance of using models of the past.

> Any instance of this (nonviolent direct action) even if it fails, is
> proof of the feasibility of the pacifist position, for it shows that
> sensible and moral individual and small-group action is possible,
> and thereby it diminishes our masochistic paralysis in the face
> of an approaching doom 'too big for men to cope with. . . . what
> is needed is stories, examples, and opportunities for action con-
> crete in the experience of the audience.[31]

To help people visualize how to use noncooperation as a political tool, various past actions could be dramatized. For example,
the Norwegian teachers strike against the Nazis in the 1940s.*
This is an excellent historical example of noncooperation on a
national scale. The material is all there, and with skilled handling,
a human drama could be reenacted. The method of resisting
could be spelled out and connections could be made to present-
day situation. Knowing of the success of this resistance would
make people more confident about pursuing civilian nonviolent
defense rather than military defense.

In the economic area, we could help people visualize how to
move toward alternative ways of organizing around work. The
takeover by the workers of the watch factory in Lip, France, would
provide an exciting story of cooperation, resistance, and a creative
approach to building a worker-controlled enterprise. The venture
did not succeed, but it sparked the imagination of people around
the world.

The Scott Bader Company in England provides another example of moving towards worker-controlled business. Ernst Bader
began his company in 1920, and 30 years later, had a very successful enterprise which was a leading producer of polyester res-
ins. He found himself very wealthy, but because he had not
forgotten how he had resented the way labor was organized when
he was an employee, he decided to change his organization. The
result was that ownership was transferred so that everyone working at the plant held ownership in common, and the business
functioned under a constitution. This story of conscience, creativity and success could be a drama that would educate people in
alternative methods of corporation ownership and organization.

The concept of "intermediate technology" could be treated.
This is E. F. Schumacher's term which he discusses in his book

*Editor's note: see Paul Wehr's discussion of this experience in Chapter Ten.

Small Is Beautiful, a plea for the return of human economic organization to a small scale in order for the world to regain its humanity. Part of the problem of a developing country is that it must depend on a technologically advanced country for technological answers to its dilemmas. These advanced countries lean toward technically complex solutions. Water for drought-stricken areas is one example. The solution considered possible by "technocrats" is desalination of ocean water. This process which included a nuclear-powered plant and the pumping of the water to where it was needed cost about $14,000 per irrigated acre. Intermediate technology searches for ways that are simple and can be decentralized, rather than dependant on a huge centralized industrial unit. A solution was found for the country of Botswana by making catchment basins. The idea was over a thousand years old, but the technology of today found a very inexpensive material to line the basins so that they would be waterproof. The cost of this project was close to $40 per irrigated acre. This is a human story—people have moved from being in a situation of dependency on the big powers toward independence. This affects the lives of real people. The solution is in line with simplicity and decentralization. The people have achieved liberation from dependency on large mechanical systems beyond the control of those using them and therefore, have achieved liberation from domination by those who might control a large complex unit. Dramatization of this process would be an appropriate subject for nonviolent theater.

The nonviolent process itself, including personal biography, could be the focus of theater pieces. Barbara Deming in her book *Prison Notes* wrote of her inner and outer experiences on a walk she and others took through the South on behalf of disarmament and civil rights.* Her encounters with city officials, sheriffs and jailers are filled with drama. She has a nonviolent viewpoint from which she sees the encounters. Martin Luther King, Jr.'s life and writings provide a wealth of material from which to draw. Gandhi's life would seem to provide endless material. Thich Nhat Hanh's play "The Path of Return Continues the Journey," called a "tone-poem" by Daniel Berrigan, is about the self-immolation

---

*Editor's Note: See Chapter six on civil rights march in Albany, Georgia, by Katz and Hunt.

of Chi Mai, a young Buddhist nun. The play is an exposition of a Buddhist view of nonviolent action and life after death.

Outreach is essential if we are going to build a nonviolent movement. A way of achieving this is to put into theater form the practically limitless material on nonviolent social change available. Time would be well spent in finding those who are good writers for stage, television or cinema and urging them to draw from these materials. Community groups could begin to write their own plays based on nonviolent actions, or could experiment through improvisation with the material. The writings could be circulated in high schools, colleges, churches, community theater groups, and so on.

In considering how materials can be developed with the product reflecting the goal desired, I suggest the following as the beginnings of a set of ethics for theater, theater which addresses itself to the nonviolent revolution:

1. Incidents in a documentary or "factual theater" piece must be based on truth.

2. If aroused, anger at an oppressor should be the type that desires to transform the oppressor rather than to destroy him or her. If destruction is called for, it should be aimed at systems, not people, with an alternative system suggested to replace it.

3. Efforts must be made to understand the audience. One must know for whom the work is intended and the most effective ways of communicating with that audience must be discovered and pursued.

4. The audience must be considered a responsible part of the whole production. It must not be played "at" or played "upon" but rather given the role of responsible decision maker and participant.

5. The conclusion of a play, theater piece, or film, should leave one with a sense of needed action, a design by which to act, energy with which to struggle, and hope to support one in the struggle.

Conclusion

To sum up, the directions for social change are toward liberation from all forms of oppression. With liberation goes the discipline of caring for others as much as for oneself. It is important that the process of change be in line with the end desired; therefore, the process should be nonviolent. Process should be based on the ideal of transforming rather than destroying the oppressor.

Using George Lakey's framework, I have suggested ways in which theater can be an aid to the nonviolent revolution. Theater can be used to awaken people's consciousness of their oppression. It can be used for organization—in the sense of helping groups find community and articulate their oppression through theater, and in the sense of bringing theater groups together in order to learn from each other, through criticism and self-criticism, how to better communicate the ideas of the nonviolent revolution. We've explored how "propaganda of the deed" can *be* theater and how theater can further the ends of "propaganda of the deed." We've explored how theater can aid resistance and noncooperation. And finally, we've explored how, by methods and models, theater can better lead people into alternative ways of living.

Notes

1. John M. Swomley, Jr., *Liberation Ethics*, New York: MacMillan Company, 1972, p. 1.

2. Utpal Dutt, "Theatre as a Weapon," *The Drama Review*, New York: New York University, Spring, 1971, p. 225.

3. Ibid., p. 225, 227.

4. Ibid., p. 227.

5. Richard B. Gregg, *The Power of Nonviolence*, Nyack, N.Y.: Fellowship Publications, 1959, pp. 50—51.

6. Swomley, op. cit., p. 1.

7. E. F. Schumacher, *Small Is Beautiful*, New York: Harper and Row Publishers, 1973, p. 55.

8. *Boston Globe*, September 3, 1974.

9. Ibid.

10. Gene Sharp, *The Politics of Nonviolent Action*, Boston: Porter Sargent Publisher, 1973, p. 633—634.

11. Maxine Klein, "A Country of Cruelty and its Theatre." *Drama Survey*, Dennis Hurrell, University of Minnesota Press, 1966, p. 167.

12. Carol Benglesdorf, "Cultural Foco in the Mountains," New York: Cuban Resource Center, p. 8.

13. *Proposal for a Project for Training for Street Theatre as a Tool for Nonviolent Action*, Quaker Project on Community Conflict, 13 East 17 Street, New York, N.Y., Sept. 1972, p. 2.

14. Lawrence Apsey, *The Work of Transforming Power*, Quaker Project on Community Conflict, 13 East 17th St., New York, N.Y., p. 1.

15. Paul Ryder Ryan, "The Living Theatre's Money Tower," *The Drama Review*, New York: New York University, June, 1974, p. 33.

16. David Copelin, "Chicano Theatre," *The Drama Review*, New York: New York University, December, 1973, p. 84.

17. Ibid., p. 88.

18. George Lakey, *Strategy for a Living Revolution*, San Francisco: W. H. Freeman and Co., 1973, p. 102.

19. Ibid., p. 107.

20. Ibid., p. 107.

21. Ibid., p. 108.

22. Gregg, op. cit., p. 39.

23. Lakey, op. cit., p. 123.

24. Ibid., op. cit., p. 146.

25. Karen Malpede Taylor, *People's Theatre in Amerika*, New York: Drama Book Specialists Publishers, 1972, p. 232.

26. Lakey, op. cit., p. 148.

27. Paul Goodman, *Utopian Essays and Practical Proposals*, New York: Random House, 1962, p. 74.

28. Ibid., p. 75, 76.

29. Ibid., p. 76.

30. Daniel Berrigan, *The Trial of the Catonsville Nine*, Boston: Beacon Press, 1970, p. vii.

31. Goodman, op. cit., p. 77.

BIBLIOGRAPHY

Definitions and Concepts

Arendt, Hannah. *On Violence*. New York, Harcourt, Brace & World, 1969.

Dr. Arendt reflects philosophically on violence, a subject whose existence has long been acknowledged but has not been examined in its own right until recently. She draws distinctions between modern warfare and politics, between violence and power.

Camus, Albert. "Neither Victims nor Executioners." Reprinted in *Seeds of Liberation*, Paul Goodman, (ed.), New York, Braziller, 1964.

In this powerful essay against murder and violence Camus explains why he can no longer adhere to a theory which may directly or indirectly require the taking of a man's life. He warns against elevating the ends above the means. "All I ask is that, in the midst of a murderous world, we agree to reflect on murder and make a choice."

Dellinger, David. "The Future of Nonviolence," in his *Revolutionary Nonviolence*. New York, Bobbs-Merrill, 1970.

In the most interesting essay in this collection from the standpoint of theoretical nonviolence, Dellinger states that the theory and practice of nonviolence are still in a primitive stage. This new source of power has been crudely utilized in a limited context but we must still discuss its applicability as a solution to a wider range of critical tasks.

Deming, Barbara. *On Revolution and Equilibrium*. New York, Grossman, 1971.

Taking as a point of departure Fanon's *Wretched of the Earth*, often cited as a call for violent tactics, Deming argues that only nonviolent change is truly revolutionary. Nonviolence involves a "life-serving balance . . . (an) equilibrium between self-assertion and respect for others." Deming meets the usual objections to non-violence with arguments that are both intellectually challenging and empirically convincing.

Mayer, Peter, (ed.), *The Pacifist Conscience*. New York, Holt, Ri-nehart and Winston, 1966.

The great classics of pacifist theory—including works by Gandhi, Einstein, Lao Tzu, Buddha, Kant, Russell, and Freud—are brought together in one volume, where they can be compared both for basic similarities and for variety of approach. Peter Mayer's introduction is a concise summary of the history of pac-ifism. This valuable source book also includes William Robert Miller's extensive bibliography and bibliographic index.

Niebuhr, Rheinhold. *Moral Man and Immoral Society*. New York, Scribner's, 1960.

One of the most important philosophical works in the debate between violence and pacifism. Niebuhr contends that there are important differences to be understood in the moral and social behavior of groups and individuals.

Sharp, Gene. *The Politics of Nonviolent Action*. Volumes I—III, Bos-ton, Porter Sargent, 1974.

Provides a full analysis of the politics, dynamics and methods of nonviolent action.

Sibley, Mulford Q., (ed.), *The Quiet Battle: Writings on the Theory and Practice of Non-violent Resistance*. Garden City, N.Y., Double-day, 1963.

Sibley grouped this well-known collection of readings into three sections. "Foundations of nonviolence and nonviolent resistance" includes writings by Thoreau and Gandhi; "Nonviolent power without express principle" includes Josephus' account of Jewish nonviolence and Roman power, and the account of Norway's re-sistance against the Nazis. In Part III, "Nonviolent power with express principle," are writings on nonviolence and the American Negro, and an account of colonial Pennsylvania.

Thoreau, Henry David. On Civil Disobedience. Westwood, N.J., F. H. Revell 1964.

Thoreau's classic statement on the necessity of civil disobedience to combat an unjust government, and of nonviolent resistance to an unjust war. Speaks also of the problems of having any government at all, and of the problems of majority rule.

Tolstoi, Leo. Tolstoy's Writings on Civil Disobedience and Nonviolence. New York, Bergman, 1967.

In his later life, after the publication of his most famous works, Tolstoi came to reject organized religion and the institutions of government. His writings from 1890 on call for an absolute pacifism and for the placing of the individual conscience above the demands of the state. This anthology includes "Notes for Soldiers," "Patriotism or Peace," "Letter to a Non-Commissioned Officer," and excerpts from "The Kingdom of God."

Gandhian Philosophy

Bondurant, Joan V. *Conquest of Violence*, rev. ed. Berkeley, University of California Press, 1965.

The author seeks to explain Gandhi's philosophy of *Satyagraha* as meaning something more profound and spiritual than simple civil disobedience and mass action. *Satyagraha* transcends the limitations of civil disobedience which is a method of resistance to a given law, to become an instrument of struggle for fundamental change.

Gandhi, Mohandas Karamchand. *Non-Violence in Peace and War*. Ahmedabad, Navajiwan Press, 1944—49. 2nd ed. 2 vols.

This book is of interest both to the serious student of Gandhi and to the individual who merely wants to sample Gandhi's thought. It is a comprehensive collection from Gandhi's speeches and writings, including analysis of specific events and situations as well as discussion of nonviolence and its applications on a more general, theoretical level.

Gregg, Richard. *The Power of Non-violence*. 2nd ed., rev. New York,

Fellowship Press, 1959.

Gregg explains the non-violent method in modern Western concepts and terminology, showing how nonviolent persuasion can be applied in any country, at any time, and for any cause, with more powerful and permanent results than physical coercion. This has long been a standard work on the philosophical and practical aspects of nonviolence, especially as related to Gandhi's movement.

Fisher, Louis, The Life of Mahatma Gandhi. Harper 1950.

An insightful biography of Gandhi, covering his conception of nonviolent action and the historical context of its development.

Nonviolent Action in the United States

Berrigan, Daniel. *The Trial of the Catonsville Nine*. Boston, Beacon Press, 1970.

Dan Berrigan's "factual theatre" rendition, in verse, of the trial of the nine men and women who burned draftboard records with home-made napalm as an act of nonviolent civil disobedience. A moving record.

Cooney, Robert and Michalowski, Helen, *The Power of the People*, California Peace Press, 1977.

A pictorial and overall look at the history of active nonviolence in the United States covering the American Revolution through the 1970s.

Hentoff, Nat. *Peace Agitator: The Story of A. J. Muste*. New York, Macmillan, 1963.

A J. Muste, a minister, labor leader and organizer of nonviolent pacifist action until his death in 1967, has been called "a devastating reminder to young pacifists of what a real radical is" (John Oliver Nelson). *Peace Agitator* describes Muste the activist and demonstrator.

Lynd, Staughton, ed. Nonviolence in America: A Documentary

History. Indianapolis, Bobbs-Merrill, 1966.

An excellent anthology of letters and historical documents by a long-time antiwar activist. Lynd's purpose in selecting the chronological format was to show that nonviolence is an indigenous American tradition with roots as far back as the 17th century.

United Farm Workers

Levy, Jacques E. *Caesar Chavez. Autobiography of La Causa.* New York: W. W. Norton, 1975.

Interviews with Chavez and intimates, collected over several years, immediate and very useful, especially on the subject of nonviolence.

Meister, Dick and Loftis, Anne. *A Long Time Coming. The Struggle to Unionize America's Farm Workers.* New York: MacMillan, 1977.

The most up-to-date study, astute and comprehensive, with a close look at earlier organizing efforts. Highly recommended.

Taylor, Ronald B. *Chavez and the Farm Workers. A Study in the Acquisition and Use of Power.* Boston: Beacon Press (paperback), 1975.

Emphasis on strategy. Highly recommended. People with time to read only one book about the UFW should read this.

Civil Rights Movement

Bell, Inge Powell. *CORE and the Strategy of Non-violence.* New York, Random House Studies in Sociology.

A historical-sociological study of CORE which shows the development of the philosophy of nonviolence, and its degeneration and defeat as part of the civl rights movement.

Deming, Barbara. *Prison Notes.* New York: Grossman, 1964.

A moving personal account of the peacewalkers struggle in Albany, Georgia.

King, Martin Luther. *Stride Towards Freedom, The Montgomery Story*. New York, Harper & Brothers, 1958.

King describes the growth of his philosophy of nonviolence, and the translation of that philosophy into action during the Montgomery bus boycott.

Disarmament and Nuclear Power

Boulding, Kenneth (ed.), *Peace and the War Industry*. Aldine, Transaction Books, 1970.

Readings on the effect of a large defense establishment on the economy and possibilities for change.

Lovins, Amory, "The Road Not Taken", *Foreign Affairs*, October, 1976.

An excellent account of the dangers of nuclear power and the need to develop alternative reusable resources.

Melman, Seymour (ed.), *Conversion of Industry from a Military to a Civilian Economy*, series of 6 volumes, Praeger, 1970.

A comprehensive and technical view of economic conversion.

International Dimension

Bristol, James, *Nonviolence: Not First For Export*. American Friends Service Committee, Philadelphia, 1972.

An eloquent analysis of the relationship between struggles for social justice and nonviolent movements.

Lakey, George. *Strategy for a Living Revolution*. World Order Book, New York, 1973.

Discussion of a nonviolent path to world-wide social transformation.

Mahadevan, T. K.; Roberts, Adam, and Sharp, Gene. New Delhi Gandhi Peace Foundation, 1967. *Civilian Defense: An Introduction*.

An important collection of essays defining a nonviolent defense policy for a national state.

Nute, Betty Richardson, *Helder Camara's Latin American*. London, Friends House, 1974.

Outlines history of Latin America's Martin Luther King.

INDEX

305